Cutting Back City Hall

Cutting Back City Hall

ROBERT W. POOLE, JR.

Foreword by
William E. Simon

A Free Life Editions Book

UNIVERSE BOOKS
New York

Published in the United States of America in 1980
by Universe Books
381 Park Avenue South, New York, N.Y. 10016

An earlier version of Chapter 15 appeared in *The Futurist*,
December 1978.

80 81 82 83/ 10 9 8 7 6 5 4 3 2 1

Printed in the United States of America

LIBRARY OF CONGRESS CATALOGING IN PUBLICATION DATA

Poole, Robert W 1944-
  Cutting back City Hall.

  "A Free life editions book."
  Bibliography: p.
  Includes index.
    1. Municipal finance—United States. 2. Local
taxation—United States.   3. Real property tax—
California. I. Title.
HJ9145.P66   336.73   79-6411
ISBN 0-87663-266-5

For Nancy

Contents

Foreword by
William E. Simon

There is a perverse assumption made by many people (and in politicians it almost seems inherent) that the solutions to today's problems lie only at the federal level. I remember vividly the effort by New York City's political establishment to hide its financial sins in federal largess and guarantees. A more recent example is Chrysler's campaign for federal loan guarantees.

In fact, I think it is fair to say that the national scene in general, and the federal government in particular, are the focus of most political and citizen efforts today. Liberals still call for massive federal infusions of inflation-generated dollars to solve every conceivable problem. Even conservative and libertarian critics increasingly fall into the trap of focusing almost exclusively on the national scene—both as the source of our problems and as the place to make a difference. It is time to question that assumption *and* to prove that it is wrong.

What makes CUTTING BACK CITY HALL so impressive is that it addresses the problems and opportunities of local government from a local level. There are no appeals for massive federal solutions. Instead, Robert Poole demonstrates how dozens of local governments are using free-market and businesslike methods to solve the problems of big local government.

Local governments have grown tremendously over the last decade, providing everything from fire protection to tennis courts. In many instances, we have a form of local socialism. And with it has come a bigger tax bite, a sluggish and unresponsive bureaucracy, and more and more obvious inefficiencies. What some thought of as a disease particular to New York City—financial collapse—has now spread to many other cities, Cleveland and Chicago being the most conspicuous.

Poole's aim is truly to subvert—"to turn from beneath"—to develop local and free-market solutions to local problems. Local governments affect us all very directly. But, most important, we can *do* something about the problems of local government. In fact, as Poole so carefully shows, many important, exciting, and practical things are being done throughout the country to cut taxes, improve services, and increase the freedom of citizens to choose the services they want and the ways in which they wish to spend their money.

Partially inspired by the tax revolt that gave birth to California's Proposition 13, CUTTING BACK CITY HALL goes considerably beyond calling for reduced taxes. Poole shows how cities can cut, and are cutting, the costs of local services by as much as 40% without the wholesale curtailing of services that many people fear. In fact, he shows, again and again, how the practices he suggests often *improve* service and make it much more *responsive* to citizen desires.

People have been bamboozled for too long into believing the myths that government holds the keys to the economic kingdom and that government alone serves the public interest. These myths have been used to excuse gross inefficiencies, high costs, and inflated bureaucracies. Since many of the services government provides are necessary, the cry of the tax revolt leads some people to fear they will have to go without them. Poole shows this just isn't so.

Many of these so-called public goods are goods like any others and can be more efficiently and economically provided by the private sector. Private organizations—both nonprofit and profit-making organizations—usually do the job better and at less cost because they have the discipline of the real-world marketplace. Poole demonstrates this theoretically and then with numerous examples, ranging from private profit-making fire protection to superior private transportation systems. He cites case after case, with specifics and cost figures, to show how and where private contracting is used and how much it can save. And those savings are impressive: from 10% to 40% and more. In many cases, besides being cheaper the services are actually of better quality when provided by innovative, profit-seeking companies.

Poole's examples show what is being done in towns across the country. Much more needs to be done. The task will be difficult because many entrenched interests are involved. But I think that this book will go a long way toward starting a movement to revamp the way we look at local governments and the services they provide and will inspire interested citizens, legislators, and administrators to work toward these changes.

The changes that Poole suggests will reduce local tax burdens and raise the standards of local services. Citizens will have more money to spend the way *they* choose. But most important, these changes will result in greater self-reliance, choice, and citizen control over our lives and local environment.

CUTTING BACK CITY HALL is a constructive and hopeful guide to dealing with the problems of high local taxes, inefficiency, and bureaucracy. Coming in the wake of the tax revolt, it is a call for the next step: the positive reconstruction of our local governments through free-market alternatives. Not only will these changes effect a revolution in local government, but I hope they will serve as a wellspring for changes that reach state and federal government, as well.

Acknowledgments

This book had its earliest origins in the consulting work I carried out as a staff member of Public Safety Systems, Inc., a now-defunct subsidiary of General Research Corporation in Santa Barbara. As a PSSI staffer from 1970 through 1974 I had the opportunity to work with local governments in five states, learning of a number of the innovations discussed in this book (and in a few cases helping cities or counties to implement them). That experience paved the way for my subsequent work as an independent consultant and cofounder of the Local Government Center.

One of the most important people I met during the PSSI years was Louis A. Witzeman, founder and president of Rural/Metro Fire Department, Inc., of Scottsdale, Arizona. It was seeing Witzeman's operation up close in 1971 that made me aware that public services really *could* be carried out by private enterprise—and could very well end up being done better and at less cost.

But the specific impetus for this book came from two individuals, Mark Frazier and Chuck Hamilton. Mark moved to Santa Barbara in 1976, impressed with the research and writing I'd done on privatization. More entrepreneurial than I, he asked me, "If you put your mind to it, could you show a city how to cut its budget by 25% or 30%—without crippling public services?" When I replied in the affirmative, he challenged me to write a handbook showing local officials how to do just that. Together we worked up an outline, and while I did the writing, Mark arranged for the National Taxpayers Union to publish and distribute it. The resulting 46-page handbook, *Cut Local Taxes—Without Reducing Essential Services*, has sold nearly 15,000 copies with virtually no advertising. Mark was also the cofounder with me of the Local Government Center.

Chuck Hamilton of New York's Free Life Editions was very impressed with *Cut Local Taxes*. In the summer of 1977 he proposed that I write a full-length book along the same lines as the handbook, this time providing a theoretical framework as well as specific examples, and covering in depth all municipal services. Over the two years during which this book was being written, Chuck has provided guidance, ideas, encouragement—and best of all, a publisher.

Beyond these key people, numerous others assisted me in obtaining specific items of information: people in city and county governments, at private firms, at research organizations. To list them all would be very difficult and would almost certainly risk leaving out some whose contributions were just as valuable as those included. I do wish to thank the Reason Foundation for allowing me to use their facilities during much of the time this book was in preparation.

Santa Barbara, California
November 1979

Cutting Back City Hall

1

Cities in Trouble

June 6, 1978 may well go down in history as the dawning of a new era for local government in America. It was on that day that the citizens of California enacted, by a two-to-one margin, Proposition 13. At one stroke California's city and county governments lost an average of 57% of their property tax revenues, their second-largest source of income. After the legislature allocated $4.1 billion of the $5.3-billion state surplus to bail out local governments, the net effect was a cutback in total (state and local) tax take of about 8%.

While 8% doesn't sound like much of a "slash" in government, in point of fact it represented a startling reversal of what had been an era of heedless growth. From 1967 through 1976 city government revenues nationwide increased 187%—that's an average increase of nearly 19% each year! By causing government revenue to actually *decrease* by 8%, Proposition 13 did what decades of urban experts had considered unthinkable. It actually reversed the ever-upward spiral of government spending.

Of course if Proposition 13 were simply an isolated phenomenon, it would be relatively easy to dismiss as just another example of California craziness. But events of the following year demonstrated unequivocally that California had again been a harbinger of things to come. Consider the victory of ballot initiative measures by the citizenry in the November 1978 elections. Property taxes were cut in Alabama, Idaho, Massachusetts, and Nevada. North Dakota cut income taxes. And spending limits were imposed in Arizona, Hawaii, Illinois, Michigan, and Texas.

These popular initiatives were followed by a plethora of legislative actions in 1979. A 50-state *New York Times* survey released in August 1979 found that 37 states had cut taxes or imposed spending limits in 1979 (see Table 1):

- Twenty-two states cut property taxes.
- Eighteen states cut income taxes.
- Fifteen states cut sales taxes.
- Eight states enacted spending limits.
- Twelve states repealed or reduced other taxes.

The tax revolt, in other words, is here to stay.

And that, in turn, means an end to business as usual for local governments. Property taxes have been cut back more often than other taxes, and property taxes *do* constitute the largest *local* source of city and county revenues. However, the largest overall factor in local government budgets is revenue from other levels of government. State sales tax monies, state income tax funds, and various forms of federal aid constitute some 40% of local government revenue. Thus, when the tax revolt hits income or sales taxes, it is also threatening the coffers of local government, perhaps more drastically than a cut in property taxes.

It should be clear, then, that the cities' era of free spending is over. This has been made even clearer by the spectacle of two of our major cities— New York and Cleveland—reaching a condition of bankruptcy. Successive administrations of both cities thought they could spend their way out of trouble, only to discover the era of limits in an especially painful way.

Table 1

STATES CUTTING TAXES IN 1979

PROPERTY TAX CUTS—22

Arkansas, Florida, Idaho, Iowa, Kansas, Kentucky, Maryland, Massachusetts, Minnesota, Missouri, Montana, Nevada, New Mexico, North Dakota, Ohio, Oregon, South Dakota, Tennessee, Utah, Washington, Wisconsin, Wyoming.

INCOME TAX REDUCTIONS—18

Arizona, Colorado, Delaware, Indiana, Iowa, Kansas, Minnesota, Mississippi, Montana, New Mexico, New York, North Carolina, Oklahoma, Oregon, Rhode Island, Vermont, Virginia, Wisconsin.

SALES TAX REDUCTIONS—15

Kansas, Kentucky, Maine, Maryland, Michigan, Minnesota, Mississippi, Nevada, New York, South Dakota, Tennessee, Virginia, Washington, West Virginia, Wisconsin.

SPENDING LIMITS—8

Florida, Massachusetts, Montana, Nebraska, Oregon, Rhode Island, South Carolina, Utah.

PROPERTY ASSESSMENT CURBS—4

Arizona, Iowa, Maryland, Oregon.

Note: Most states in which there was no action passed tax reduction laws or amendments or spending limits during 1978. New Jersey, for example, has been struggling for several years to live under ceilings on government spending for state and local governments, first enacted by the Legislature in 1976.

Source: *New York Times*, August 5, 1979

We don't have to suffer more New Yorks and Clevelands. There are better ways of coping with reduced local tax revenues than demanding still more federal aid, playing games with the city's books, or defaulting on municipal bonds.

Bits and pieces of these better ways already exist in scattered cities across the country. But because they do not yet form a readily identifiable pattern, no one has put the pieces together into a coherent design for the future. Doing so involves taking a whole new look at local governments, at the myriad services they provide, and at how these services are paid for. That is what we'll do in this book.

Before we begin, it's important to get a clear understanding of just how rapidly local governments have been expanding in recent years. So much attention has been focused on federal spending that few people realize how rapidly state and local governments have been growing by comparison. In terms of employees, for instance, from 1960 to 1975 total federal employment increased by only 19%, while local government employees increased by 114%.

With that kind of increase in employees, it's no wonder that the cost of local government has soared. But the fact is that local governments have been taking in money much faster than they've been adding people. In just ten years, from 1967 to 1976, total city government revenues increased from $19.4 billion to $55.6 billion, according to figures collected by the U.S. Census Bureau. (In the same period, the Consumer Price Index went from 100 to 170.5. Thus, while inflation increased by 70.5%, local government's take increased 186.6%—2.65 times as rapidly as inflation!) Besides increasing in numbers, municipal employees have become substantially better paid. Some surveys show city and county employees receiving 10% to 20% more than people in equivalent jobs in the private sector. In the City of Los Angeles, municipal refuse workers make as much as $787 per month more than private collectors' employees.

Voters, of course, do not keep track of statistics of this sort. They just know that the tax that is most visible—their property tax—keeps rising and rising. Overall, city property taxes increased by 95% in the decade—from $7.3 billion to $14.2 billion. The *big* growth, however—the money that has fueled such huge increases in spending without triggering a taxpayer revolt until now—has come from the *other* three major sources of revenue.

As Table 2 shows, other (less visible) local taxes increased 187.5% over the decade 1967–76, and charges for services and miscellaneous revenues (fines, permit fees, etc.) increased 160.5%. But the really large increase has come in the category called "intergovernmental revenue"—allocations of state-collected taxes (e.g., sales, income, and liquor taxes) to cities and counties, plus federal aid (revenue sharing, CETA programs, model cities, etc.). These funds soared from $5.1 billion in 1967 to $22.3 billion in 1976— an increase of 337%. As a result, while the property tax has shrunk to only a quarter of city revenues, tax money from elsewhere now provides over 40%, as noted earlier.

Table 2

TRENDS IN CITY GOVERNMENT REVENUE
1967-76 (billions of dollars)

	PROPERTY TAXES		NONPROPERTY TAXES		INTERGOVERNMENTAL REVENUE		SERVICE CHARGES & MISCELLANEOUS		TOTALS
	AMOUNT	PERCENT	AMOUNT	PERCENT	AMOUNT	PERCENT	AMOUNT	PERCENT	
1967	$7.3	37.6	$3.2	16.5	$5.1	26.3	$3.8	19.6	$19.4
1968	7.8	36.8	3.4	16.0	6.0	28.3	4.0	18.9	21.2
1969	8.3	34.4	3.9	16.2	7.3	30.3	4.6	19.1	24.1
1970	9.2	34.5	4.5	16.8	7.8	29.2	5.2	19.5	26.7
1971	10.1	32.9	5.0	16.3	9.8	31.9	5.8	18.9	30.7
1972	11.0	31.5	6.1	17.5	11.4	32.7	6.4	18.3	34.9
1973	11.8	29.2	6.6	16.3	14.8	36.7	7.2	17.8	40.4
1974	12.2	27.5	7.2	16.2	16.7	37.7	8.2	18.5	44.3
1975	13.0	26.1	8.1	16.3	19.5	39.2	9.2	18.5	49.8
1976	14.2	25.5	9.2	16.5	22.3	40.1	9.9	17.8	55.6
10-year increase	94.5%		187.5%		337.3%		160.5%		186.6%

Source: U.S. Census Bureau

In some cases local government has expanded so rapidly because there is a genuine need for expansion of existing services to meet the needs of the new population. Far more typical, however, is the case of Los Angeles County, whose population increased from 6.7 million to only 7.0 million people between 1965 and 1975 but whose budget soared from $951 million to $3.07 billion in the same period. That increased the cost per capita from $142 to $439—a tripling of the tax burden on every man, woman, and child.

Local governments have ballooned in this fashion for several reasons. First, people heedlessly expected new services without questioning whether it really made sense to ask *local governments* to provide them. Second, local bureaucracies and interest groups succeeded in thinking up new things to do. Third, liberal academics provided support for ever-more spending; John Kenneth Galbraith told a *New York Times* symposium in 1975 that "no problem associated with New York City could not be solved by providing more money." Finally, for a long time the money was readily available, thanks largely to the nearly invisible growth in federal and state aid.

New York City, at one extreme, spent and spent, creating a vast municipal hospital system, a city university system open to all at no charge, the highest welfare benefits in the country, and a civil service system unparalleled in its solicitude toward employees (e.g., 45 vacation and "chart" days off each year for police officers, a 36-hour work week for everyone)—all without concern for its increasingly hard-pressed taxpayers. At the other end of the spectrum, even Petaluma, California, with a population of only 32,000, spent $9,000 of its taxpayers' money each year to subsidize the World Wrist Wrestling Championships. Fostering the arts, aiding the handicapped, employing the down-and-out, filling up people's leisure hours, demonstrating solar technology—you name it and some local government somewhere has done it.

It is only with the advent of the tax revolt that people are starting to question whether many of these things (as important as some of them are) are really appropriate *government* functions. There is, after all, only so much money available. Taking money from individuals and businesses to spend on frills drains not only the taxpayer but also the whole economy. This money might have been used much more productively in the private economy. (The $6.4 billion left in private hands by Proposition 13's first year, for example, helped lead to the creation of 552,000 new jobs in the private sector—far more than the 100,000 jobs lost from the public sector. California's unemployment was cut to its lowest level in 15 years!)

Moreover, even when it is providing essential services (like police, fire protection, and garbage collection), there is no reason to believe that government is an *efficient* provider of services. Governments *are* good at collecting revenue, notes political scientist William Niskanen, but nothing in current political or economic theory gives local governments any particular advantage as *providers* of services. Indeed, when we do find side-by-side comparisons of government and the private sector performing the very same services, it's invariably the private sector that's more efficient. Columbia University management professor Emmanuel Savas, for example, found that in cities of over 50,000 population it costs the average municipal sanitation department *68% more* to collect the garbage than it costs a private firm.

Besides being wasteful and inefficient, local governments have a tendency to expand into areas the private sector is already handling. More and more city fire departments are getting into the paramedic rescue business, for example, frequently in competition with efficient, competent private firms. Other cities do things like tying up millions of dollars in little-used, special-purpose equipment, rather than renting the equipment or the service, when needed, from private operators.

Many city work forces are notorious for featherbedding. New technology that permits greater productivity—more work being accomplished by the same number of people or the same work accomplished by fewer people—is all too often stubbornly resisted. In many cities three-fourths (or more) of all fire calls can be handled adequately by two-place, lightweight "attack trucks." But most fire departments cling tenaciously to gas-guzzling triple-combination pumpers staffed with three, four, or even five firefighters.

Then there's the bureaucracy and its civil service system. Originally conceived to protect employees from political patronage, civil service nowadays grants them what amounts to lifetime tenure. Civil service was developed before the advent of strong municipal employees unions—which have added their own layer of job protection on top of what is provided by civil service. What's being "protected" by these duplicative systems is mostly outmoded, inefficient work methods and a calcified bureaucracy.

A key factor in the poor performance of government services is their lack of incentive. A private firm engaged in providing a service (e.g., tree trimming) is organized in hopes of making a profit. But it has no guarantee of doing so. Its managers must therefore continually analyze its operations so as to keep its costs within the limits of the revenues it is able to generate. Municipal agencies, with guaranteed customers and guaranteed revenues (taxes), have no such incentive. As a result, they tend to do the same thing in the same way, year after year, with little real effort to innovate so as to accomplish more for less. Dean Dick Netzer of NYU's Graduate School of Public Administration has pointed out that "*none* of the major services performed by local governments is performed in ways that differ significantly from the methods and approaches used 50 years ago." How many private firms of 50 years ago would still be in business if that were how they operated?

Yet another problem with what Professor Savas calls "municipal monopolies" is that they don't offer citizens any choice. The consumer of food and the consumer of clothing have a tremendous variety from which to choose; not so the consumer of police protection or garbage collection or ambulance service—at least in most cities where these services are government monopolies. Voting once every few years for city council members gives a citizen very little impact on the type and quality of public services provided. Yet the same citizen's daily vote at the supermarket, with each purchase, can determine the fate, not only of Swift and Del Monte, but of Safeway and A&P as well.

For all these reasons, we should be very cautious—much more cautious than we've been—in giving to local government the task of delivering public services.

Even before the tax revolt, some cities—notably New York and Cleveland—were in serious trouble. A number of other large cities, especially in the Midwest and Northeast, are considered "declining" cities; they are losing population and industry and were doing so before the tax revolt. Now, with the prospect of revenues actually shrinking, not just these problem cities but all local governments are in potential trouble. What is the way out of this trouble?

For years we were told by reformers that the solution to our urban problems lay in (1) spending more tax money and (2) eliminating wasteful duplication of services by consolidating smaller suburbs and districts into area-wide metropolitan governments. But the reformers failed to disclose—perhaps because they themselves did not appreciate—the true costs of these proposals. Spending more tax money on facilities and services increases the tax burden—which can have the effect of driving out both businesses and individuals. An important reason for the exodus from the Snowbelt to the Sunbelt in the past 20 years has been the former's significantly higher tax burden, especially on employers.

Creating metro governments does indeed reduce duplication—but at the price of a much larger, more costly administrative structure (bureaucracy) and a reduction in the responsiveness of services to local desires and needs. The much-maligned "chaos" of small towns and overlapping service districts in many cases is far more responsive (and, it turns out, less costly) than a massive metropolitan government. That was the conclusion of California's 1974 Task Force on Local Government Reform[1] and of several other recent studies,[2,3] as well as of several detailed studies of police services (see Chapter 3).

In addition, both of these conventional solutions fail to reckon with the obvious and growing desire of the citizens to reduce taxes and have greater control over what they earn.

What is needed is a fundamental rethinking of what it is we expect local government to do, and how we should go about paying for it. Much of what cities and counties do is essentially the operation of service businesses. But they very seldom operate these services like businesses. Where an occasional innovator runs a department somewhat like a business, the cost savings can be impressive. Other cities are going further, charging users of specific services (instead of taxing everyone), and even inviting private firms to bid on supplying the services.

Numerous private firms have already gotten into the public service business, sometimes on a nonprofit basis but more often on a regular, profit-making basis. As a rule, they figure out less-costly, more efficient ways to operate and end up delivering more service for less money. When services are delivered on a fee-for-service basis (even if provided by local government), there are important long-term implications for the kinds and amounts of services provided. Making services available at a price provides a way of greatly expanding consumer choice—without increasing taxes.

It is this kind of orientation to public services that offers the key to coping with the tax revolt. And it is this approach—reexamining our bloated city halls and privatizing services where it makes sense to do so—that we will explore in this book. Chapter 2 presents the case for three reforms—privatization, user charges, and what I call "thinking smarter"—in some detail, explaining what each means, when each is appropriate, and how they all fit together. The next 12 chapters apply these concepts to the principal service areas of local government, one by one: police, criminal justice, fire, etc., all the way through schools. In Chapter 15 we will put these ideas all together and take a flight of fancy into the future, to see what a truly cut-back city hall could look like by the year 2000. Chapter 16 then provides some ideas and suggestions on how to put the ideas in this book into practice. Finally, three appendixes are included for further exploration of the concepts and examples used in the text.

2

Keys to Cutting Taxes

The key to cutting local taxes is cutting the cost of the services provided by local governments. One way to do this is the meat-axe approach: simply slash each agency's budget an arbitrary percentage and let the chips fall where they may. This approach "works" but is often self-defeating. Besides maximizing the odds of labor troubles, it also virtually guarantees cutbacks in the level of public services people have learned to expect. For both reasons, public support for the meat-axe approach is usually short lived. There are better ways of cutting back city hall.

These alternatives to the meat-axe approach include ways of providing public services more efficiently. Necessary services are provided *and* taxpayers' money is saved. And the improved efficiency benefits everyone in the long run because less of society's total resources need to be spent on public services, leaving more available for other purposes (such as building new factories and providing more service industry jobs).

There are three principal ways of improving the efficiency of local services: (1) *privatization*—delivery of the service by more efficient private providers; (2) *user charges*—having only the users of a particular service pay for it, so that providers have to tailor the service to actual user needs instead of bureaucratic convenience; and (3) *thinking smarter*—applying analytical and businesslike methods to the production of public services. We'll explore each of these approaches in this chapter.

Before getting into these techniques, it is important to clear up a common misunderstanding concerning the justification for government involvement in those things we normally think of as public services. Consider for a moment: Why do people assume that fire protection is a proper function of local government but fire insurance is not? Why are sewer lines provided by government but electric lines by a private firm?

Why are baseball diamonds provided by the city but miniature golf courses by private enterprise? What about garbage collection, which in about half our cities is provided by private firms and in the other half by government?

For the most part, there is no particular theoretical justification for consigning one set of these services to the public sector and another set to the private sector. Economists *do* recognize one category of service which most of them consider inherently governmental, and they call that type a "public good." They define a public good as an activity or service whose very nature is such that if it is provided at all, everybody in the general area benefits, whether or not they pay for it. The classic example is national defense. If some people were to get together and put up the money for an army, navy, and air force to defend the country against attack, to the extent that the effort were successful, everyone in the country would benefit. Historically, therefore, most economists have argued that such services should be funded by taxes imposed on everyone.

But most economists and political scientists have gone on from there to apply this concept uncritically to local services, *without* carefully considering whether the defining characteristics of a public good really apply. When we look closely at garbage collection, recreation programs, paramedic service, water and sewer systems, and even many aspects of police and fire protection, we *don't* find classic examples of public goods. On the contrary, we find services with specific, identifiable users who benefit from the service, with nonusers either not benefiting at all or benefiting to a much smaller extent than users. (About the only local services that come close to looking like classical public goods are mosquito abatement and other public health measures and certain preventive aspects of police and fire protection.)

If most public services are not really public goods, there is no theoretical case for them to be provided exclusively by government or funded by compulsory taxation of all the residents. The fact is that most public services *can* be provided by private organizations. Most *can* be paid for by their customers. In every region of the country—and especially in the Sunbelt, where tradition holds less sway—numerous public services *are* being provided by private organizations: volunteer agencies, nonprofit corporations, and ordinary profit-seeking firms. Likewise individual services—and not just ones provided by private organizations—*are* being charged for instead of being funded by taxes.

PRIVATIZATION

Perhaps the most important key to cutting costs is privatization—the provision of a service by one or more private-sector organizations instead of by local government. Virtually every category of public service has been or is being provided by a private organization somewhere in the United States: police, fire, paramedics, roads, water, parks, recreation, garbage— even tax assessment.

There are several forms of privatization. In some cases, the market provides whatever services suppliers and consumers decide on and the local government is simply not involved. Garbage service in the unincorporated portions of Los Angeles County follows this model, as does fire protection in the unincorporated areas of a number of states. In other cases the city or county may control the market by franchising a limited number of firms to provide the service—taxi service often follows this pattern. In still other cases the local government selects a single firm to serve an exclusive territory (either the whole city or a specific district) for a limited number of years. The well-known private fire department in Scottsdale, Arizona, is provided in this manner. Still another model is quasi-privatization, in which the local government contracts not with a private firm but with a nearby city or county agency. Many California cities contract with the county sheriff's office for their police protection.

Privatization can save taxpayers money in many ways. To begin with, our first type of privatization—where the local government stands aside—may lead to volunteer services being developed. Even today the vast majority of American fire departments are manned by volunteers, costing the taxpayer not a penny. Some of the country's best emergency ambulance service is provided by a large volunteer rescue squad in the Bethesda/ Chevy Chase area of Maryland adjoining Washington, D.C. Volunteer groups can provide valuable services in schools, recreation, and social services as well. And in many big cities, volunteer block associations are providing security patrol services that take some of the patrol burden from hard-pressed police departments.

Privatization more commonly involves the substitution of private (usually profit-seeking) firms for government service providers. Does this change save money? Doesn't the firm's private character lead to added *costs*, such as advertising and profits, that are passed on to the consumer? It turns out, in fact, that in nearly every case that's been studied, private firms are *less* costly than public agencies for delivering the *same* level of service. Documented cost savings range from 50% (fire service in Scottsdale, Arizona) to 40% (national average saving for private garbage service in cities of over 50,000 population) to 33% (data processing in Orange County, California) to 10%–20% for services like tree-trimming, pavement striping, and park maintenance.

Private firms tend to be efficient precisely *because* they have to make a profit. A municipal agency, for instance, has permanent, guaranteed access to tax funds and a guaranteed monopoly on the service. There is little incentive for it to be efficient and save money. A private firm, on the other hand, has no long-term guarantee of funds. If it is one of many firms competing for individual customers in a city, this fact is obvious. But even where it has an exclusive franchise for two or three years, the private firm faces competition from potential suppliers when its contract expires. If they wish it to make money, the firm's managers must price its services low enough to be competitive but high enough to yield a return on its investment. *That*, in turn, *forces* them to figure out better ways of doing business. "We have the greatest incentive in the world to innovate, to pioneer, to analyze every little step," says Lou Witzeman, president of Arizona's Rural/Metro Fire Department, Inc. "Sheer survival."

What economists call "economies of scale" is another factor leading to efficiency in privatization. Just as in manufacturing, some of the costs of producing a specific public service decrease, per unit of service delivered, as the scale at which the service is provided increases. This principle is not valid without limit, however. For most services, once the city becomes *very* large, unit costs actually become higher and higher. (This effect is due to the increased layers of bureaucracy that tend to be added in large cities.)

Perhaps the only general rule we can draw from this is that the costs of producing a public service *do* vary with the size of the area and the number of people served. And the costs vary *differently* for each of the different services provided. Thus, the "optimum size" city for minimizing the per capita cost of police protection may be quite different from the optimum size for minimum per capita water system or recreation department costs. *Whatever* the size of the city or county, it's not likely to be the optimum (most efficient) size for producing more than one or two of its public services—if that.

Hence, if cost minimization is the goal, citizens are likely to be much better off purchasing their services from suppliers who can be an efficient size, rather than being constrained by the boundaries of the city. This may mean that some services are purchased from a single supplier that serves a number of communities (e.g., a water or sewer system) while others are purchased from a multitude of small suppliers either competing within the same area or allocated to districts (e.g., garbage or taxi service). Still other services (but not most) may indeed be purchased from suppliers who serve all of the city and *only* the city.

Because of this effect, services purchased from other local governments can also be money-savers in those cases where the supplier agency can realize economies by serving a larger area. For instance, Robert Deacon, an economist at the University of California at Santa Barbara, found that 23 cities in Southern California that contract with other local governments for police services pay an average of 42% less, per capita, than comparable cities which provide their own police services.[1]

Besides saving money directly (for a given level of service), there are other important advantages to privatization. To begin with, if a well-defined service is purchased from a supplier for a limited period of time, the slate is wiped clean at the end of the contract and the process begins again from scratch. In a recent report on privatization,[2] the Urban Institute listed eight other advantages:

• *Providing specialized skills.* In cases where a city may not need highly specialized persons on a full-time basis, contracting offers a lower-cost way to obtain their services. The same applies to costly, special-purpose equipment. This advantage is especially applicable to smaller cities.

- *Limiting the growth of government.* The total size of government, as measured by the number of permanent full-time employees, can be held down or cut back by using contracting. This may save additional money (beyond the lower costs of the service itself) by reducing the city's need for general administrative staff (e.g., the payroll and personnel departments).
- *Avoiding large initial costs.* Contracting can permit large new projects to begin (e.g., adding a garbage recycling plant) without a large initial investment in land, facilities, or equipment—if the private supplier has made or will make these investments on its own.
- *Permitting greater flexibility in program size.* When services are provided under contract, the city administration will have an easier time specifying reductions in or additions to service levels—without getting bogged down in complex labor negotiations. The private firm is usually not dependent solely on the city for its income, and is used to expanding and contracting its work force to meet changing demands for its services.
- *Providing a yardstick for comparison.* When a service is provided in part of the city by private firms and in part of it by a city agency (e.g., garbage collection in Minneapolis), the side-by-side operation provides a means of comparing costs and performance, so that either can be measured against the other.
- *Promoting increased objectivity.* Too often city administrators have difficulty being objective about the performance of their own agencies. When operational responsibilities are in a separate, outside organization, the city managers can be expected to take a more objective look at its performance and cost. The likelihood of better service at less cost is thereby increased.
- *Producing better management.* When operations are separated from control, as in contracting, the city's managers can devote more attention to planning and monitoring, rather than being preoccupied with the day-to-day problems of running the agency and providing its services.
- *Producing better management information.* Drafting a contract for provision of a public service focuses attention on an exact specification of the services to be carried out and the performance levels required. Properly written, such a contract also provides for monitoring of the services actually provided, to be sure the terms of the contract are met. In many cities this is the first time information of this type has ever been provided.

To be sure, contracting is not a panacea, and there *can* be problems. It is vital that the contract be carefully and specifically drafted, to spell out precisely what services are to be provided. And it is equally important that the contractor's performance be monitored throughout the life of the contract. Instances of corruption have occurred, in cases where the selection process was not an openly competitive situation. But well-defined procedures exist, and are in widespread use, to keep the bidding process open and aboveboard. One factor in doing so is avoiding excessively narrow bid specifications that may artificially limit the eligible bidders to one or two favored firms.

Unfortunately, no comprehensive data exist on the full extent of privatization. The Urban Institute has reviewed the few existing surveys and studies. It concluded that, in 1975, state and local governments purchased $36 billion worth of services from private firms and from other units of government. That amounted to 24% of all state and local expenditures. One detailed study—of Philadelphia in 1972—revealed that 26% of local expenditures in that year went for purchases of services.

Despite the lack of recent survey data, there are strong indications that privatization is on the rise. The Local Government Center, a nonprofit research organization based in Santa Barbara, California, began collecting information on privatization in 1976. In its first three years its researchers uncovered case after case of cities and counties switching to private firms. Many of these cases are discussed in the chapters that follow. As cities face continuing financial difficulties, and as taxpayer revolts spread, local officials will be under increasing pressure to turn to privatization in order to cut costs without impairing services.

USER CHARGES

The second method of saving taxpayers' money and increasing efficiency is to substitute user charges for taxation. At first glance it may appear that, since money is still being collected for local services provided by government, all that is done is to shift from one form of revenue raising to another, with no savings at all. But as we shall see, while user charges do not guarantee savings for every taxpayer, they can provide important tax savings for many of them—*and* can promote greater efficiency in service delivery.

To begin with, let's be clear what we mean by a user charge. We define a user charge (or user fee) as a charge imposed for a governmentally provided service based on the amount or level of service demanded by or provided to the user. User charges are, in the words of Urban Institute researcher Selma Mushkin, "public prices for public products," very much like the prices charged for services in the private sector. Indeed, for many services provided by both the public and the private sector (golf courses, trash collection), it is possible to compare public and private prices directly.

A user charge is *voluntary*, in contrast to taxes, since payment occurs only when a citizen *chooses* to use a particular service, and the amount is proportional to that person's use. Not all citizens play tennis, for example. Charging for use of tennis courts puts the cost only on those who benefit, rather than on every taxpayer. User charges also differ from license charges or permit fees, since these latter are regulatory in nature—they are payments for governmental permission to engage in an activity (run a business, build a garage, etc.) rather than a payment for a particular service.

Economists and political scientists have defined two criteria by which to judge when a public service is a good candidate for user-charge funding rather than general tax funding. The service must, first of all, have *readily identifiable users* who must benefit substantially more from the service than nonusers. And, second, it must be possible to ensure that *nonusers can be excluded* from the benefits of the service, or that benefits to nonusers are minimal. When these two criteria (which essentially guarantee that the service is not a public good) are satisfied, the service will closely resemble an ordinary private service and can easily be charged for.

Because cities and counties vary considerably in which services they in fact charge for, readers in one locality may be accustomed to "having to pay for" one group of public services which is provided "free" as a matter of course in another locality. There seems to be little rhyme or reason across the country why certain services are funded by taxation rather than by user charges. Tradition, rather than the neat, logical criteria of economists, seems to be the primary deciding factor.

Thus, although in most cities we find water, sewer, and other utility services paid for largely by user charges, in many areas only the *operating* costs are paid via monthly bills, while the *capital* costs are derived from general obligation bonds, paid off out of general property-tax revenues. In a few cities (including much of New York City) there are no water meters at all and the entire cost is met out of general tax revenues. Garbage service, when provided by government rather than by private haulers, may be fully user-paid (as in most cities) or partially or totally subsidized out of general tax revenues (as in the City of Los Angeles). Many public beaches, campgrounds, and parks are "free" while others charge admission. City parking lots usually charge their users, but not always enough to cover costs. Some cities charge for paramedic service, while others make this very costly service available at no charge to users. Mass transit systems nearly always charge fares, but usually not enough to cover their costs.

U.S. Census Bureau data for 1975/76 show the extent of user charges being used by local governments. Utility charges (water, gas, electricity) accounted for $10.7 billion in city government revenues—about 40% of the amount raised by taxes. Charges for *other* current services—parks, recreation, parking, school lunches, hospitals—amounted to another $6.9 billion, 26% of the amount raised by taxes. Thus, total user charges provided two-thirds as much revenue as taxation. The portion of total city revenues provided by user charges increased from 56% of tax revenues to 68% over the period 1957-77. The growth would probably have been larger, except that there was little pressure on local officials to come up with new revenue sources, due to the explosive growth of federal and state aid during this period.

But today, when citizens are balking at soaring property taxes and outside funding is being cut, officials across the country are taking a much closer look at expanded user-charge funding. In California the first year following passage of Proposition 13 saw an explosion of user charges (and of new fees masquerading as user charges). By June 1, 1979, cities and counties had raised $125 million in new or increased user fees—about 19% of what they had lost in property-tax revenues.

Besides being a replacement for lost tax revenues, user charges have some powerful economic and political advantages. They make public services more efficient. Economist Selma Mushkin points out what tends to happen when public services are *not* charged for:

> Under present resource allocation practices within the public sector itself the wrong product is sometimes produced, in the wrong quantity, and with no (or inappropriate) quality differentiation. If it is feasible to determine benefit values and to identify the beneficiaries of a public program, pricing [i.e., user charges] becomes a viable means of ensuring that the allocation of public resources becomes more efficient.[3]

In other words, if citizens are treated as consumers and given choices of various types and levels of public services—instead of being presented with a standardized service on a like-it-or-lump-it basis—local agencies will find out much more precisely what services people want and what they don't want. Voting via the price system is far more sensitive to the infinite varieties of consumer demand than all-or-nothing voting in the political process.

For example, by charging for trash collection, with different rates for different levels of service (once-a-week curbside, twice-a-week backyard, etc.), the supplier can determine what levels of service people really want, as they express those preferences by voting with their dollars. There is, in fact, some empirical evidence that municipal garbage-collection agencies tend to overproduce. When people are given a choice, they generally prefer a somewhat less-abundant level of service at a lower price. Thus, user charges tend to discourage the wasteful provision of excess service.

But the economic benefits don't stop there. Another benefit is the reduction of congestion and crowding. It's a truism that when something is perceived as being free, people demand far more of it than if they have to make direct payments. Public services like beaches, parks, and tennis courts that are provided without charge tend to get overcrowded at times when many people wish to use them. (Imagine the crowding if movie theaters operated without charge on Saturday nights!) Imposing charges at times of peak demand, or imposing higher charges at peak times than at off-peak hours, gives users an incentive to weigh alternative uses of their time. Many will decide to reschedule their use to off-peak hours when the price is lower, or to engage in some other activity that costs less (e.g., playing miniature golf rather than playing tennis). In this way, over-crowding is relieved and the total use of the facility is spread out more evenly. (This also makes it easier to staff the facility.)

User charges can also motivate more cost-effective behavior by users. A good example is fire protection. Economic studies by William Pollack and others indicate that less total money would have to be spent on fire protection if more property owners invested in protective measures such as sprinkler systems. The provision of municipal fire protection as a "free" public service has had the side effect of causing an overinvestment in fire *suppression* capability and an underinvestment in fire *prevention* capability—a classic case of locking the barn door after the horse has escaped. Pollack and others have devised various structures of fire service user charges that would remedy this situation.[4] Since the charge would be based on the overall fire risk presented by each property, owners would have a direct economic incentive to invest in fire prevention. A charge of this sort was implemented by Inglewood, California, in the wake of Proposition 13.

Besides the economic case for user charges, there is a powerful political and social case for them. To date, neither department heads nor elected officials have taken this case to the public, but it is, nonetheless, one that *can* be sold. There are six political and social advantages to user charges, as follows.

1. *Fairness.* Why are tennis courts, beaches, and golf courses provided "free" by the public sector but bowling alleys, movie theaters, and miniature golf provided at market prices by the private sector? *Both* sets of services are used by particular subsets of the population. There is no good reason why the general taxpayer should be taxed so as to subsidize either group. But that is precisely what happens when the former set of services is provided without charge. Even worse, these subsidies are frequently from the poor to the rich. Everyone, rich or poor, pays property taxes—the poor as a large fraction of their rent, middle-income people and the rich directly as taxes on their homes. Thus, in many cities low-income renters are paying property taxes in order that the well-to-do can have "free" tennis courts, beaches, and marinas.

It would be far more equitable to provide such services on a user-pays basis, so that only those who benefit directly end up paying. To the extent that some members of the community may be too poor to afford these charges, it is quite possible to provide free passes or other forms of explicit subsidy *only* for them. Subsidizing *everybody* because a few can't afford to pay simply doesn't make sense.

2. *Flexibility.* Public services can be much more flexible and responsive when they are priced. Changes in programs and services can be made more readily when the users, rather than all the taxpayers, are footing the bill. To take full advantage of this benefit, cities should let department managers initiate new programs and terminate old ones in response to the demand revealed by the user-charge "market"—instead of deciding such issues in political forums like the city council chambers. There is no need to go through the charade of justifying a new program as being in the interest of the taxpaying public as a whole (which it usually isn't, anyway) if the specific users are willing to pay for it.

3. *Freedom.* A hallmark of the past decade (and especially of the past few years) has been the growth of people's desire to be left alone by the government. The tax revolt is at least as much a revolt against oppressive, intrusive government as it is against high levels of taxes. People increasingly

wish to make their own decisions and control their own lives and resources.

The substitution of user charges for taxes fits in well with this desire. User charges reduce the government's coerced "take," returning the spending decisions to the citizen rather than the government. *If* people want to play tennis, they pay for tennis; if not, they don't. *If* people wish more intensive police patrols, they pay for them; if not, not. If they buy a boat and berth it in the city marina, they pay for the marina, but if they don't, they're spared this expense and can spend the money as they choose.

4. *Expansion of services*. Here's an advantage from the department head's standpoint. Since success and prestige are measured by the size of the department and the extent of its programs, user charges are a way for the department head to expand *despite* citizen-demanded tax cuts. As long as the department makes new programs fully user-supported, why should the general taxpayer complain? Thus, department heads have a clear motivation to get behind the shift to user charges.

5. *Commuter solution*. One of the problems plaguing many big cities is the feeling that they are being ripped off by suburbanites—people who have fled the city to comfortable homes in the lower-taxed suburbs but still come to the city to work and play. There, they take advantage of the city's costly public services—which the poor people and businesses left behind in the city must struggle to pay for via their property taxes.

User charges neatly solve this problem by charging everyone—resident, commuter, and tourist—who uses the services. No longer need cities be impoverished by a shrinking tax base as citizens move to the suburbs. When users pay their own way, the commuter problem pretty much disappears.

6. *Growth solution*. In many suburban areas and smaller cities, the most divisive local issue is growth versus no-growth. A key aspect of this issue is the provision of costly new services (water, sewers, fire protection, schools) to newly developed areas. Efforts to cope with this problem have led to water/sewer hookup moratoriums, downzoning, construction permit limits, and other measures of sometimes questionable constitutionality— as well as of great emotion and divisiveness.

User charges can solve this problem, as well. Developers are made responsible for constructing the new "infrastructure" of public facilities necessitated by their developments, and the costs of these facilities are incorporated into the price of the properties. Then only the users pay for the costs attendant on their addition to the community. The resulting higher housing prices will provide a solution somewhere between the extremes urged by the pro- and anti-growth factions: Some development *will* take place, but because of higher costs it is likely to be less than if the rest of the taxpayers were subsidizing the new public facilities.

Combined with the economic benefits of more efficient service production, these six advantages—fairness, flexibility, freedom, expansion of services, commuter solutions, and growth solutions—constitute a powerful case for user charges.

THINKING SMARTER

The third category of money-saving methods is something of a catchall. When, rarely, a public agency operates in a way that mimics the behavior of an innovative, profit-seeking firm, chances are it has figured out some smarter way of organizing the delivery of its services. Thinking smarter can produce significant savings in many areas of local government operations. Numerous examples are given in the chapters that follow; a few are described here just to give the general idea.

Your city's police force can nearly double its strength during high-crime hours without increasing the police budget. A few police departments are doing just that, because they've thought up a smarter way to schedule their patrol officers. Analyzing the records of calls for service by hour of the day, they saw that in most cases demand for police response was three or four times higher in the evening hours than in the early hours of the morning and twice as high as in morning and afternoon hours. In cooperation with their officers, they devised a new shift schedule based on a ten-hour day, four days a week. Using ten-hour shifts they could arrange things so that six of the 24 hours in a day were covered by overlapping shifts—putting twice as many officers on duty during the overlap. This overlap, of course, was programmed to occur during the high-crime peak hours. Although most existing "ten plans" were adopted as a means of raising service levels without increasing the budget, they could also be used as a means of preserving an existing level of service while permitting a budget cut.

The above example illustrates what *analysis* can do to improve public services. Many other examples illustrate the same point. A technique called "work measurement" has been applied to a great variety of municipal jobs—typically bringing 15% to 20% savings. There's no magic to work measurement. Essentially, it involves only taking a careful, objective look at how the work is performed and redesigning the whole process for greater efficiency. The reason work measurement almost invariably produces savings when applied to a public service agency is that the jobs involved have usually not been designed or analyzed before at all—they have just grown, like Topsy, in a haphazard fashion.

Technology is another key to thinking smarter. When a fire department switches from 2½-inch to 4-inch hose, doubling the volume of water a group of men can direct onto a fire, this simple technological improvement has made it possible for the same number of firefighters to accomplish more work. Likewise, a group of adjacent police departments that coordinate their radio frequencies and share the use of a minicomputer to help manage the allocation of patrol forces is able to replace a multitude of dispatch centers with a single one staffed with considerably fewer people.

Unfortunately, examples of thinking smarter in the public sector are relatively rare. The reason why goes back to a point mentioned early in this chapter. Lacking a profit incentive, and virtually guaranteed access to the taxpayers' wallets, local public service agencies have had the luxury of continuing to operate in traditional, inefficient ways.

Until now, that is. Hard-pressed local taxpayers finally seem to have had enough. The initial reaction from local government has been to threaten meat-axe cuts that will cause taxpayers to repent the error of their ways. But, as we've just seen, numerous innovative means exist to deliver quality services to local citizens—at less cost. In the chapters that follow, we'll explore the application of our three principles—privatization, user charges, and thinking smarter—to the principal agencies of local government. And the results, as you will see, can be quite impressive: in terms of savings, efficiency, and better living.

3

Police

The police department is the most fundamental city agency, representing the ultimate power of government to enforce certain rules within its areas of jurisdiction. Because of this, and because of people's fear of crime, the police budget tends to be virtually immune to questioning by economy-minded citizens.

This insulation is unfortunate because law enforcement, like any other service, is essentially a business activity. It requires allocating scarce resources, setting priorities, and controlling costs. Without this kind of businesslike orientation, a police department can consume huge amounts of resources while accomplishing very little. During the past decade police budgets have frequently doubled, tripled, or quadrupled, far outstripping the rate of inflation. And as every citizen knows, the crime rate has continued to climb.

Cushioned by this sacred-cow atmosphere and guaranteed access to tax money, police departments have operated largely on the basis of myths and intuition. Recent research has tested many of the assumptions on which policing has been based. These studies tell us that the capability of the police to prevent and solve crimes is far more limited than commonly supposed. Among the myth-busting findings have been the following:

- Routine preventive patrol in marked police cars has little value, either in preventing crime or in making citizens feel safe. (Police Foundation study in Kansas City, Missouri.[1])
- Cutting seconds or even minutes from the average police response time makes little difference in whether or not a criminal is apprehended. (Studies by the Police Foundation and the National Institute of Law Enforcement and Criminal Justice in Kansas City, Missouri.[2])
- Most serious crimes are solved through information obtained directly

from the victim or witness, rather than from leads developed by detectives. (Nationwide study by Rand Corporation.[3])

- A large number of felony crimes essentially solve themselves based on information given to the responding officer; massive data collection systems (modus operandi files) are probably not worth what they cost. (Stanford Research Institute study.[4])

Our streets are relatively safe and orderly *not* because of a massive police presence but because of the ordinary mechanisms of social control employed in daily life by the people who live there. The police serve basically in a back-up role, to apprehend (where possible) those who forcibly interfere with the lives and property of others. To expect them to do much more is to embark on an endless quest for higher budgets that can produce little in the way of tangible results.

When police departments are taken off their pedestal and are looked at from this more realistic perspective, the police budget becomes an area in which significant economies are possible. At the same time, communities can be safer if citizens *themselves* get involved rather than naively expecting the police to do everything.

WHO SHOULD PAY?

All of us benefit in a vague, generalized way from having criminals apprehended and brought to justice. But if we remove from consideration the now questionable crime-prevention function, then we can see that most police activities (investigation, arrests, etc.) involve specific crimes with specific victims—that is, identifiable beneficiaries of police action. Much police activity, we find, is not really a public good after all.

That being the case, it is legitimate to question the idea of all police services being provided by the government and funded by tax money. It becomes worthwhile to identify and separate out as many of the specialized services as possible, reducing the tax-funded part to a minimum. In this way, those who benefit from a particular specialized service can be asked to pay for it, whether it is provided by the city police or by some other body. In other words, we can introduce *user charges* into policing, with all the benefits we noted in Chapter 2.

People are already starting to pay for specific police services. Dissatisfied with the protection they receive from the city police department, residents of numerous New York neighborhoods are hiring security firms or setting up their own citizen patrol units. Typical of the latter is the East Midwood Patrol in Brooklyn. Its 120 members volunteer their time to offer all-night patrol, 365 days a year. Their main efforts involve teaching householders good security practices, along with watching for prowlers and muggers from their patrol car. If trouble is spotted, they contact the city police via CB radio. Crime in East Midwood dropped sharply after the Patrol began operations. The Patrol asks all households in the 25-block area to donate $10 a year toward patrol expenses—and 85% of them pay. Out of some 39,000 city blocks in New York City, 10,000 have functioning block associations, aimed at compensating for inadequate city services. Nearly all include some kind of security patrol.

The Rand Corporation has found that similar citizen patrols have been organized since 1970 in Boston, Baltimore, St. Louis, Chicago, San Jose, and Norfolk. Others, partly spawned by racial troubles in the 1960s, exist in such cities as Newark, Detroit, Washington, New Orleans, and Los Angeles. Many block associations in these cities hire professional security guard companies at annual fees of $125 per household. Many affluent suburbs likewise hire private patrols, via their homeowners' associations. One example is wealthy Rancho Santa Fe, north of San Diego. Its six-member patrol, organized in 1976 because county sheriff's patrols were deemed inadequate by residents, boasts a computerized dispatch center equipped with the "911" emergency telephone system.

Over time, the net effect of these private patrol activities—whether paid or volunteer—is to reduce the demand for city police services and therefore to reduce the police budget. What occurs is a transfer of the patrol function from the public sector to the private sector, leaving the investigation and apprehension functions largely in the city's hands.

Perhaps the most extensive example of such a transfer occurs in San Francisco. Stretched across the city's northern section are 62 private police beats, "owned" by private police officers who are paid by their customers— the businesses, apartment owners, and homeowners.[5] The "Patrol Specials," as the officers are called, receive a complete police academy training, carry guns, and have full arrest powers. But they are fully private entrepreneurs who receive not a penny of tax money. Instead, once a Special "purchases" a beat (from its previous "owner")—generally for ten times its monthly revenue—it is up to him to negotiate contracts with as many of the beat's property owners as wish to purchase his services. Depending on what is provided, the fees can range from $10 to $1,000 per month.

Some customers, such as the Japan Trade Center, want and pay for 24-hour-a-day foot patrol. Others want only periodic drive-by checks. Special Roger Levit charges homeowners from $10 to $20 a month to watch a house while the occupants are on vacation—rotating house lights, taking in newspapers and mail, etc. For another $30 his men will make regular on-foot backyard checks. Small retail stores may pay as little as $35 a month, while a large apartment house wanting three to six nightly inspections may pay $450.

The San Francisco system thus provides a vast diversity of police services, tailored to the needs of the individual customers who pay for what they want. As in most big cities, the city's own police force has its hands full trying to apprehend serious criminals. The taxpayers can neither afford to provide the specialized patrol services, nor should they have to. The user-pays principle is far more equitable. And in San Francisco it has stood the test of time. The city's private beats date back to the city's beginnings in the 1850s, and were formalized in its 1899 city charter.

In most conventionally policed cities, the idea of user charges is not completely unheard of. Many departments charge for funeral escorts, crowd control at large special events, directing traffic in front of large commercial and industrial developments, serving civil papers, and taking fingerprints. Each of these services has a specific beneficiary. The existence of user charges in these areas sets a precedent for extending the user-pays principle into every other area where a beneficiary can be identified. And as we have seen, this includes a large portion of all police activity.

PRIVATE CONTRACTING

In many cases it may not be politically feasible, at this time, to shift large portions of police activity to a user-pays basis. But the cost of policing may still be reduced, by having the city purchase the service from the private sector. Tax money would still be involved, but the efficiency with which the service is produced may well be greater than if the city police did the job. Because a private firm must *compete* for the business—either against the city police or against other firms—it has a much greater incentive to think up more efficient ways of operating.

There are many firms able and willing to provide some form of police service. The private security industry—typified by industry leaders Burns, Globe, Pinkerton's, and Wackenhut—has grown very rapidly over the past decade. As of 1979, estimates of the number of private security people in uniform ranged from 500,000 to over 1 million, compared with around 500,000 state and local police. The private security industry is growing at a rate of 11% to 12% a year, and the two largest firms grossed $215 million (Pinkerton's) and $200 million (Burns) in 1978. Despite the professionalism of the larger firms, there are still enough security firms employing poorly trained, low-paid people to give the industry something of a bad reputation. A 1971 Rand Corporation report[6] documented these problems as of 1970. The industry has come a long way since then, as competition, stricter regulation, and increasing customer sophistication have put many of the slipshod operators out of business. Recognizing the industry's progress, and the tremendous need for more resources in the fight against crime, the administrator of the Law Enforcement Assistance Administration several years ago called for a partnership between local government and the private security industry.

This partnership has gotten under way in the past few years in a number of large cities. The most common pattern has been for a city to hire a security firm to perform some particular task which requires a higher level of service than can be provided with expensive city police officers. Thus, Lexington, Kentucky, hired one such company to patrol its high-crime housing projects. St. Petersburg, Florida, hired a guard service to patrol its parks. Houston has a private firm guarding its city hall area. Most cities have hired private security firms to provide the security inspections at their airports.

A similar trend has also been occurring in West Germany, especially in

Bavaria. Various government agencies have hired private firms to provide security services at the Olympic Park grounds, the various university sports arenas, and a huge mental hospital in the suburbs of Munich. In addition, private police patrol the stations of Munich's new subway system.

Most German private police are armed, as are many (but not all) American ones. But very few American private police have the authority to make arrests—other than a citizen's arrest. Lacking arrest authority, they can still carry out such activities as patrol and investigation, leaving formal arrests to the city police force. But in a few cases, private firms have begun sending their employees to city or state police academies for training, so that they can be "sworn in" as full-fledged peace officers with arrest powers. (Until recently, the San Francisco Patrol Specials were the only private police with arrest authority.) Once its officers are sworn in as peace officers, a private firm can compete with government police agencies for a city's entire police business.

Just such a competition took place in Arizona in 1975. Officials of the newly incorporated city of Oro Valley were not interested in setting up their own city police force, preferring instead to hire outside expertise. During its first year as an incorporated city, Oro Valley had received nearly all its services from Pima County under contract. After that year was up, the city and the county could not agree on a price for continuation of patrol service by the county sheriff's department. Rural/Metro Fire Department, Inc., which was already providing fire service in Oro Valley, offered to provide police patrol for $35,000 a year. When its offer was accepted in July 1975, the company began providing the service, using six officers. Three were already certified as police officers under state law, having transferred from police departments in other cities. The other three were planning to enroll in the Arizona Law Enforcement Officers Association Council (ALEOAC) training program within the required six-month period. Unfortunately, when they attempted to do so, ALEOAC refused to accept them because they did not work for a government agency. Rural/Metro appealed to the state attorney general—who upheld ALEOAC in February 1976. As a result, the officers had to be officially hired by the city, though the company continued to operate the department as a management contractor.

There are several other instances of cities contracting for complete police services. Guardsmark, Inc., one of the industry's larger firms, has provided policing under contract for the town of Buffalo Creek, West Virginia. In 1976 it held discussions with Del Mar, California, about replacing that city's contract with the San Diego County Sheriff's Department, but the city decided to continue with the sheriff after reaching more agreeable contract terms. The Wackenhut Corporation (which has the most extensive private sector experience with police work) provides the entire police force for the Energy Research and Development Administration's 1,600-square-mile Mercury Test Site in Nevada. Its officers carry out patrol, traffic, investigation, and technical security duties for this huge nuclear weapons test area. Wackenhut also provides full police services at the

Kennedy Space Center in Florida, along with fire and rescue services. In addition, it has had contracts to police three separate jurisdictions in Florida. One contract, with the village of Indian Creek, provided a 15-person police department for five years. At the end of that period, for reasons of "civic pride," city officials hired the officers as permanent city employees, constituting a regular city police force.

Whether full-fledged private contracting for police services will become more prevalent remains to be seen. To date, it appears to have been confined either to government installations or to very small cities which wanted a "real" police force but didn't yet feel able to provide one. What seems to be involved is an attitude problem—that somehow only government should be providing police services and that private firms are at best a temporary expedient or a supplement. Yet the San Francisco experience clearly proves otherwise. Guardsmark chairman Ira Lipman says he is confident his company may be operating full-fledged police forces under contract to cities within ten years. He may well be right.

ECONOMIES OF SCALE

One of the problems many smaller cities face is that certain aspects of a police department are expensive in relation to the total police budget. There is far more to a police department than just officers and cars. Twenty-four-hour-a-day telephone answering and radio dispatching is needed, as well as a training program, a crime lab, and some sort of holding facility for prisoners. Small towns and cities frequently can't afford such items, which in larger cities make up a much smaller proportion of the total police budget.

The fact that there are economies of scale in *some* areas of law enforcement has led many people to advocate the consolidation of smaller departments into large-scale regional police departments. This, they say, will take advantage of these inherent economies of larger size and will provide for a more professional and better-equipped force. Thus, citizens will get better—and cheaper—law enforcement. Among the prestigious bodies urging police consolidation were the 1967 President's Commission on Law Enforcement and the Administration of Justice and the 1973 National Advisory Commission on Criminal Justice Standards and Goals.

Here again, we are apparently facing a case of policy recommendations based more on myth than on hard facts. Everybody "just knew" that small police departments are inefficient and unprofessional. Until, that is, somebody started doing some actual research on the question. In 1972 Elinor Ostrom and four other political scientists studied police services in the Indianapolis metropolitan area.[7] Although most of the Marion County public services were merged with those of Indianapolis in 1969, creating Unigov, police services were not consolidated. The area thus included the three small departments of Beech Grove, Lawrence, and Speedway (all cities of from 13,000 to 16,000 people), together with the large Indianapolis Police Department. Ostrom and her associates selected three neighborhoods within Indianapolis that were as similar as possible (in housing, land use, population, etc.) with the three small cities, and compared the cost and quality of police services in each. They found that on every measure in their surveys the citizens of the small cities felt better served than the residents of comparable areas in Indianapolis. However, the per capita cost of policing in Indianapolis was almost *double* that of the small cities—$21.33 against an average of $12.76 in the small cities.

Other studies have come up with similar results. Samir IsHak compared police performance and cost in Grand Rapids, Michigan, with that of three nearby small cities, with essentially the same results.[8] Another study by Ostrom compared police performance in three black neighborhoods in Chicago and two independent black communities in southern Cook County—Phoenix and East Chicago Heights.[9] Although the cost of service within Chicago was 14 times greater, the residents of the independent communities expressed equal satisfaction with their police service—and actually rated their police higher in terms of honesty, fairness, and trustworthiness. Ostrom and Dennis C. Smith went on to study police cost and performance in the St. Louis metropolitan area, where they surveyed residents in 44 neighborhoods served by 29 jurisdictions.[10] They found that on nearly every performance measure, the *larger* the department the *lower* it scored. They found *no* evidence of larger size being linked with lower costs and, indeed, found major *diseconomies* in areas larger than 250,000 because of the increased cost of administering such a large organization.

Thus, consolidating small departments into a large metropolitan police agency will more than likely create a large bureaucratic department that provides *less* service at a *higher* cost than the small departments it replaces. This does not mean that *all* small departments are necessarily efficient. *Very* small departments may not be able to afford such costly features as 24-hour dispatching or even 24-hour patrol service. In these cases, some form of consolidation may make sense.

In York County, Pennsylvania, for example, five small communities ranging in size from 380 to 10,500 formed the Northern County Regional Police Department in 1972. Prior to the consolidation three of the five had no police department at all, relying on on-call service from the state police, and one had on-call service from a neighboring police department. The consolidated department now provides 24-hour service in all five communities, at a greater cost than before (for a higher level of service) but at less cost than any of them could have managed on its own.

Many small and medium-size cities are consolidating, not entire police *departments*, but only the costly support services—dispatching, record systems, crime labs, jails. This type of *functional* consolidation provides the promised cost savings of economies of scale without giving up the small department's autonomy and responsiveness to local needs—and without creating a costly administrative structure.

Dispatching, which requires 24-hour manning, expensive equipment, and a secure facility, can often be done far more economicaly on a shared basis. Five small cities in Texas—Port Neches, Groves, Nederland, Pear Ridge, and Griffin Park—set up a joint dispatch system in 1971. The cities pay for the system on the basis of their relative populations. A similar arrangement was set up in 1969 among eight police departments in Muskegon County, Michigan. Prior to the Centralized Police Dispatch program, only three of the departments could afford 24-hour communications, though among them they employed 19 uniformed officers as dispatchers. Today, after a 1972 reorganization, the program operates a modern 24-hour-a-day dispatch center with five radio frequencies and eight incoming 911 telephone lines. The use of civilian dispatchers combined with the economies inherent in a shared system have reduced personnel costs by 42%. The eight agencies pay for the system in accordance with a formula based on population, assessed valuation, and calls for service. A similar eight-city dispatching system is under development in the South Bay area of Los Angeles County, including the cities of Inglewood, El Segundo, and Redondo Beach.

Dodge City and Ford County, Kansas, have combined their law enforcement dispatching, records system, and headquarters into one facility, as well as their courts and jails. In Connecticut, 14 police departments, including New Haven's, have developed a computerized regional information system known as the Case Incident Reporting System (CIRS). The system allows officers in each department complete access to the records on cases and individuals of all the other participating departments. This saves a great deal of time and effort, improving the investigative capabilities of each one. It also provides for automatic preparation of statistical reports for management information purposes. The three Illinois cities of Batavia, Geneva, and St. Charles established a joint emergency dispatch center for all emergency services (police, fire, ambulance) in 1976. That consolidation was so successful that in 1979 they announced plans for a joint headquarters building. While the three departments will remain autonomous, they will share a central records system, training facilities, detention cells, locker rooms, and vault and evidence rooms. The cities each expect to save about $30,000 a year by this move.

Yet another way for a small or medium-size city to obtain high-quality, responsive law enforcement at reasonable cost is similar to private contracting, except that the city contracts with a nearby, larger police department. The best-known example of police contracting is the "Lakewood Plan" in Los Angeles County. When the city of Lakewood incorporated in 1954, its founding fathers negotiated a contract with the County Sheriff's Department to provide a specified level and type of police services, for an agreed-upon price, on a year-to-year basis. The cost was far less than the cost of setting up a whole new police department. This fact was not lost on other incorporating cities in the area. Today there are 29 cities in Los Angeles County obtaining service under contract from the Sheriff. And the idea has spread to 16 other counties in California, with a total of 61 cities under contract. Similar contract service exists in Atlanta, where the city police department provides contract policing to areas in surrounding Fulton County. In Connecticut the state police provide contract policing for 46 towns under that state's "resident trooper" plan. Other states where contract law enforcement takes place include New York, New Jersey, Pennsylvania, Maryland, Wisconsin, Michigan, Minnesota, and Illinois. The one city in Illinois policed under contract is Burbank, a suburb of Chicago. Its 31-officer force from the Cook County Sheriff's Department costs $800,000 a year. Independent studies have estimated that for Burbank to have its own 31-officer department the cost would be $1.2 million—50% more.

Contract law enforcement usually saves money, because the larger agency can spread the costs of support services over many users. In addition, the departments that provide contract services usually price their service at the *marginal cost* of providing additional cars and officers, rather than including a fully allocated share of their overhead expenses. Thus, even though a large metropolitan sheriff's department may be costly to its own constituents, it can save money for those fortunate enough to deal with it on a contractual basis.

Besides saving money, the purchasing city retains control over the level of service provided. The basic unit of patrol service is a patrol car on 24-hour duty, seven days a week. The contract city can purchase any multiple or fraction of this basic unit. Rather than coping with a bureaucracy in its own city government (which *must* be supported every year), the city is dealing at arm's length with a supplier of services—which must be responsive or lose the business. The supplier agency therefore has an incentive to operate efficiently and provide the type of service desired by the purchasing city. The city always has the option of not renewing the contract and either setting up its own police department or seeking an alternative supplier. A small city in a large metropolitan area may be able to choose among several nearby cities, the county sheriff, or a private firm.

THINKING SMARTER

Significant savings can be achieved in police departments by thinking smarter. Some departments are beginning to take advantage of recent research findings and methods of analysis. A few of the many examples will give a sense of what is possible.

What a department decides about its police cars can result in cost differences of up to 100% between otherwise similar departments. One of the most important factors is whether to assign *one* or *two* officers per car. For the same total number of on-duty patrol units, a two-man-car department will spend 100% more on field officer salaries than one using one man per car. Until recently, controversy simmered over the relative adequacy of one-man cars. Many people assumed that two-man cars meant officers would be more efficient in dealing with incidents, less likely to be attacked, and less likely to behave in ways that could lead to citizen complaints.

But all these apparently obvious points turn out to be incorrect. In 1977, the Police Foundation released the results of an intensive study of one-versus two-man patrol cars in San Diego.[11] City police were divided into 22 one-man and 22 two-man cars, and assigned evenly throughout the city. Careful records were kept on all aspects of their operations for one year. Police Foundation president Patrick Murphy summed up the results this way: ". . . clearly and unequivocally it is more efficient, safer, and at least as effective for the police to staff patrol cars with one officer." Significantly, the total annual cost to the San Diego department was 83% greater for a two-man car.

Overall performance of the units was about the same, in terms of calls for service and officer-initiated activity. The only differences were that the two-man units wrote somewhat more traffic tickets and that one-man units received notably *fewer* citizen complaints about the way they handled incidents. The overall efficiency of the one-man units was greater. They did require back-up assistance more often, but not nearly enough to justify having the second man in the car to begin with. As far as officer safety is concerned, there were actually fewer cases of resisting arrest and assaults on officers in one-man units. The San Diego study thus demonstrates that one-man units are clearly preferable, unless a city's crime conditions are so hazardous that one-man back-up units would be needed most of the time.

Using compacts rather than full-size sedans for patrol cars can result in savings of 33% per year in vehicle operating costs. This has also been a controversial idea. Although a number of cities have made the switch, others have held back, feeling that compacts were somehow not adequate for police work. But this reservation, too, has been shown to lack merit.

In 1977 the Los Angeles Sheriff's Department conducted a detailed evaluation of eight police sedans. Three were full-size, two were intermediates, and three were compacts. All were 1977 models. Specialist Reserve Deputy John Christy, who is also executive editor of *Motor Trend* magazine, devised the testing procedure of seven separate evaluations. There was a slow- and high-speed performance and handling trial, conducted by test drivers, and an instrumented performance run. Other tests included a fuel economy run, a comprehensive mechanical evaluation to rate the ease of maintenance, a human factors check, and a radio suitability test.

When all eight cars had been rated, the clear-cut winner was the Chevy Nova, a compact. The next two vehicles, nearly tied, were the Pontiac LeMans and the AMC Matador, both intermediates. Only one full-size car finished in the top five and that was a 1977 Pontiac Catalina—one of GM's "downsized" standard sedans. Careful design of the test by the department assured that the highest scoring vehicle would be "not only the best-suited but also the most cost-effective," according to LASD Captain W. F. Kennedy. In previous experience with 1975 and 1976 Novas, the department found that total operating costs, including fuel, tires, and maintenance, averaged less than 8 cents per mile—a far cry from the 12-13 cents that many departments were paying for full-size sedans.

A potential money-saving vehicle approach is the take-home police car. Instead of buying only as many patrol cars as there are beats—and using them essentially 24 hours a day—the department buys a car for each and every patrol officer. A specific car is permanently assigned to each one, and the officers are encouraged to commute to and from the job in the patrol car. Since the cars are in use only 8 to 9 hours a day, instead of 24, they last *much* longer—up to four years instead of only one. Over a period of years, therefore, a take-home car department will need to buy fewer cars than a conventional department.

A number of police and sheriff's departments have tried out this idea, and many of them are reaping benefits over and above the initial cost saving. The Sheriff's Department in Whatcom County, Washington, for example, has found that its deputies take much better care of their "personal" cars, leading to less wear and tear that's reflected in much lower maintenance costs. Other benefits include greater visibility of the police force and possible deterrent effects of a more widespread dispersal of police cars in the community. Departments now using the take-home concept include Prince George's County, Maryland; Portsmouth, Ohio; St. Paul, Minnesota; Indianapolis, Indiana; Lexington, Kentucky; and Albuquerque, New Mexico.

But the evidence is not all positive on whether take-home cars are always money-savers. A lot depends on how much better the cars are maintained under this approach and on whether off-duty officers refrain from extensive personal use of the car (which would make it wear out sooner). A study by the National Bureau of Standards[12] concluded that take-home car programs could easily end up costing more than the conventional approach. It suggested that much of the reported saving may have been due to inadequate cost analysis by the departments involved.

The same report analyzed the cost effectiveness of contracting out police vehicle maintenance. Based on a number of assumptions (including an in-house labor cost only two-thirds as high as that of private shops), the analysis found that for fleets of 90 cars or smaller, it is less expensive to contract the maintenance to an outside supplier. If the labor costs are about the same, even fleets of 100 or more cars can be maintained for less money via contracting. That's because the police department could do without the large investment in facilities and equipment (which the private firm can amortize over all its customers).

Vehicles, though, are not the major police department expense—people are. Over 90% of a typical police department budget consists of salaries and fringe benefits. Thus, most measures for economizing must in some way reduce personnel costs. There are many ways of doing so.

Many departments are using increased numbers of civilians. Switching to civilians can reduce costs for two reasons. First, many police tasks are not dangerous and do not require the skill and training typical of sworn officers. Hence, lower-paid employees may be used in these positions. Second, even when the task would require an equivalent salary level, most cities provide higher-level fringe benefits (as much as 50% higher) for sworn personnel that they do for civilians. Replacement of an officer by a civilian thus saves money even at identical salary levels.

Civilians are now playing an important role in dispatching operations. Frequently, when a city sets up a new dispatching center combining police and fire dispatching under the "911" emergency telephone number concept, uniformed dispatchers of the separate departments are replaced with civilians. Such systems have been set up recently in Seattle and in Monterey County, California, and civilianization of complaint-board and radio-operator positions in the Los Angeles Police Department is estimated to yield annual savings of $735,000. Among the police departments which have switched to civilian dispatchers are those of Huntington Beach and Garden Grove, California, and Phoenix, Arizona.

In Fort Lauderdale, Florida, civilians have been hired to investigate traffic accidents and enforce traffic laws. Through the Selective Traffic Enforcement Program (STEP), the 16 civilian traffic-safety aides have been empowered by the state legislature to issue traffic citations. An additional benefit of the program is that it has relieved police officers of 75% of the tedious and time-consuming traffic work.

A large percentage of the time of a typical police officer goes to activities of a public service nature. These duties reduce the time each officer has for crime control work and can thereby lead to employing more officers than the level of crime requires. Some cities are coping with this problem by hiring civilian aides to relieve sworn officers of much of this workload. The Scottsdale, Arizona, Police Department has developed a Police Assistant (PA) program in which 18- to 20-year-old civilians respond in patrol cars to noncrime calls for service. The assistants must meet the same entry requirements as officers but receive only about half the hours of training. Scottsdale's PA program has become the department's primary source of new recruits. Over its first six years in operation, 37 PAs became regular police officers. The department's present 13 PAs save about $100,000 and 2,500 man-hours per year, compared with having regular officers carry out PA duties.

In Miami, Florida, a similar program recruits 19- and 20-year-olds as Public Service Aides (PSAs). After a ten-week classroom training course, the PSAs go through seven weeks of in-service training with a senior officer before receiving street assignments. The PSAs handle traffic at accident sites, write reports, refer citizens to various public agencies, perform first aid, and carry out crime prevention programs. In 1975 PSAs handled 80% of the calls received by the department. A survey by the Law Enforcement Assistance Administration (LEAA) of eight such community service officer (CSO) programs found that the average cost of employing CSOs was 49% less than that of employing regular officers.

Cutting down on the hundreds or thousands of hours that officers typically spend in court waiting to testify as witnesses can reduce the need for sworn officers. Tacoma, Washington, reschedules traffic cases according to which officers are required as witnesses, to allow an officer to testify in several cases on the same day. Fort Lauderdale has assigned a court liaison officer to the prosecutor's office. Officers are allowed to remain on call with the liaison officer and don't have to spend all day in court waiting for their cases to be heard.

Similar reductions can be made by scheduling patrol shifts more in accordance with varying demands for service. Since the evening hours usually generate far more calls than other times of day, a number of departments have adopted overlapping shift plans to increase the number of on-duty officers in the evening without increasing the size of the force. Often such plans involve changing to ten-hour shifts—hence the designation "ten plans." In North Charleston, South Carolina, such a plan was begun in 1973. The 24-hour day is divided into three ten-hour shifts: one from 6 A.M. to 4 P.M., a second from 4 P.M. to 2 A.M., and the third from 8 P.M. to 6 A.M. Thus, between 8 P.M. and 2 A.M. the number of officers on duty is doubled. Every officer is assigned to one of five squads, which works either four or five ten-hour shifts per week, averaging a 42-hour work week. A similar plan has been in operation in Huntington Beach, California, since 1970. Officer acceptance is high, and there are indications that the increased nighttime manning reduces crime and permits better response to calls for service.

Another way to hold down the need for officers is to exercise greater discipline in assigning officers to calls. Some departments still send out patrol cars to virtually every type of call, regardless of how trivial. Others have begun defining specific dispatch priority systems, which provide, in many cases, for taking a report over the telephone instead of dispatching a unit. A system of this kind is in use in the combined dispatch center operated by the City of Portland (Oregon) and Multnomah County. Each dispatcher is given a manual setting forth in detail the types of calls for which units are to be dispatched and those for which reports are to be taken by phone. By having routine reports and other matters taken over the phone, this policy frees police units for crime fighting and other emergency matters—and thereby reduces the need for additional officers.

The innovations discussed here are disarmingly simple. Yet most have been adopted in only a handful of police departments and only in the last five to ten years. Why? Unfortunately, police departments—like government agencies generally—are very resistant to change. Insulated from outside scrutiny by a public which is awed by the importance of police work, and therefore immune from budgetary pressure, police departments all too frequently have continued to operate in the same manner, year after year, decade after decade. And that insulation from criticism is on top of the inherent disadvantage, shared with other government agencies, of lacking the profit-and-loss incentives of the private marketplace, which *force* a business to adapt and innovate—or die. Today's tax revolt has the potential to motivate some fresh thinking in our police departments. The more that policing can be operated like a business—which, in fact, it is— the better off all of us will be, both as citizens seeking relief from crime and as taxpayers.

4

Criminal Justice

Once someone has been arrested, various agencies of local government have the responsibility of deciding what to do with him or her. The agencies involved in this process—the sheriff's department, prosecutor's office, public defender, the courts, probation department, and jail—are referred to as the criminal justice system. Their job is to assess the guilt or innocence of the suspect and, if guilty, to impose and carry out an appropriate sentence.

It is necessary to gain some perspective on this system's limitations before discussing ways to make it more efficient. For the fact is, the criminal justice system deals with only a small fraction of all criminals. Research conducted by the author in Alameda County, California, illustrates this point. In 1973 there were 98,218 felonies reported to the police in that county. Since victimization studies conducted by LEAA and the U.S. Census Bureau show that actual crime is two to three times greater than reported crime, we can estimate actual felonies at 245,545. For all these crimes, the police arrested only 13,695 adults and 6,798 juveniles. Of the 13,695 adults, the police released 2,377 on grounds of insufficient evidence, requested misdemeanor complaints against 1,315, and requested actual felony complaints against 10,043. But the district attorney's office found that in only 4,946 of the felony cases was there sufficient evidence to warrant felony prosecution. Of these 4,946, the municipal court dismissed or processed as misdemeanants 2,714, sending only 2,232 to superior court for felony trials. Of these, 1,656 were convicted of felonies—that means 12% of those arrested as felons, 1.7% of all reported felonies, or 0.7% of all actual felonies.

Although a felony is defined as a crime punishable by imprisonment in the state prison system, only 329 of those 1,656 went to prison. A few were sentenced to state youth authority facilities or to mental institutions, but 1,172 received local (misdemeanor-type) sentences—about half went to jail for less than a year plus probation, 62 got straight jail terms, 3 got off with fines, and about half received only probation.

These figures are fairly typical. A 1977 study by the Institute for Law and Social Research (ILSR) found that fewer than 30% of felony arrestees in Washington, D.C., were convicted, either as felons *or* as misdemeanants.[1] Similar results were obtained in a District of Columbia Bar Association study of nine jurisdictions across the country. The biggest single cause of the high dropout rate is lack of evidence that will stand up in court. Brian Forst, chief investigator of the ILSR study, summed up the situation as follows: "It is likely to be difficult for many persons to see how justice is done in a system in which the majority of offenders are not arrested, the majority of the arrestees are not convicted, and the majority of convicted defendants are not incarcerated." Yet that is exactly the kind of system we have.

Beyond providing low odds of a criminal getting caught or being punished, the system has several other major shortcomings. Studies of deterrence show that to be effective in deterring future criminal acts, it is far more important that the imposition of legal sanctions be swift and certain rather than harsh. Yet the criminal justice system is neither swift nor certain. Delay in processing cases is the rule, not the exception. Cases drag on for months because of legal technicalities and bureaucratic incompetence. Worse still, there is little or no consistency within the system. Even within the same county a defendant's probability of being prosecuted as a felon, misdemeanant, or not at all—or of being sentenced to prison, jail, or just probation—depends mostly on which particular district attorney deputy and which particular judge deals with the case. In one study, the Rand Corporation found that "there are large disparities within Los Angeles County in the exercise of prosecutorial discretion and in the disposition of felony defendants . . . the large differences should be cause for concern . . . because they mean that justice is not meted out evenhandedly in the county."[2]

In short, we have a criminal justice system that is not doing its job effectively. The chances of a criminal getting caught or being punished are very low. If he or she is caught, justice is slow and inconsistent. The costs to taxpayers of this system are quite high, and, as we shall see, unnecessarily so. One of the results of all this is that the crime rate continues to rise and people feel less and less safe.

At first glance one would assume that to reduce the "costs" of a large criminal population we must spend far more on the criminal justice system. In fact, however, there are many ways in which the direct cost of the system can be *reduced*, while at the same time *increasing* its effectiveness. Here are some of the basic elements of such a strategy:

- Reduce the system's scope of concern, eliminating trivia and limiting it to serious criminal matters.

- Increase the efficiency with which it operates, by using modern management methods.
- Make justice swift and sure.
- Make the users (i.e., the criminals) pay the costs, wherever possible.

We'll examine these elements in the sections to follow.

REDUCING THE SYSTEM'S SCOPE

One reason that the police catch so few real criminals and our courts are so backlogged is that a large proportion—estimates range from 30% to 50%—of the efforts and resources of the criminal justice system are directed at people who merely annoy or offend other people but have not caused actual harm to persons or property. These people are the victims of our so-called victimless crime laws—laws which make it a crime to engage in voluntary acts that violate the rights of no one. Thus, a system intended to protect people from aggressions against their persons or property must spend huge amounts of time and money arresting and prosecuting prostitutes, dope smokers, bingo players, and dirty-book sellers. A study by the author found that a medium-size California county spent $6.3 million of its $19-million annual criminal justice budget—33%—dealing with victimless crimes.

Over the past decade numerous criminal justice authorities have called for decriminalization of most or all of these crimes—as a matter of simple justice as well as to free additional resources for dealing with real crimes. Among the groups supporting decriminalization of some or all of these "crimes" are the National Council on Crime and Delinquency, the National Advisory Commission on Criminal Justice Standards and Goals, the American Medical Association, and the American Bar Association. Various civic organizations have picked up on this theme, including the San Francisco Committee on Crime and the Alliance for a Safer New York. Even in the highly emotional area of hard drugs, most of these authorities agree that making drugs illegal simply creates a highly profitable black market—and leads to additional real crime as some percentage of addicts find they must steal to support their habits. Increasing numbers of judges and attorneys privately support complete decriminalization of all drugs.

Unfortunately, the criminal law is defined by state legislatures, not by city or county officials. But this does not mean local officials' hands are tied. It is possible to formulate and implement a coherent policy of downgrading victimless crimes to the lowest level of priority, by using the legally available discretion built into the criminal justice system. For example, in 1971 the Los Angeles district attorney's office began filing all marijuana possession cases as misdemeanors rather than felonies (as permitted by state law). As a result, there were 10,000 fewer felony cases filed in 1971/72 than in the previous year—a reduction of 25%. Those victimless crime cases still winding up in court can receive minimum rather than maximum sentences (e.g., small fines rather than incarceration).

Changes of this kind save money by tying up less of the system's resources; those resources can either be shifted to serious crimes *or* be reflected in budget cuts. Either way, the citizen/taxpayer will be better off. Citizens concerned about justice and economy should demand this kind of policy from their local officials, while urging their legislatures to repeal the victimless crime laws.

Another way of reducing the costs of courts and corrections is *diversion*. In the past decade a number of cities and counties have set up programs that divert first-time offenders from formal criminal processing to less costly alternatives. What happens is that the prosecutor's office agrees to refrain from pressing charges if the defendant agrees to participate in some form of educational or rehabilitative program. If he or she completes the program successfully, all charges are dropped and the record of arrest is erased or sealed. If he or she refuses, regular criminal proceedings can be resumed. The advantage to the defendant is the chance to avoid the stigma of a criminal record. The advantage to the criminal justice system—and the taxpayer—is avoidance of all the costs of prosecution and corrections. Diversion has been used for many kinds of juvenile offenses, for drunk driving, for many minor misdemeanors, and for a number of victimless crimes, especially drug possession.

Typical of diversion projects is The Court Resource Project (TCRP). TCRP operates in 13 district courts in three Boston-area counties. Each day project personnel review the day's arraignment list for detainees between 17 and 22 years of age who have committed misdemeanors or minor felonies. Those meeting certain criteria receive a 14-day continuance of the arraignment, during which counselors attempt to work out a service plan featuring work, school, or some other kind of training. If the plan is accepted by TCRP, the court is asked for a 90-day continuance to allow the plan to be implemented. If the client lives up to the plan, the charges are dropped; if not, he or she is returned to court on the original charges. During a three-year period, of 1,800 clients screened, 1,000 were accepted into the program. At the time of arrest, 68% were unemployed but after 90 days in the program 97% were employed, in school, or in training. Only 8% of those completing the program were rearrested. The cost per client was $1,000, compared with about $12,000 for court processing and incarceration.

Yet another way to reduce costly court processing is to settle various kinds of minor cases outside of court via arbitration. Arbitration is a kind of privatization, which substitutes a voluntary, user-funded settlement process in place of the mandatory, tax-supported one. Spearheading the trend is the American Arbitration Association (founded in 1926). In 1978 the AAA helped settle more than 48,000 disputes, nearly four times as many as a decade earlier. Since the association's founding, whole classes of legal disputes—such as claims between insurance companies and labor contract arbitrations—have been removed from the courts altogether. In the past decade AAA has become increasingly involved in minor criminal and civil disputes: neighborhood fights, juvenile offenses, etc. Its Community Dispute Service is AAA's fastest-growing division, as more and more communities recognize the advantages of bypassing the courts—low cost, rapid settlement, and an atmosphere of conciliation rather than confrontation. In 1976 AAA began offering its services in divorce cases, and it sees a big future in this field as more and more states enact "no-fault" divorce laws.

Another arbitration service is lawyer Carl Person's National Private Court (NPC), based in New York City.[3] Contending that "Court congestion has cost us a loss of our right to a jury trial," Person organized his system for civil case arbitration late in 1977. Designed to operate on a nationwide basis, NPC makes use of the services of experienced attorneys and judges, who serve in a private capacity as its own "judges" and are selected jointly by the parties on the basis of their areas of expertise. Conventional arbitration follows informal procedures and evidence rules; consequently, appeal to the courts is frequently infeasible. NPC follows the federal rules of evidence and civil procedure, to facilitate nationwide operations and permit appeals when necessary (though the submission agreement generally provides only for a one-time private appeal). Litigation, including one appeal, must be completed within three months, compared with several years in the civil court system. NPC currently has 35 judges signed up but has not been able to raise the funds needed to market its services nationwide, as planned.

The success of arbitration as a low-cost speedy alternative to the courts has begun to influence local criminal justice systems, leading to a sort of quasi-privatization within the system. In Minneapolis, domestic and neighborhood disputes may now be resolved without police or court participation thanks to the Citizens Dispute Settling Project. Operating via the city attorney's office, the project aims at settling disputes quickly and nonviolently, with minimum government involvement. Disputes come to the project's attention in one of two ways: Either a participant comes in requesting help or an arrested person may be interviewed in court to determine if the case is one the project can handle. The project will take the case only if both parties voluntarily agree to participate. Each is counseled individually by a trained counselor before being brought together in a mediation session. When a settlement is reached, it is written up as a contract between the parties. Project counselors engage in follow-up, and if either party violates the contract, the case is referred to court for prosecution. A similar project is operating in Orlando, Florida.

In Los Angeles the superior court in 1971 began a voluntary arbitration program for personal injury and other civil cases. Simple arbitration hearings are conducted by volunteer attorneys, thus avoiding jury trial and other costly court proceedings. In its first year the program handled 346 cases and saved nearly $1 million in court costs. San Francisco's courts now offer a similar program.

Yet another arbitration example concerns minor criminal cases. Columbus, Ohio's Night Prosecutor Program diverts misdemeanants before formal arrest charges are filed and allows them to confront their victims in a "mediation-conciliation" process. Most cases referred to the program are interpersonal conflicts involving assault and battery or menacing threats. The confrontation takes place in an administrative hearing staffed by a representative of the city attorney's office and volunteer law students from Capital University. During its first six months the program diverted 1,400 cases, only 18 of which were not resolvable in the informal hearing and had to go on to court. Moreover, once the program had been in operation for a year, the rate of occurrence of crimes like assault and battery actually dropped by 20%.

In short, what is happening in the courts is similar to the situation with citizen patrols (Chapter 3). Citizens are increasingly taking responsibility for routine dispute settlements, shifting this function from the public to the private sector and leaving the criminal justice system with the serious cases. The more types of cases—both civil and criminal—that get shifted to arbitration, the less pressure there will be for bigger court budgets, and the more resources the courts will have to focus on serious criminals.

INCREASING EFFICIENCY AND EFFECTIVENESS

Removing the bulk of minor matters from the courts and narrowing the scope of the criminal law will do a great deal to lessen the courts' burden. But there is much that must also be done to increase the efficiency of the court system. As is true of the police, courts have operated mostly by intuition and tradition. The very concept of *court management* was virtually unheard of a decade ago. In part, this situation stems from the fact that the courts are run by lawyers, and lawyers are trained to think in terms of particulars, not *systems*. (It also stems from the general nature of bureaucratic endeavors, operating outside the discipline of the market, generously supported by tax money.)

But all this has begun to change. Increasing court congestion, the availability of computers and of federal funds, and fortuitous communication between and among enlightened judges, industrial engineers, and systems analysts, has led to a growing acceptance of the need for court management—"thinking smarter" applied to the courts. Despite the fact that the court system's "product" is determining guilt or innocence and specifying a sentence, the mechanics of preparing efficient schedules and matching resources with needs are quite amenable to systems analysis. Thanks to the pioneering efforts of the Institute of Court Management in Denver and various consulting firms, many large and medium-size court systems now employ professional court administrators. And many large court systems are developing computer-based information systems which keep track of cases, provide ready access to all needed records, and assist in producing efficient schedules.

The Los Angeles municipal courts illustrate the improvements that are possible by simple reforms. They cut the waiting time for civil cases from 16 months to only 6–12 weeks. How? The calendaring judge simply made and enforced a rule permitting no more than three continuances. In San Francisco, reform of civil court procedures, including a switch to eight-member civil juries, speeded up civil proceedings so much that four courts previously used for civil cases were transferred to the criminal division. This helped reduce the criminal case backlog by 25%.

Pittsburgh, too, has increased the efficiency of its courts. Its professional court administrator pushed through a number of time-saving reforms, including a tough policy on continuances, pre-selection of Monday morning's jurors on Friday, pre-trial conciliation conferences (which settle 25% of the cases), and last-chance settlement conferences. Even troubled New York City was able to make a major improvement in its court system, thanks to the efforts of the Economic Development Council and a professional court administrator. By designing a new organizational structure with a clear chain of command, ending judge-shopping, and enacting other reforms, the criminal court backlog was cut 58% in ten months.

One of the areas in greatest need is the prosecutor's office. Especially in large cities, inadequate managerial capabilities in the prosecutor's office lead to large numbers of cases being lost needlessly—meaning that the guilty go free. A 1975 study by the U.S. Justice Department showed that in 94% of Washington, D.C., cases dismissed because of an "uncooperative witness," the real cause was foul-ups in the prosecutor's office which prevented the witness from being notified when to appear. This cause accounted for nearly 40% of all dismissals in District of Columbia courts in 1974.

Most large prosecutor's offices work in an assembly-line fashion, due to the massive caseload. Each prosecutor is responsible for cases at a given stage of proceedings. Hence, no one is in overall control of a case from beginning to end. As a result, files get misplaced, witnesses fail to appear, and repeated continuances lead to dismissals. An experienced repeat offender can take advantage of this fragmentation, seeking continuances in hopes that witnesses and attorneys will be inconvenienced and exasperated and hoping that his prior record will go unnoticed. All too often this is exactly what happens.

In the past five years, however, a whole new approach to prosecution has been developed. With federal funding the Institute for Law and Social Research developed a computerized system called PROMIS—Prosecutor's Management Information System.[4] Tested in the District of Columbia courts, it has since been adopted in a number of medium and large cities across the country. PROMIS is used to identify the more serious cases for special attention. It assigns a numerical rating to each case, based on (1) the seriousness of the offense, (2) the seriousness of the defendant's record, (3) the number of times the case has already been delayed, and (4) the prosecutor's initial assessment of the likelihood of conviction. What this does is to select the 15% to 20% who are "bad guys"—experienced criminals who might otherwise slip through the system unnoticed. Their cases are handed over to a Special Litigation Unit—prosecutors who will stay with a case from start to finish.

The results of using PROMIS are impressive. In Washington, cases singled out and handled by the Special Litigation Unit result in conviction 25% more often than average. In New York, where a similar system called MOB (Major Offense Bureau) is in operation, processing time for serious cases has been cut from many months to about eight weeks. Notes Bronx District Attorney Mario Merola, "With MOB the certainty of justice is there—and that's more of a deterrent to crime than a severe sentence."

Besides singling out hard-core criminals, PROMIS offers other benefits. Its computer capabilities automatically produce subpoenas, witness and victim telephone number lists, and notices for expert witnesses, so as to reduce or eliminate scheduling problems. PROMIS monitors the even-handedness and consistency of the decisions made by individual prosecutors, thus enabling the chief prosecutor to keep track of how discretion is being exercised. And it provides extensive data which researchers and policy makers can use to assess the performance of the judicial system.

CORRECTIONS THAT CORRECT

What happens once a criminal has been found guilty is our next consideration. In most cases the criminal is either thrown in jail for a few months or put on probation for several years. In the former case, it means spending 24 hours a day immersed in a criminal subculture, with very little to do, and with room and board paid for by the taxpayers. In the latter case, it means being released back to the conditions from which the criminal came, with instructions to check in every so often at the office of a very overburdened probation officer. Neither type of sentence does much to change the offender's behavior, and both, especially jail, cost the taxpayers a lot of money.

Fortunately, some better alternatives have been developed. One of the first to become popular was work release or work furlough. Under this plan, jail inmates are given assistance in finding jobs in the community. They are released to go to the jobs during the day and they must return to the secure facility at night. In some cases this facility is the jail; in others it is a minimum-security motel-like facility located closer to the jobs.

From his or her employment earnings the inmate pays a percentage to the county for room and board and is allowed to use the after-tax remainder either for family support or as a nest egg. Thus, the taxpayers' burden is relieved because the inmate is at least partially self-supporting. And because he or she has found a job and is earning money, the inmate has something of a stake in society—a motivation to remain out of trouble in the future. In the work-furlough project of Santa Barbara County, California, only 18.7% of those who completed it returned to jail on new charges within a year, compared with a general California recidivism rate of about 40%.

An even more promising concept is *restitution* (payment of compensation by the offender to the victim), an idea that has been largely forgotten in the development of American criminal law. Instead, criminal proceedings have become contests between the State and the criminal, with the victim largely ignored. Any attempt to collect damages from the criminal involves drawn-out criminal proceedings and then, if guilt is pronounced, a time-consuming civil suit—at the victim's own expense. It's no wonder that few victims take the trouble.

But a new wave of restitution programs is changing all that. The heart of such a program is a contract negotiated between the offender and the victim, and sanctioned by the court. As a condition of release from jail, the offender agrees to go to work under supervised conditions, with his or her earnings divided among several uses: compensating the victim, supporting the offender's own family, paying taxes, and defraying the costs of the program.

Some restitution programs operate out of a facility to which the offender must return at night and on weekends. Others, like probation, permit the offender to live at home, under the supervision of a probation officer. Failure to live up to the contractual obligations is grounds for returning the offender to the lockup.

Fortunately, restitution programs appear to be quite successful. The Georgia Department of Offender Rehabilitation began a pilot residential restitution program in 1975. It operated out of four centers located in Albany, Atlanta, Macon, and Rome, each capable of housing 25-30 offenders. Staff at each center provided assistance in finding jobs, did counseling, and assisted in budget planning. In some cases the offenders performed community service work instead of or in addition to gainful employment.

In the first 18 months of the program, the offenders (85% of whom had committed felonies) paid back $127,000 to their victims; paid $242,000 in state and federal taxes; returned $343,000 to the government for their room and board; spent $432,000 in the community on food, clothing, and other expenses; paid $139,000 to support their families; saved $84,000 as nest eggs; and contributed 4,212 hours of unpaid public service work. Fully two thirds of those admitted to the program completed it successfully and were released.

The Georgia program is only one of a series of experimental restitution programs in operation across the country. The Minnesota Restitution Center began operating in Minneapolis in 1972. Like the Georgia program, it experienced a two-thirds success rate with its mostly felony clients. It is now being expanded statewide on a nonresidential basis.

Other restitution programs show similarly encouraging results. For dealing with petty crimes, the Columbus, Ohio, city attorney operates a program in which law students help work out restitution agreements between misdemeanants and their victims. The average cost per case is about $20, compared with $100 for a normal court hearing. A Pima

County, Arizona, project seeks to work out felony restitution contracts without going to court. By doing so it ends up costing only $304 per case, compared with $1,566 to process a normal felony court case.

The benefits of restitution have not been lost on the federal government. In 1977 LEAA parceled out $2 million to seven cities—Boston, Augusta (Maine), Hartford, San Bernardino, Denver, Atlanta, and Portland (Oregon)—to set up pilot programs and test various details. From these programs LEAA has collected extensive documentation on how best to set up such programs and how much they can really save.

Most formal restitution projects have thus far concentrated on crimes involving property loss. But here and there judges have begun applying the idea to crimes against persons, as well. In 1972 Maryland Judge George B. Rasin sentenced a murderer to a life term (eligible for parole in 15 years) with the proviso that upon parole he must pay 40% of his income for the rest of his life to the sons of the woman he killed. In 1973 Miami Judge Dan Satin put a 19-year-old murderer on partial probation so he could support his victim's widow and five children. And in 1977 Judge Clifton Kelley of Sebring, Florida, sentenced a construction worker who had put out another man's eye to pay him either $5,000 or a new eye. He could have received 15 years in prison, but Kelley pointed out that sending him there would help no one, least of all the victim, and would cost the taxpayers money. The potential of restitution is thus very broad.

Restitution represents an application of the user-pays principle to the criminal justice system—with the "user" in this case being the system's "client," the criminal. Yet although restitution offers some relief to the specific *victims* of crime, it does little to unburden the taxpayers, who must still foot the bill for the costs of operating the criminal court system. That is not always the rule in *civil* cases, where the losing party is frequently assessed court costs. (That these user charges often do not represent the fully allocated costs of making use of the courts is yet another area for taxpayer-initiated reform.) To date, it has always been assumed that the taxpayers must assume the full burden of court costs in criminal matters. But once the idea that the criminal is responsible for the costs imposed on the victim is established, the next logical step is to extend the idea to court costs. In March 1979 Los Angeles City Councilman Arthur Snyder suggested just that. In discussing new user fees during city budget hearings, Snyder asked city staff to study the idea of assessing convicted criminals for the costs of arrest and prosecution. Thus far, however, the idea has remained buried within the city's bureaucracy; the City Attorney's Office will say only that it is "studying" the idea.

An additional way of saving taxpayers money is to bring computer systems to probation problems. In a large metropolitan area, with many courts and police departments, a shoplifter can be caught and plead guilty in one community, then while on probation steal again in a nearby city and again plead guilty, repeat the process a third time in another city—and each time be treated leniently as a first offender. Local judges have no way of knowing about the previous offenses. Just this situation was occurring in the Los Angeles area. "The net result is that summary probation and formal (supervised) probation have become a long-standing joke with criminal defendants," says Judge Clarence A. Stromwall of the Los Angeles Municipal Court.

But in 1977 that situation changed dramatically when a new computer system came into being. Called PASS (Probation and Sentencing Subsystem), it provides computer terminals in 31 courthouses throughout the county, giving each one access to up-to-date probation records. PASS lets one court know what another one has done. As a result, instead of treating a probationer as a first offender and holding a trial, the prosecutor need only hold a probation revocation hearing. The cost difference is substantial: about $100 for the hearing, compared with $1,086 for a misdemeanor trial. PASS is expected to avoid an average of 1,610 trials per year, thereby saving the taxpayers $1.3 million annually. In addition to making probation credible, it is expected to act as a deterrent to further crime by those on probation.

There are many ways to make the local criminal justice system less costly and more effective. We have explored some of them here. The system should be restricted in scope to focus on serious crimes, not wasting money enforcing some people's morality on others. Disputes and minor crimes should be shifted from the courts to arbitration. And first-time offenders should be diverted from court if they agree to engage in responsible activities. Courts and prosecutors' offices must be run by skilled administrators, taking full advantage of techniques like systems analysis and special-purpose computer-based information and scheduling systems. Criminal proceedings should be as swift as possible, consistent with due process. Sentences should be consistent and aimed at making offenders responsible to repair the harm they have caused their victims. And where used, probation must be taken seriously, not allowed to become a mere slap on the wrist.

Policies such as these will reduce the cost of crime by reducing recidivism, as well as cutting the financial cost of the criminal justice system. Most important, these changes will help to make each locality a safer place to live.

5

Fire Protection

Most people think of fire protection as a typical public good—a service that must be paid for by taxes and provided by a government agency. But there is far more to fire protection than simply waiting for a fire to occur and then dousing it with water. A great deal of fire protection is inherently a private, rather than a public, responsibility. The way a building is designed, built, and maintained is important. The owner's investment in protective features (e.g., alarms, sprinkers) has a great deal to do with the probability and seriousness of fires. As we noted in Chapter 2, analysts like William Pollack at the Urban Institute have concluded that the provision of fire protection by government—that is, produced by a bureaucracy and offered to the public at no direct charge—has led to an overinvestment in fire *suppression* and an underinvestment in fire *prevention*. A 1974 study by Public Technology Inc. of the fire department grading system administered by the insurance industry reached the same conclusion.[1]

Pollack seems to have been the first to propose that this situation be remedied by means of user charges. The typical city fire department is supported by property taxes. Consequently, each owner's bill is proportional only to the assessed value of the property, regardless of how fire resistant it may or may not be. Pollack proposed a fee based on a formula including the property value, size, number of occupants, and probability of fire. The latter would be based on the building's structural characteristics, age, and use of protective systems (fire doors, smoke detectors, sprinklers). Under this system owners would have an economic incentive to invest in improvements that reduce the risk and severity of fire.

Proposition 13 helped spur the first actual use of such a fee in 1978. The pioneering city was Inglewood, California. Threatened with a loss of revenue because of property-tax cuts, its fire department analyzed its operating costs and came up with a new financing plan. Some $1.6 million of the fire department's budget was necessitated solely by the additional personnel and equipment needed to cope with large-scale blazes in the city's commercial and industrial buildings. (This determination was based on well-established analytical procedures whereby the required "fire flow" for a particular building can be computed, based on its size, materials, fire-resistive features, etc.). Thus, it was decided to fund only the "basic" level of fire protection—fire flow adequate for single-family houses—from the property tax. The remaining $1.6 million would come from a fire-service fee, based on each building's excess fire-flow requirement.

The fire-service fee went into effect in the second half of 1978. Some property owners, whose net cost went up, challenged the fee system in court. Others, however, whose commercial structures are fire resistant, benefited handsomely. The Forum, a large auditorium/stadium, for instance, used to pay $60,000 in property taxes for fire protection. After the change it paid only $3,700 in fees. "We're encouraging people to invest in their own fire protection," said Fire Chief Dale Hill.

Nearby Culver City and Commerce also adopted user-fee ordinances. And a number of other California cities have considered doing so. The 1979 legislature passed a bill to permit fire protection districts to enact such fees—with a two-thirds vote of their citizens. But the fees have proved politically unpopular thus far. With the apartment owners' suit still pending, Inglewood suspended use of the fee system after the 1978/79 fiscal year. The Culver City and Commerce fees, though on the books, have not yet been implemented. Thus, tradition is proving to be stronger than many people anticipated.

Nevertheless, we can see how far removed fire protection actually is from being a public good. Not only can fire protection be charged for, it can also be provided by the private sector. In fact, the traditional tax-funded government fire department is the rule only in a minority of American communities (though they contain the majority of the population). The many forms of privatization—volunteer departments, subscription service, contracting, etc.—vary considerably in organization and sophistication but share one characteristic in common: *Almost without exception they are less costly than conventional government fire departments.* Nor is this lower cost an accident. We shall see how and why it comes about, and how a few government fire departments have learned some things from their private competitors.

VOLUNTEER FIRE DEPARTMENTS

According to the National Fire Protection Association, 87% of America's 24,500 fire departments are manned by volunteers. Volunteers supplement the paid employees at many of the remaining departments, to the point where 91% of the nation's 2.2 million firefighters are volunteers. Most volunteer departments are in rural or semirural areas, but in some states many small and medium-size towns and cities have volunteer departments. New York State, for example, has only 62 paid fire departments—and more than 1,800 volunteer departments. In Iowa there are 900 volunteer departments and only 23 paid ones. California is one of the few states with more paid than volunteer departments—571 to 462.

Volunteer departments vary greatly in the quality of service they provide. Some are highly professional, with a high level of personnel, extensive training, and modern equipment. Others are little more than social clubs with a hand-me-down 1940s pumper. Some form of objective comparison *can* be made, however, thanks to the rating service developed by the fire insurance industry. The Insurance Services Office sends teams of fire engineers to inspect the level of fire protection in every community in the country. Each is graded on a four-part scale which rates its water supply, fire department, communications system, and prevention efforts. The community's total score determines which ratings class it ends up in, from Class 1 (best) to Class 10 (worst). Most cities with paid departments are in Classes 3 to 6. Despite the fact that for many years ISO's Grading Schedule was biased against volunteer departments (e.g., it counted *three* volunteers or paid reservists as equivalent to *one* regular firefighter), many of them rank as high as paid departments. Unfortunately for our purposes, however, there are no overall statistics comparing the ISO ratings of paid and volunteer departments. Individual case studies, however, provide numerous examples of volunteer departments every bit the equal of paid departments, even in cities as large as Reading, Pennsylvania (pop. 300,000).[2]

Auburn, California, provides an example of a professional volunteer department. This community of 7,000 has a 75-member fire department dating back to 1852. It has three stations and $350,000 worth of modern equipment. Chief Henry Gietzen reports that the department has a waiting list, and always has had, since serving in the department is a mark of prestige in the community. Auburn has a Class 5 rating from ISO. Similarly well qualified is the McMinnville, Oregon, volunteer fire department. This department operates with a core of six paid men plus 72 volunteers. Its volunteers are alerted by portable radio paging units, to assure rapid response. And its extensive training program requires volunteers to train for a full year before getting a permanent assignment. McMinnville has a Class 4 rating.

Volunteer fire departments are substantial money savers for the taxpayers in their communities. About 90% of the budget of a typical paid department is spent on salaries and fringe benefits. Since volunteer departments for the most part eliminate this expense, they need only about 10% of the budget of paid departments—for facilities, equipment, and maintenance. A few raise this amount by taxation, as does Auburn. But most are financed voluntarily, either by direct contributions or via fund-raising events.

Anthropologist John Lozier studied volunteer fire departments in rural West Virginia.[3] He found that the more professional ones are highly skilled at fund-raising while the more traditional ones rely on community activities to raise funds. Members of the traditionalist Gray's Forge volunteer department take part in a wide variety of community service activities. The department is financed by dances, bake sales, and a major summer festival (which also raises funds for other community organizations).

The more professional departments, like that of Foster, West Virginia, stress technical excellence and virtually eliminate social fund-raising activities. Instead, the Foster department calculates an annual fee for each household in the area and sends it members door to door asking citizens to contribute. Each paid-up household receives a license-plate-size sign bearing a house number keyed to the department's custom-designed response system. In a rural area these signs are helpful in locating the house in the event of a fire call. In addition, they are evidence of which householders have met their "obligation" to support the community's fire department.

Door-to-door solicitation provides a way for the firefighters to become familiar with each building and resident in the community. It also makes it more difficult for residents to refuse their support. But coercion is not involved. Reports John Lozier, "The ultimate sanction, a threat to refuse fire service, is occasionally implied but never applied. The effective sanction is a threat of damage to an individual's standing in the community." And interestingly, poor people in towns like Foster, though they can't contribute as much as others, are often among the most regular contributors.

Thus, volunteer fire departments *can* be professionally run, highly rated, and financed entirely by voluntary means. Far from being a thing of the past, volunteer departments remain a vital force in American fire protection. Indeed, there are signs of a swing *back* to volunteer departments. "I'm sure some cities can and must get back to on-call and volunteer firefighters," says McMinnville Chief Jerry Smith. "It's becoming more obvious every year that the people cannot and will not pay for some of the services they feel they should get." Indeed, in 1975 the town of Orcutt, California (pop. 27,000), switched to an "on-call" fire department. Up until then it had contracted with the Santa Barbara County Fire Department for a paid engine company to supplement its 23-man, four-truck on-call force (trained men who are paid only for time spent responding to calls). But Orcutt's taxpayers decided that the $67,000 annual contract cost was excessive and that they could do the job more economically themselves. Now they use only their paid reservists. Other departments with a mix of paid and on-call men may well decide likewise, as the tax revolt continues.

PRIVATE SUBSCRIPTION SERVICES

In some rural and unincorporated suburban areas—especially areas of rapid growth—a different kind of fire service exists. This is paid subscription service, provided to individual customers by a private, profit-making fire protection company. Fire service of this type exists in at least five states: Arizona, Georgia, Oregon, Montana, and Tennessee. Counties in these states do not automatically provide fire departments in unincorporated areas, as is the case in many other states. Hence, a market for such service exists.

In Arizona that market is well served by Rural/Metro Fire Department, Inc.—the company we encountered providing contract security and police service in Chapter 3. Since 1948 Rural/Metro has been providing fire protection to individual subscribers in Arizona. It currently operates out of 30 locations in five counties. As of 1979 Rural/Metro had 55,000 subscription customers, most of them homeowners.

It's little wonder that Rural/Metro's customers are satisfied. Thanks to many efficiencies developed by the company (which we will discuss later in this chapter), its costs of operation are amazingly low. A typical 1,200-sq.-ft. house pays only $23 per year for fire protection—even though it may be out in the country far from any fire hydrant. The 1977 national average cost for city fire protection is $35.39 per person, or about $103 per house (since there is an average of 2.9 persons per household). Thus, Rural/Metro customers pay only 22% of the national average. Rates for commercial and industrial property are based on square footage, except that schools and hospitals are served at no charge. All subscribers also receive, free of charge, emergency first aid service, rescue and resuscitation service, fire-safety inspections, inspection service when on vacation, emergency utility shutoff and removal of excess water in event of burst pipes, and "removal of desert reptiles from your premises."

If a nonsubscriber's property catches fire, the company's policy is one of professional public service: protect life and property first and ask questions later. The state Corporation Commission permits the company to send nonsubscribers a bill for its services. The charge is 14 times what the annual subscription rate for the property would have been, plus $50/hour for each firefighting vehicle, $10/hour for each command vehicle, and $15/hour for each firefighter. This policy has the effect of deterring free riders. At the same time, though, no one is forced to subscribe. Those who prefer to take their own protective measures or trust their luck are still free to do so.

In many cases individual subscriber service occurs for a limited number of years, as an area develops. When it reaches a certain stage, citizens often wish to incorporate it as a city, enacting local property taxes and setting up government services. Once this occurs, of course, everyone receives fire protection and pays for it via taxes. Although this has happened in several of Rural/Metro's former service areas, it is a tribute to the quality of the company's service that in two newly incorporated cities—Oro Valley and Paradise Valley—such a high percentage of people were subscribers at the time the city incorporated, and were satisfied with the service, that they saw no need to get the newly formed city government into the act.

Rural/Metro achieves its amazingly low costs by thinking smarter. As noted earlier, labor-related expenses constitute about 90% of a fire department's costs. Hence, the greatest potential for saving lies in reducing the cost of personnel. R/M's philosophy is that it is unnecessary and wasteful to have only full-time firefighters, who must sit around and wait for a fire to occur. It therefore relies on a relatively small core staff of paid regulars, supplemented by a well-trained group of paid reservists called Auxiliary Firefighters.

In its home city of Scottsdale, Arizona, the Auxiliaries are 25 employees from various city departments—mostly from parks and public works—trained to double as on-call firefighters. They must pass the same initial tests and go through the first 20 hours of regular firefighting training. Once trained, the Auxiliaries are paid a monthly retainer of from $35 to $70 plus $6.34 per hour for any on-duty time outside normal working hours. Each Auxiliary is assigned to one of four shifts, which are on duty one week out of four. During working hours of his on-duty week, the Auxiliary is authorized (and required) to leave his regular city job when summoned by a portable radio pager to respond to a fire. He is also required to respond after hours, 24 hours a day, during his on-duty week.

The Auxiliary program is an outstanding success. The Auxiliaries are trained as general-purpose firefighters, proficient at from half to two-thirds of the fireground tasks—laying lines, doing nozzle work, and conducting salvage and ladder work. They are required by contract to respond, just like full-time employees. And statistics demonstrate that they do. In a recent study, Auxiliaries accounted for 44% of the total personnel responding to alarms. That same study showed that during a six-month period each Auxiliary was required to be away from his normal city job only 6.28 hours—only a bit over one hour per month. Thus, the city loses a negligible amount of employee time, while saving substantial sums on its fire protection costs.

Besides using a mix of full-time and part-time people, the company uses a number of other "manpower multiplication" techniques to reduce the need for excessive staffing. First, some of the off-duty paid Auxiliaries are provided with paging radios, so that they can be called for major fires, even though not on duty. Second, since the company serves a number of adjacent areas outside Scottsdale, it can call on a large number of additional *on-duty* personnel, trained to the same standards and using the same type of equipment but not paid for by Scottsdale residents. This points out another advantage of the private firm over government fire departments; even though the latter frequently render "mutual aid," their equipment, procedures, radio frequencies, training, and even terminology are often very different, leading to significant coordination problems.

The company has also developed a number of technological innovations that reduce the number of personnel needed to perform a given function. For example, R/M has pioneered the use of attack trucks (mini-pumpers).

They are smaller, lighter, and more maneuverable than regular pumpers and respond with regular pumpers to most fires. For the 75% of incidents that are minor, the attack truck (with its onboard water tank, pump, and hose) can handle the job alone, permitting the pumper and its crew to return to "available" status. If the incident is major, the faster attack truck usually gets there first, carrying an officer who can size up the situation before the other units arrive, organize the placement of pumpers and hose lines, and thereby save time and make more efficient use of the men and equipment.

Another R/M innovation is the Snail—a tread-mounted, remote-controlled robot which can drag a 2½-inch hose line into areas too hot (up to 700° F) or too dangerous for firefighters to enter. The Snail, which cost only $3,000 to build, is controlled by one firefighter but can do the work of four.

Rural/Metro makes its dollars go further when it comes to equipment acquisition, as well. It is a licensed manufacturer of fire apparatus, building pumpers and attack trucks both for its own use and occasionally for sale to other fire departments. This enables it to obtain its equipment for about half the price of commercial, overly chromed engines, while also incorporating the company's own design innovations. One of R/M's most impressive vehicles is Engine 21, flagship of the Scottsdale fleet. It was designed "as if we had never seen a fire truck, but knew water in the proper quantities at the proper pressure would put out a fire," says Louis A. Witzeman, president of the company. Unique in the industry, Engine 21 carries a portable pump that can be dropped off at one hydrant, while the truck continues on to a second hydrant (thereby serving as two pumpers in one). Its design is modular, with interchangeable equipment bays for water tanks, ladders, or hose lines. Engine 21 was designed and built by Rural/Metro for only $25,000, compared with $50,000–$75,000 for a conventional 1,000-gallon-per-minute pumper (at that time—today's pumpers cost more than $90,000).

Engine 21 makes use of lightweight plastic 4-inch hose, rather than the heavy canvas 2½-inch hose most common in the fire service. The 4-inch hose permits fewer firefighters to deliver a quantity of water to a fire. It has also permitted fire hydrant spacing twice as great as usual in residential areas, at considerable saving to the taxpayers. To save valuable time at fires, the hose is equipped with quarter-turn, quick-disconnect couplings, instead of garden-hose-type threaded couplings. Four-inch hose and quarter-turn couplings are beginning to be used by other American fire departments, but originally Rural/Metro had to import both from Germany.

Rural/Metro, although the largest, is not the only firm engaged in private fire protection. Another is the Grant's Pass Rural Fire Department and Ambulance Service. This firm serves all of unincorporated Josephine County, Oregon, outside the city limits of Grant's Pass. The company serves 10,000 subscribers and is growing rapidly. It charges $35 a year for single-family residences and from $50 to $300 a year for businesses. Nonsubscribers are charged $100/hour plus $5 per firefighter. For their basic annual fee, subscribers also receive free ambulance service.

The company operates from six stations with 12 full-time, paid employees and a large number of volunteers. It is rated class 9 by ISO. The neighboring Grant's Pass Fire Department has "no comment" about the quality of the company's service, and refuses to conduct mutual aid operations with it. "The politicians don't like us," says owner and Chief Bertha Miller, "but every time they speak out against us, we pick up more customers."

Outside Billings, Montana, a similar friction exists between the O'Donnell Fire Service and the city fire department. O'Donnell serves 5,000 subscribers from three stations, using 11 full-time, paid staff and 10 reservists. It charges homeowners $42 per year; nonsubscribers pay $75 per hour for each fire unit involved. The company has a Class 6 ISO rating in areas with water supply and Class 8 elsewhere.

O'Donnell offers residents a considerable cost advantage. Citizens of nearby Billings pay about $250 per household to support their city fire department, compared with the company's $42 annual charge. O'Donnell gains its cost advantage in two ways: paying fewer full-time firefighters and using innovative equipment (custom-designed trucks, high expansion foam). The firm's major problem is that the city keeps expanding outward, annexing away its customer base. Consequently, it must continually seek new customers just to stay even. Despite this obstacle, it has more than doubled its customer base in the past three years.

Tennessee provides the setting for additional subscription service. Five small subscription fire-service firms were recently merged to form the Tennessee Rural/Metro Fire Department, Inc. The new company, partially owned by Rural/Metro of Arizona, serves 6,000 subscribers on the outskirts of Knoxville. In its first two years of operation it upgraded the largely rural service from Class 10 to Class 9, giving its customers significant fire insurance savings. Another subscription company serves about 6,500 customers in East Ridge, Tennessee. It has signed up over 90% of the homes in its area, charging only $15 per year. Altogether, there are ten subscription fire companies in various parts of Tennessee.

Subscription fire service is also thriving in Georgia. There are five subscription firms in Chatham County. The largest of these is the Southside Fire Department, located in the suburbs of Savannah. Begun in 1962, Southside serves some 8,000 subscribers and is growing rapidly. Its service area encompasses 220 square miles. It covers this area from five stations, using a force of 20 paid and 110 volunteer firefighters and 18 vehicles. Single-family homes under $20,000 in value pay $30 per year; over that value the rate is $35 per year. Much of Southside's service area is graded Class 6, though some areas without fire hydrants are Class 8 or Class 9. Over the years the company has been asked to take over several areas formerly served by volunteer departments. When this occurs, the firm moves in its own personnel and equipment and recruits the existing volunteers as well.

Another Georgia firm is the West Richmond County Fire Department just outside Augusta. Begun in 1975 with 6,000 customers the first year, the firm ended 1977 with more than 10,000 subscribers and continues to grow rapidly. In most areas it has a Class 6 rating and is working to upgrade it to Class 5. The company charges homeowners $1 per $1,000 of valuation. Thus, on a $30,000 home the annual charge is $30. The company's Class 6 rating results in an insurance premium saving of $65 a year on a $30,000 home. By subscribing, then, an owner saves $35 a year. Not surprisingly, a high percentage of homeowners in the county subscribe.

The existence of subscription fire protection provides additional evidence that fire protection is not a public good. As we have seen, in five states individual homeowners and businesses find it to their advantage to pay for professional, private fire-protection services. Problems with free riders are minimal; the firms' principal problem is city-government annexation or incorporation that takes away their customer base.

A further example of private fire protection is the industrial fire department. Many large industrial installations, instead of socializing the cost of their unusually large fire-protection needs by demanding an oversize city fire department, choose to provide their own protection. Some are even getting together to provide shared protection. In Bayway, New Jersey, seven large firms have joined together to create the Linden Industrial Mutual Aid Council. The driving force behind the council is Exxon, whose Bayway refinery has long had its own 12-man fire department. Another large industrial fire service is the 57-member Channel Industries Mutual Aid (CIMA) organization, to which all the major plants on the Houston Ship Channel belong. CIMA represents the largest collection of petroleum and petrochemical fire-fighting expertise and equipment in the world. Its resources include 25 fire trucks, two fire boats, numerous pieces of special equipment, and hundreds of trained industrial firefighters. Citizens in cities with large industrial installations should take a careful look at how much of their fire department's size and cost are due to the special requirements of these industries. The public good argument can be rhetoric that disguises a large and unnecessary subsidy.

PRIVATE CONTRACTING BY GOVERNMENT

If you live in an incorporated city which collects taxes and views fire protection as a public good, there are ways to minimize the cost and maximize the efficiency of the fire service. One way is to contract with a private firm, instead of operating a city fire department. As in the case of police protection, contracting provides a city with a choice among suppliers and gives the providing company an incentive to be efficient. The leader in fire-service contracting is our old friend, Rural/Metro Fire Department, Inc. Its service within the Scottsdale city limits is via contract with the city, and it also provides contractual fire service to four fire districts and two developer-owned new towns in Arizona.

Scottsdale, the company's home base, is a showcase of the benefits of private fire protection. Rural/Metro grew up with the city, providing subscriber service before the city incorporated. When Scottsdale became a city in 1952, city officials decided that there was no need to create a city fire department. Instead, following the example of the many cities which contract for such services as garbage collection and street sweeping, they decided to use the city tax funds to hire Rural/Metro on a renewable contract basis. Over the succeeding years the contract has been renegotiated and renewed a number of times. Both parties continue to be highly satisfied with the arrangement.

The bottom line when it comes to evaluating Rural/Metro is its cost and performance. First of all its low cost is quite impressive. The per capita cost of fire protection in Scottsdale, a city of over 90,000 people, is about one-fourth the national average for cities of 50,000–100,000. Because the costs of fire protection vary, depending on the types of structures, their age, and weather conditions, it is more meaningful to compare cities that are as similar as possible. Economist Roger Ahlbrandt, Jr., made a theoretical study of this sort in 1972.[4] In 1976 the Institute for Local Self-Government (ILSG) made an actual on-the-scene, side-by-side evaluation.[5]

As part of a research project on contract public services, ILSG made a detailed comparison of fire protection in Scottsdale and its three very similar neighbors—Glendale, Mesa, and Tempe—all of which have conventional city fire departments. Over the years 1971–75, the average per capita cost in Scottsdale was only $6.48, about half as much as in Glendale ($12.62), Mesa ($11.43), and Tempe ($10.68).

But is it as good as its neighbors' fire service? The Institute examined this question in detail. A key indicator of fire department performance is response time. Although Scottsdale has twice the land area of the others (72 square miles versus 24.5 for Glendale, 48 for Mesa, and 30.2 for Tempe), Scottsdale had the best average response time: 2.96 minutes, compared with 3.0 for Glendale, 3.0 for Mesa, and 3.8 for Tempe. Another key indicator is the ISO grading. Scottsdale has earned a Class 5 rating, the same as Glendale, while Mesa is Class 3 and Tempe is Class 4. Thus, Scottsdale's fire protection is judged acceptable by ISO's conservative standards. And its residents pay no more for fire insurance since homeowners' policies cost the same in Classes 3, 4, and 5. Finally another indicator is the actual fire loss. The Institute found that the average annual per capita loss was $5.45 in Scottsdale—quite comparable to the $5.19 figure for Glendale and $5.26 for Mesa, and far below Tempe's $9.60.

Rural/Metro is not the only firm engaged in contracting with cities and fire districts. New contract service came into existence in 1977. When voters in the Nashville, Tennessee, area created a metro government, five small subscription fire companies were hired by the new government on contract to serve the formerly unincorporated county areas. Whether this will be just an interim step or a permanent move to contract service remains to be seen.

Two more contracts came into being in 1979. On January 1, American Emergency Services Corporation began operating Illinois's first private fire service. The 5,000 residents of Elk Grove Township, adjacent to O'Hare Airport, had voted the previous month by a 9-to-1 margin to contract with the private firm rather than to renew their 22-year contract with adjacent Mount Prospect. Like Rural/Metro (on which it is modeled), Gary Jensen's firm relies on 25 paid reservists to supplement his nine full-time firefighters. All of the latter have Emergency Medical Technician certificates and two are trained as full-fledged paramedics. The firm operates two fully equipped emergency ambulances as well as two pumpers and a ladder truck. Based on the industrial/commercial township's average daily population of 20,000, the first-year cost was $15 per capita—compared with an estimated 1979 national average of more than $29 for cities that size.

Also in January 1979, Rural/Metro was hired by the county commission of Hall County, Georgia, to replace its county fire department. Delayed by a court challenge over the legality of contracting (which was upheld), operations began on March 1. The $862,000 first-year contract for fire and ambulance service saved county taxpayers $100,000, and Rural/Metro projected a somewhat greater saving for the second year. Angry fire union members, whose court challenge failed, next organized an election to recall the county commissioners. That move succeeded, but the new commissioners—impressed by the firm's performance and cost saving—made no move to change the contract. (Incidentally, R/M offered jobs to all the former firefighters, but only about 20% applied, and of those, all but one were hired.)

Contract fire protection is not limited to the United States. Denmark's Falck Company has been providing contract fire protection to Danish municipalities since 1926. It currently has fire equipment based in 90 stations across Denmark, providing fire protection for about half the country. Like Rural/Metro, Falck operates with a core staff of full-time paid men supplemented by paid reservists. Falck responds to about 30,000 fire calls per year, and derives 70% of its income from fire protection services. (The rest of its activities involve ambulance and rescue work, as we'll see in Chapter 6.)

INTERGOVERNMENTAL COOPERATION

In many states it is possible to contract with another governmental unit for fire service. As we saw in the case of law enforcement, contracting with another government agency permits a city to take advantage of whatever economies of scale may exist. It also gives the purchasing city greater flexibility since it can negotiate for the type of service it desires and may switch to an alternative supplier (including a private firm, should one later become available) if not satisfied.

Government contracting for fire services is especially common in California. In Los Angeles County the county fire department contracts with 35 of the county's 77 cities, saving them the trouble and expense of operating their own departments. Since the program began (with the city of Lakewood, in 1954), only three cities have dropped out and started their own departments. In Orange County eight cities, including the "new town" of Irvine, have for many years contracted for fire service with the California Division of Forestry (CDF). The contracting arrangements were considered as long-term, stable relationships rather than as interim steps. One of the eight cities, Placentia, made history in 1975 by abolishing its city fire department, in response to a wildcat strike by firefighters, and contracting with CDF. But late in 1978 CDF gave notice that it would no longer provide urban fire protection in Orange County after June 30, 1980. As this book went to press, city and county officials were considering whether to (1) create new departments, (2) contract with other cities, or (3) contract with the private sector.

Other California counties with intergovernmental contract fire service include Monterey, San Bernardino, Santa Barbara, Riverside, and Ventura. Such contracting also exists in Kentucky, Maryland, Minnesota, New Jersey, Ohio, Tennessee, and Virginia.

Some of the cost advantages of contracting can be obtained by consolidating adjacent small fire departments in urbanized areas. The potential advantages include elimination of overlapping or redundant response areas, reduced administrative positions, centralized dispatch, and greater flexibility in using personnel and equipment. All of these translate into hard dollar savings. Huntington Beach, California, in 1968 enacted a joint powers agreement with three adjacent cities to consolidate dispatching and to coordinate fire station location policies. The joint operation requires 14 rather than 18 stations and six rather than eight ladder companies. The savings total over $1 million a year. A similar functional consolidation was achieved among six cities in California's Contra Costa County.

SPRUCING UP THE CITY DEPARTMENT

Many innovative methods have been developed by private fire-protection companies and a handful of progressive municipal fire departments. These can be applied by any city or county fire department. For the most part they have *not* been tried because the fire service over the years has become the most tradition-bound of all local public services. This is partly because of its being, like the police, a sacred-cow function of government and therefore not subject to critical scrutiny at budget time. It is also because of the conservatism of the insurance industry and its relatively unchanging ISO standards. These have tended, like building codes, to retard innovation rather than to encourage it. Whatever the reason, the fire service has lagged far behind the technological state of the art. What follows is a sampling of these innovative ideas.

Personnel Utilization

Although Rural/Metro pioneered the large-scale use of paid reservists, there is no inherent reason why this approach cannot be used in any fire department—government or private. The use of portable radio-paging units (about $300 each) makes this idea more feasible in both urban and rural areas. And while the exact mix of full-timers and reservists may vary with local conditions, the reservist concept makes technical and economic sense across the board.

Cottage Grove, Oregon, is a small community 25 miles from Eugene. The city's fire department operates with a mix of paid men and volunteers but had the problem of reduced volunteer turnout during working hours. It recently organized its 13 public works employees into a paid reservist unit—the Public Works Fire Department Support Unit. The Support Unit's members are required to respond during regular working hours, thus solving the turnout problem. The members each receive four hours of fire training every six months, covering hose and nozzle work, salvage, traffic control, etc.

Other departments that utilize paid reservists include Orange County (California Division of Forestry), Riverside County, Visalia, Santa Maria, and Lompoc in California, and Denison, Texas. In each case the reservists receive regular fire training but are paid only for the time spent actually responding (plus, in some cases, a small monthly retainer). Savings to the city, depending on the extent of reservist use, range from 20% to 40%.

Other personnel changes can lead to additional cost savings. Using volunteers or reservists at night can provide important cost reductions. The Citrus Heights Fire Protection District in Sacramento County, California, uses college students as night reservists. They attend school during the day, pay rent for city-owned living quarters, and receive the minimum wage for on-duty time at night. Downers Grove, Illinois, uses a similar concept for its night staff and estimates its savings at 33% of all personnel costs. Orange, California, does not fully staff its six fire stations. Instead, it operates a two-person "flying squad," based at the central station, which is sent as needed throughout the city to supplement each station's assigned personnel. Savings are estimated at $50,000 a year.

Productive use of firefighters' on-duty time is another avenue for savings. The Rural/Metro employees in Scottsdale spend some of their time building new fire engines, repairing city water meters, and assembling the specialized refuse containers used by the city. Glenview, Illinois, and Visalia, California, firefighters operate the city's printing department. In other cities firefighters issue bicycle licenses or carry out city inspections.

Facilities

Although fire stations and other facilities account for only a small fraction of a fire department's average annual cost, significant economies are possible here as well. One California department has found a way to build stations for less than half price by converting ordinary tract houses. In 1971 the city of Garden Grove purchased a surplus house in a street-widening project. Rather than construct a needed fire station at 1211 Chapman Avenue, the city moved the house to the site, enlarged its garage to fit a pumper, and added a hose rack in the backyard. The total cost for what became Station No. 6 was only $42,000, compared with about $135,000 for building a new station, at 1971 prices. When another station was needed the following year, the department went shopping for a suitable tract house in the area to be served. A three-bedroom, two-bath house at 14162 Forsyth Lane was purchased new for $25,625. Adding a garage and hose rack plus furnishing and landscaping brought the total cost to $58,629. Firefighters find the tract homes more comfortable than typical fire station dormitories, and the neighbors like the way the station blends in with its surroundings.

Major economies can result from more careful placement of fire stations. Eliminating an unnecessary station saves not only the construction and maintenance costs, but also the far larger costs of unneeded personnel and equipment. In large metropolitan areas, adjacent jurisdictions often have fire stations located quite close together. Mutual-aid agreements can sometimes permit one city's border station to be closed. In other cases, stations may be located too close together within a city, possibly due to changing land-use patterns. By agreeing to make joint use of an Arlington Heights, Illinois, fire station, the city of Rolling Meadows saved the $350,000 cost of constructing a second station of its own.

Some larger cities are now using a sophisticated computer program to determine the optimum number and location of fire stations. Developed by nonprofit Public Technology, Inc. (PTI), the program uses such factors as street layouts and alarm histories to specify how many stations are necessary, where they should best be located, the predicted response time, and the predicted number of alarms at each. The PTI program is being used by several dozen cities, including New Orleans, Dallas, Long Beach, San Diego, Wichita, and Eugene, Oregon. Not all are using it to reduce costs, but those that are, such as San Bernardino, California, expect "major" savings in both capital and operating costs.

In Denver, researchers from the University of Colorado and the Denver Urban Observatory developed their own mathematical model to determine optimum station location. Their results showed that the present level of service could be maintained with a reduction of two engine companies and three ladder companies, by suitable rearrangement of equipment and stations. The city/county Budget and Management Office has prepared a multi-year fire-service plan which calls for phasing out the surplus companies, saving $2.8 million over the six-year phase-out period, and $1.2 million a year thereafter.

Another area for cost savings is removal of obsolescent firebox alarm systems. Many years ago the firebox on the street corner was the principal means of reporting a fire. Today, though, most fires are reported by telephone (and pay phones generally outnumber fireboxes on the streets). Moreover, in most cities the firebox has become a target for pranksters, who delight in turning in false alarms.

As a result, many cities have begun to reevaluate the need for a firebox alarm system. Los Angeles took the lead in this area several years ago. Poring over departmental records in an intensive study, the city fire department found that 92% of the alarms received via street boxes were false. Moreover, nearly 89% of the valid box alarms were also reported by telephone. Further analysis showed that only 1.4% of the box alarms were for *real* fires that were not also reported by telephone.

Despite the meager benefits of the system, it was costing the taxpayers a lot of money. Simple maintenance cost over $100,000 a year. And every response to a false alarm led to $80 in direct costs, besides tying up personnel and equipment and increasing the risk of accidents involving responding units. Because 7,000 false alarms were being turned in annually, the needless response cost was running $560,000 per year. Based on these figures the department decided to scrap the entire system. Some 300 boxes had already been removed from areas of chronic false alarms, and the remaining 1,400 were taken out in 1975. As antiques, the boxes themselves proved extremely popular. The city salvage department priced them at $73 each, and all were quickly sold. Rumor has it that many were immediately resold at much higher prices.

Removing fireboxes is a step that some cities still hesitate to take, despite the impressive cost savings. They have two worries: public safety and insurance rates. As far as public safety is concerned, the Los Angeles statistics are fairly typical. Most firebox alarm systems bring in mostly false alarms, and nearly all true alarms are reported by telephone. Public access to telephones for emergency reporting is being upgraded all across the country, as phone companies introduce the three-digit "911" emergency number. In many cases pay phones are then modified to permit dialing 911 without having to insert a coin.

It is true that the ISO grading system penalizes a city for not having a box alarm system. But the penalty affects only 100 out of a possible 5,000 points of the grading scales. Other improvements—in communications or in other aspects of fire protection—can offset any penalty for removing the boxes. And it is only a matter of time until ISO revises its standards to reflect the reality of modern-day telephone communications.

These facts are becoming apparent to city officials. In 1977 San Diego and Santa Barbara, California, decided to scrap their box alarm systems. Both cities are putting in "911" telephone systems. Joining the parade in 1978, Oakland, California, removed its 1,250 alarm boxes at an annual saving of $80,000.

Equipment Innovations

Most fire trucks and equipment have changed little since the 1920s when motorized trucks completed the replacement of horse-drawn wagons.

Most departments rely exclusively on two types of trucks, pumpers and ladder trucks, produced virtually custom-made to each city's specifications at $75,000–$100,000 each. As we have seen, Rural/Metro and several other private firms have led the way in producing less expensive, standardized fire engines using many off-the-shelf components and innovative design ideas. Not many of these ideas have yet found favor with municipal fire departments.

One that *is* slowly making headway is the mini-pumper or attack truck.[6] Depending on the locality, anywhere from 40% to 80% of all calls can be handled with two firefighters and a minimum of equipment—a van or one-ton truck with its own water tank and hose. Use of a mini-pumper at small incidents (grass and rubbish fires, lock-out calls, auto fires) tends to reduce overall personnel requirements and costs a lot less—anywhere from $6,000 to $29,000 for a complete mini-pumper.

Besides Rural/Metro, one of the pioneers in using mini-pumpers is Syracuse, New York. In 1974 Syracuse's fire department completely reorganized, in response to a state law mandating a 40-hour firefighter work week. Retaining its traditional pattern of staff and equipment would have required adding 125 firefighters to comply with the law. The new concept, based on using a mix of mini-pumpers and full-size trucks, required only 62 new employees—an annual saving of $600,000. Most Syracuse engine companies now consist of a two-person mini-pumper and a three-person maxi-pumper. Depending on the type of call, the response will be the mini alone, both together, or the maxi with all five firefighters. Other departments now using mini-pumpers include Des Moines, Iowa; Cayce, South Carolina; and University City, Missouri. The former two have constructed their minis on pickup truck chassis, while the latter converted a 1973 Dodge van.

Public Technology, Inc., has developed an infrared viewer for use by the fire service. Called Probeye, and now in production by Hughes Aircraft, the viewer permits location of fire victims and hidden fire sources by "seeing" their heat through solid walls. It is also useful in overhaul and salvage work and in routine fire inspections. Probeye costs $3,500.

PTI and Rural/Metro have separately worked on two other technical problems: control of water flow and improved breathing apparatus. Rural/Metro has spent several years working on a radio-controlled fire hydrant valve. With the unit mounted on the hydrant, the flow of water can be controlled by one of the men on the hose, rather than by an extra firefighter stationed at the hydrant. Rural/Metro's system is still under development. The PTI system provides for radio control of the pump on the pumper, from a transmitter at the hose nozzle, again eliminating the need for an extra person. It is in production at Grumman Allied Industries, Inc.

PTI has also developed a lighter-weight, longer-duration, easier-to-use, self-contained breathing apparatus for firefighters. The system was developed with NASA assistance and is entering production as this is written. Rural/Metro has taken a different approach to the limitations of present breathing gear (which typically have less than 30 minutes' air supply). At a cost of under $2,500, it has developed a firefighters' umbilical consisting of a fire-resistant Nomex braid hose ½ inch in diamater. The hose provides not only air but also a two-way communications line and an electric power line for operating hand-held lights. If the air supply fails, the firefighter can hit a quick-release latch with one hand and then rely on an auxiliary air tank bottle.

These exciting technological advances were not developed by city fire departments. Some were developed by a private firm, others by a foundation-supported nonprofit corporation. This fact only serves to underline what we've learned about the inherent disadvantages of municipal monopolies in providing public services.

6

Emergency Ambulance Service

Emergency ambulance service is a third public safety function often performed by local government. (We distinguish here between *emergency* ambulance service, which performs a life-saving, rescue function, and routine *transport* ambulance service which is frequently carried out by funeral homes in hearse-type vehicles lacking sophisticated life-support equipment used in rescue ambulances.)

Over the past decade, more and more local governments have gotten into the rescue ambulance business, spurred on by federal regulations and grant programs, and popular support generated by such TV programs as *Emergency*. In addition, the Vietnam war demonstrated the usefulness of the *paramedic* concept in saving lives—that is, providing intensive medical-type life-saving skills by nonmedical personnel. Because this training is limited to specific life-saving skills, it can be given in several hundred hours instead of the six to eight years required to obtain an M.D. degree. Consequently, paramedics can provide emergency life-saving skills at a fraction of the cost of a regular medical doctor.

Encouraged by the federal government, many states have passed laws permitting the existence of paramedics. In some cases states require paramedic training for certain types of ambulance operations. California, for example, now requires all ambulance attendants to have training equivalent to an Emergency Medical Technician I. EMT-I training consists of a 112-hour course given in conjunction with a community college and a hospital; it goes far beyond advanced first aid and includes cardiopulmonary resuscitation. A true paramedic, however, must have EMT-II training—in California this includes 1,200 hours of training and instruction. When in radio contact with a physician or registered nurse, a paramedic may administer intravenous saline solution or glucose and give various injections. Paramedic vehicles typically carry portable defibrillators, EKG monitors, and biophones. An ambulance so equipped is called a mobile intensive-care unit (MICU).

Paramedic programs are inherently very costly, and except in communities with a high proportion of elderly residents, their capabilities are needed infrequently. Nevertheless, popular enthusiasm and federal grants have led many cities into the rescue ambulance business. The most typical—and most costly—pattern is for the city to assign this function to its fire department. The fire unions have welcomed the opportunity to get into a new, exciting, glamorous business which requires sophisticated equipment and (usually) the addition of more personnel.

There are several viable alternatives to government-operated rescue ambulance service, all of which are far less costly to the taxpayers while providing excellent services to those who need them. The principal alternatives are volunteer service, subscription service, fee service, and contract service. Supporters of a government role in the rescue business frequently point to examples of nongovernmental ambulances operated without adequate equipment or properly trained personnel. They tend to *equate* private ambulance service with these carefully selected examples. Yet as in most other fields, there are both competents and incompetents in the ambulance business. And many of the incompetents stay in business thanks to favored treatment (e.g., franchises) from friendly local officials. The important point is that highly competent private rescue ambulance operations *do* exist. And this fact demonstrates that there is no necessity for local government to operate such a service. Let us see how some of the competent operations work.

VOLUNTEER AMBULANCES

America's largest and most sophisticated volunteer ambulance and rescue service operates right under the noses of our nation's lawmakers. It's the Bethesda/Chevy Chase Rescue Squad, Inc. The squad serves northwestern Washington, D.C., plus Bethesda and Chevy Chase, Maryland. It responds to about 8,000 calls per year, using a fleet of modern vehicles: six paramedic vans, an MICU, three conventional ambulances, a sophisticated crash truck, and two rescue boats. During the day its dispatch center and vehicles are staffed partly by paid personnel, but seven nights a week, from 7 P.M. to 7 A.M., the operation is staffed entirely by volunteers. There are seven crews, one for each night of the week, each consisting of 10–12 young men and women.

The Rescue Squad began inconspicuously in 1945 when a group of local businesspeople and other residents began operating a volunteer rescue service. Its first vehicle was a used ambulance housed in a borrowed garage. The dedicated service of its "men in the white hats" aroused considerable community support. As the area grew, so did the rescue squad. By 1956 when it moved into its first permanent headquarters building, it had become so popular that there was a waiting list for members. With the advent of the Vietnam war, the availability of young men volunteers decreased, making it necessary to hire the first paid staff for daytime duty. Some paid staff continue to be used because of the high volume of daytime calls. By 1975 the squad's original headquarters proved to be too small, so ground was broken for a new $1-million building, completed in 1976.

The Rescue Squad receives no government funds. It does not directly charge for its services: All are provided free of charge. It is supported entirely on a voluntary basis, largely from an annual fund drive carried out door to door each fall. It also operates bingo games and receives donations for some of its ambulance and rescue calls. Through its voluntary fund-raising the squad generates an income in excess of $300,000 a year to meet all its operating expenses and pay off its construction bonds. If the squad were a government agency, its cost would be many times that amount, just to pay for the time now put in by the 150 volunteers.

Other volunteer ambulance services operate on more of a grass-roots level. In Greencastle, Indiana, students at DePauw University organized a volunteer fire department in 1967. But a lack of fires led them to seek out the rescue ambulance business as a source of greater activity. Accordingly, several years later they created Operation Life as an emergency ambulance unit. With a $5,000 county grant plus corporate donations and proceeds from a football game concession stand, they raised a $27,000 first-year budget. Members received EMT-I training and nine of the 35 volunteers went on to full paramedic certificates. A fully equipped rescue ambulance, linked by radio to area hospitals, was put into service.

Operation Life began its rescue operations in May 1974—and promptly ran into criticism. Local funeral directors claimed that the service was putting them out of the ambulance business and that "private enterprise" should be providing ambulance service. (Why a volunteer operation is not "private" was never explained by these gentlemen.) Some city officials were distressed because the students solicit donations of $20 for local runs and $35 for runs to other localities, instead of offering the service free of charge. But these narrow-minded challenges came to naught as local officials and citizens came to appreciate the benefits of a professional ambulance/ paramedic service at a very low cost.

In 1976 the county entered into a contract with Operation Life to subsidize its operations. Currently the county picks up $30,000 of the annual $80,000 budget; another $35,000 comes from fees charged to users, and the balance is made up by donations and fund-raising activities. The students operate a paramedic van, an EMT ambulance, and various convales-cent-care vehicles. All emergency service personnel are volunteers; only the three administrators and the convalescent service drivers receive partial compensation. For $30,000 a year in tax funds, the citizens receive a service that would cost between $120,000 and $150,000 if provided directly by the county.

Another volunteer ambulance service was begun in 1978 by residents of Baker, California, a small town on Interstate 15 in the Mojave Desert.

Reacting to the auto-accident death of a local resident, 14 of the residents obtained EMT training. With a grant from the county government, they refurbished a four-year-old Dodge van ambulance and are now in operation, entirely on a volunteer basis. Money to maintain the vehicle remains a problem, however. The town of 600 people presents relatively meager opportunities for door-to-door fund raising, and the volunteers continue to hope the county government will come to their aid.

SUBSCRIPTION AMBULANCES

Ambulance services can also be provided to customers on a subscription basis. The idea is similar to taking out an insurance policy: In exchange for a relatively modest annual payment, the customer is guaranteed whatever ambulance and rescue service he or she may need that year without additional charge. This same concept is widely used by auto clubs such as the American Automobile Association and the Allstate Motor Club, which provide towing and other emergency road service as required, for a single annual payment.

In fact, the world's largest rescue service, Denmark's Falck Company, operates subscription road service *and* subscription ambulance service. The former has been so successful that the red Falck wreckers have replaced the government's highway patrol cars altogether. Over half of Denmark's 1.3 million car owners subscribe to Falck's road service, and the company answers about a million road service calls per year. It provides subscribers with first-aid kits, and its 132 stations provide hourly reports on winter highway conditions to the Danish Broadcasting Service.

Falck's subscription ambulance business is a logical extension of its road service. Although most Danish cities and towns contract with Falck to provide basic local ambulance service, more extensive coverage (including highway rescue) can be purchased by individual subscription. Typically such a subscription provides the customer with access to all types of conveyance not provided by the municipality, such as transport back home if taken ill on vacation, conveyance of long-term hospital patients home for the weekend, delivery of prescriptions from pharmacies, and, of course, rescue on the highway.

One of the largest American subscription firms serves 480,000 rural residents in nine parishes (counties) in Louisiana—the 6,000-square-mile Acadiana area. The Acadian Ambulance Service provides sophisticated paramedic rescue service as well as basic ambulance transport—and makes a profit doing it. In cooperation with hospitals in the nine parishes, it has set up the Acadiana Emergency Radio Network, a special network which can transmit medical data by radio from any paramedic vehicle to any of the region's hospitals. This permits a doctor in the hospital to work with the paramedic in assessing and stabilizing the patient's condition. The company operates a fleet of 24 ambulances based at 13 substations. They are dispatched from its Emergency Medical Dispatch Center in Lafayette. More than 60 emergency calls come into the center each day.

The key to the company's success is its subscription concept. Some 75,000 families pay $15 per year to subscribe to Acadian's service. Although the company provides basic emergency services to everyone in the region, nonsubscribers are charged directly for them. Subscribers receive free emergency response and reduced rates on routine transport. In the past decade the company has grown from two ambulances and eight employees to 24 ambulances and 100 employees.

Acadian's subscription concept was its response to the changed operating environment of the 1970s. Many smaller companies and funeral homes dropped out of the ambulance business rather than meet new federal and state requirements for training and equipment. Acadian, by contrast, conceived and successfully sold the public—and area hospitals—on the value of a sophisticated emergency care system and the benefits of the subscription concept. No federal funds were used; all funding has come from subscribers, from the Louisiana Hospital Association, and from private foundations.

Oklahoma boasts a similarly impressive subscription service, the Central Oklahoma Ambulance Trust (COAT). In 1975 the Oklahoma City mayor's office hired a consultant to study alternative ways of introducing modern emergency ambulance/paramedic service to the area. Rather than putting the city directly into the business, the consultant recommended that it act only as a catalyst to bring about the development of the service. As a result COAT was set up as a nonprofit municipal trust. Its function was to arrange for the provision of emergency services and to handle all the financial arrangements—but without using taxpayers' money.

COAT officials obtained bank loans to purchase the equipment and sought bids from private firms to supply the service. On September 10, 1976, COAT accepted the proposal of Emergency Medical Services of Central Oklahoma, a private, not-for-profit company. EMS was given a three-year contract to provide emergency ambulance and paramedic service in the 750-square-mile area of Oklahoma City and the surrounding four-county region, encompassing 750,000 people.

The company's services are paid for by a combination of subscriptions and fees for service from nonsubscribers. In addition, the Oklahoma City government has provided some interest-free loans to help with initial cash flow. In 1976 EMS signed up 32,000 households at $18 a year; in 1977 this figure climbed to 48,500 households. The COAT system operates with 18 vehicles and has 122 employees; 21 area hospitals are participating. Late in 1977, to solve a variety of managerial and coordination problems, EMS was merged into COAT. Although the operation is now quasi-governmental, it remains user-financed; subscription service remains its financial basis.

Another approach to subscription service is that of Medical Services, Inc., of Eugene, Oregon. MSI resulted from a merger of three smaller firms and is one of the largest and most sophisticated paramedic operations in the country. MSI operates entirely without tax money. The ambulance and paramedic operations are not yet offered on a subscription basis; the user pays a fee that covers all costs, averaging about $155 per call. But MSI *is* offering a unique subscription first-aid service to businesses called Aid Car.

The need for Aid Car arises out of a section of the Oregon Safe Employment Act that requires every business with two or more employees to have a written emergency medical plan, a first-aid kit, a recovery area, and a qualified first-aid person at each job location at all times. The last provision is by far the most costly, but the law provides an exception: If a physician-approved "emergency care service" is used by the company, an on-site person is not required. MSI's Aid Car qualifies as an approved emergency care service, while conventional ambulance, fire, and police services do not, since they do not respond to all minor problems. Aid Car does. For a single annual fee, based on the size of the business and its risk level, Aid Car provides a 24-hour-a-day, radio-equipped EMT to deal with minor illnesses and injuries. The service is much like an appliance service agreement, says MSI's Dennis Murphy. Aid Car will respond whenever necessary for the entire year; the only possible extra charge is if an ambulance run (rather than simply first aid) should be required.

Once the booming industrial demand for Aid Car has been met, MSI plans to offer a similar first-aid service to the general public in the Eugene/Springfield area. After that will come subscription ambulance service, like that in Louisiana and Oklahoma. The company has no plans to seek government subsidy, despite the fact that its costly paramedic service appears to be reaching the limits of customers' ability to pay. As far as MSI is concerned, the less government involvement, the better. The firm works hard at maintaining a good relationship with local government by meeting or exceeding all applicable standards and actively seeking enough sources of revenue to keep its operations self-supporting. But this does not mean putting money ahead of service. "We provide emergency care first, and worry about the billing later," says Murphy. The good will generated by this approach has kept uncollectible bills below 10% of the total—quite unusual in the emergency ambulance business.

MSI's good relationship with the powers-that-be is exemplified by its dealings with local public safety agencies. The company does all EMT training for the fire departments of Eugene and Springfield and for the 14 rural fire departments in Lane County.

MSI illustrates private ambulance service at its best. The company is highly professional, taking a very serious approach to both service and marketing. Instead of acting as if local government is its adversary, it goes out of its way to cooperate in providing high-quality service that interfaces well with local police and fire agencies. By putting service ahead of payment in its relationships with customers, it ends up with fewer payment problems than firms whose priorities are reversed. Thus MSI finds no need to seek government subsidy of money-losing paramedic operations, like some private ambulance firms. Nor does it find local governments trying to elbow their way into the ambulance business. Instead, the company is a highly respected corporate citizen.

PARAMEDIC ALTERNATIVES

We have seen several types of emergency ambulance/paramedic operations which do not involve local government or taxpayers' money: volunteer, subscription, and user fee service. Yet local governments persist in getting into the act, on the grounds that paramedic service is a unique, life-saving public service that—for some reason—local government "must" provide. Often the initial argument is that it is somehow immoral or unthinkable that people be charged for such a service and that therefore the taxpayers must put up the money so it can be provided "for free." Communities that follow this course soon find that demand for the service is expanded by all sorts of "emergencies" which don't really require the services of paramedics. But of course, if one aims to build an empire, one doesn't worry about excessive demand; one simply requests more personnel and equipment!

When a local government decides that there must be paramedic service in its jurisdiction, it has three basic choices. It can:
• operate the service itself, funded either by taxes or by user fees;
• contract with one or more private firms to operate the service, with some level of tax-funded subsidy to supplement the firm's income from fees; or
• franchise one or more firms to provide the service, on a totally user-supported basis.

Data from the Ambulance and Medical Services Association of America indicate that although 75% of all ambulances are nongovernmental (ambulance firms, volunteers, or funeral homes), only 30% to 35% of all paramedic service is private. In California, where 78% of ambulances are private, approximately 50% of paramedic service is private. Private paramedic firms operate in 19 of the 21 counties with paramedic programs and are the major or sole provider in 14 of the 21 counties.

From the standpoint of the taxpayer, a user-paid private paramedic program is obviously preferable, since the tax cost of that alternative is zero. In the Santa Barbara, California, metropolitan area that type of program is operated by 911 Emergency Services, Inc.[1] Praised by medical and public safety personnel as among the best in the state, 911's operation provides three fully equipped paramedic vans within the city and two in the suburbs. The firm responds to all emergency medical calls (dispatched by the county's unified dispatch center). If the emergency is minor, requiring only transport to a hospital, the patient is charged a base rate—the same as an ambulance charge. In 1979 this averaged $91. If specific EMT or paramedic services are required, those charges are added to the base rate; in 1979 the average bill for this type of call was $152. If the call turns out to be a "dry run" (no service required at all) no one is charged at all.

Interestingly, for all the talk about the indignity or hardship involved in paying for such service, 911 Emergency Services has found that the vast majority of its clients incur little out-of-pocket cost for its fees. That's because nearly all have some form of third-party coverage—about 64% with private insurance and another 23% with Medi-Cal (Medicaid) or Medicare. To have local taxpayers fund paramedic service when this type of coverage already exsits is absurd; as Los Angeles Fire Commissioner Jerry Field (whose paramedic services are "free") has put it, "We're saving insurance companies money at the expense of the city." Overall 911 has a no-pay rate of only 14%, far below that of most government-run paramedic programs which charge fees. (Los Angeles *does* charge a transport fee, of $35 to $40, but collects from only about 45% of its clients!)

If a completely private, user-funded paramedic program cannot be achieved, the next best alternative is a program run by the private sector under contract. A study by the Illinois Department of Transportation showed that private paramedic service costs, on average, about half that of public service. The Ambulance Medical Service Association of America found the cost of private service to be one-third that of government service. Some examples will provide specifics to illustrate the difference.

In 1975 Glendale, California, analyzed its choices and selected private enterprise. After considerable controversy, the city decided to abolish its year-old fire department paramedic unit rather than expand it to three units. Instead, it contracted with two private ambulance firms to provide the three units, at an annual cost of $146,085, compared with $519,180 which three fire department units would have cost. The city has been very satisfied with the service and recently renewed the contract for two more years.

One of the firms involved in the Glendale service, Medevac, Inc., holds two other paramedic service contracts. One is with the city of El Monte and the other covers all of populous San Mateo County. Several years ago when that county decided to implement a paramedic service, officials requested bids from local fire departments and from private ambulance companies. The cost of a fire department paramedic program was estimated at $1,875,000. Medevac's bid of $650,000 thus represented nearly a two-thirds saving to the taxpayers. The company was hired on December 1, 1976, for an eight-year period. The contract (which includes an annual inflation adjustment) provides payment to the company only for dry runs and for bills that are uncollectible after 90 days and three attempts. Due to Medevac's excellent billing efforts, its bill to the county for the first year of service was only $562,000—$88,000 less than its bid. Medevac is actively seeking business in other California cities and counties.

Even in government paramedic programs, user fees appear to be the wave of the future. A 1978 California Department of Health Services survey of 292 cities found that 81% of the government-run paramedic services charge some sort of fees, though often not the full cost of the service. Pasadena, for example, has charged for transportation and supplies (but not actual medical services) ever since its pioneering program began in 1959. Los Angeles, as noted earlier, charges for transportation only. Beverly Hills has charged for transportation *and* medical service since 1971. In the wake of Proposition 13 many of the remaining cities began charging fees, among them West Covina and Torrance.

But the fees are far from enough to cover the costs, given that (a) most of the fees cover only a portion of the services provided and (b) local governments collect only 43% of the amounts billed (according to the 1978 survey). Moreover, because the government-run programs are two to three times as expensive as private ones, it seems unlikely that fees could *ever* be set high enough to make the programs self-supporting. Full-cost fees would be way above what economists call "market-clearing levels"—that is, a level at which supply and demand are in balance. People—and insurance companies—would balk at such high levels, when they were familiar with private firms' fees of one-half or one-third as much. Thus, as long as paramedic programs remain government-run, they are likely to remain a burden on the taxpayers.

The lesson of this chapter, however, is that there's no reason *whatever* to let local government get into the paramedic business. Competent, efficient emergency ambulance/paramedic programs are in operation all across the country in the private sector—some funded by donations, others by subscriptions, and still others by user fees. Getting the taxpayers involved is totally unnecessary.

7

Garbage and Solid Waste

In the spring of 1979 writer Philip Ross accepted an assignment from *New York* magazine: Follow a city garbage truck for one full day's shift (7 A.M. to 3 P.M.) and observe what the sanitation workers do all day. Initially quite sympathetic to the working man ("I'm not going to do a hatchet job. There's no way a man can lift garbage for eight straight hours," he told *New York*), Ross ended up outraged: Altogether, the three-man crew worked *less than two hours* that day for their $16,500-a-year pay.

That vignette typifies what is wrong with many city sanitation departments. All too often they are bureaucracies gone to seed, where the prime concern is maximizing the number of jobs, never mind getting the work done or saving money. Besides, the feeling seems to be, we're talking about collecting *garbage*. It's dirty, demeaning work. How can anyone be so base as to demand eight hours of hard work from the poor souls who must labor at this job?

Yet not everyone thinks of garbage collection that way. To New York residents, garbage is a $210-million-a-year pain in the wallet, not to mention a terrible eyesore. To politicians, having to cope with both citizen complaints and militant unions, garbage is an increasing headache. Yet to hundreds of private firms across America, garbage is a growth industry, offering the potential for expanding volume and substantial profits.

Garbage service varies considerably around the country. In some places there is open competition, with any number of companies competing for the business. In other places, garbage collection is a city government function, with the sanitation department exercising a monopoly or near-monopoly. Other cities contract out collection operations to a single private firm but retain control of the billing themselves. In still other cities, the government divides the area into districts and awards short-term (several-year) franchises to private firms. This is competition *in time* rather than in *space*. Thus each firm has a monopoly in its particular area for the duration of the franchise but must compete with other firms each time the franchise is up for renewal.

In this chapter, we're going to examine these different alternatives and see which ones work best—and why. We're also going to look at what happens *after* the garbage has been collected—the growing business of recycling solid waste.

LEAST-COST COLLECTION

Before we attempt a definitive answer to which type of service is best, let's look at a few examples that are suggestive of the burdens and opportunities of the various approaches.

New York City operates the nation's largest municipal sanitation department, which provides all residential collection. (It provides commercial service as well, but most businesses, despite being taxed for refuse service, pay for private firms that are more reliable.) Columbia University Management Professor E. S. Savas studied the costs of New York's municipal garbage collection, comparing it with private collection just outside the city limits. In the Little Neck and Douglaston sections of Queens, for example, twice-a-week residential service was costing $297 a year in 1975. Just three miles away in a similar neighborhood, Bellerose, in Nassau County, a private firm was providing *three*-times-a-week service for only $72 a year. Such findings led the Citizens Budget Commission to recommend switching to private operators, at a saving of $60 to $70 million per year.

Private firms have a long history of success in collecting San Francisco's garbage. In 1932 the city was divided into 97 garbage districts, and 36 companies competed for permits to serve each one. Within a few years, however, two companies owned all the permits: Sunset Scavenger Co. and Golden Gate Disposal Co. Both companies are owned solely by their employees, each of whom is limited to 32 shares of stock. Each driver has his own truck, works his own territory (including handling all collections), and operates at his own pace. Since each is guaranteed a full nine hours' pay for covering the day's assigned territory, most crews really hustle, completing the work in about six hours. The companies operate efficiently; together, their 700 employees are supported by an office staff of only 60, including just 18 executives.

Such efficiency in operations pays off for the citizens. In 1975 San Francisco households paid about $40 a year for garbage collection. Compare that to the New York City example above! And city officials are eminently satisfied with the arrangement. San Francisco Public Works Director S. M. Tatarian told the *New York Times* a few years ago, "I shudder to think what would happen if my department was responsible for collecting garbage . . . the rates would go through the roof." Added Health

Inspection Chief Jack Coyne, "Municipal collection in this city would do nothing but promote ill will, poor service, and another bureaucracy."

In Atlanta, Georgia, the city provides residential collection but does not prohibit competition from private firms. And it funds the service via user charges rather than taxes. Thus, those who choose alternatives are not forced to pay taxes *and* for the alternative service. This became especially relevant in 1975 when the city took a number of measures to cut collection costs. It reduced residential collections from twice to once per week and increased the fee for backyard pickup from $44 to $150 per year. Those who refused to pay for backyard pickup could haul their garbage to a neighborhood dumpster for pickup.

Those moves were quite unpopular, and a number of entrepreneurs sprang into action. Mrs. Frankie Van Cleave and Mrs. Sherrie Jackson purchased a used garbage truck, hired a college student as a driver, opened an office, and before long had 300 customers signed up at $100 a year—$50 less than the city's price. Backyard Team, Inc.'s backyard service is an important marketing factor in Atlanta's Northside area, where long driveways are the rule.

Backyard Team's success illustrates an important point about the garbage collection business: There are very few economies of scale. In fact, as city sanitation departments demonstrate, there are more often *diseconomies* of scale—that is, rising unit costs as size increases, due to ever-increasing administrative costs. When garbage service is unregulated, as in sprawling Los Angeles County, the number of firms rapidly proliferates. Serving the unincorporated areas of that county are about 500 garbage collection firms, some 200 of which consist of little more than an owner and a truck. It should be noted that larger firms denounce this situation as "dog-eat-dog-competition" in which "just anybody" can get into the business. In the Los Angeles case, the larger companies' trade organization, the California Refuse Removal Council, is actively promoting stringent government regulations in order to "professionalize" the business and drive out small operators. Its proposed "limited licensing ordinance" calls for garbage truck standards, higher license fees, and a ceiling on the number of licenses granted. While the Los Angeles County Counsel views the proposed ordinance as unconstitutional, the trade group boasts of having gotten similar measures enacted in Orange, Riverside, San Bernardino, and San Diego counties, without legal challenge. If offers no figures, however, on what has happened to the rates paid by users before and after passage of such measures.

New York, San Francisco, Atlanta, and Los Angeles are not isolated cases. The hard facts are now available to answer the question of what type of service is the most economical. In 1975 and 1976 the National Science Foundation funded a massive nationwide study of the issue, led by Columbia University Professors E. S. Savas and Barbara J. Stevens.[1] Included in its survey were 1,378 communities with populations between 2,500 and 750,000. To begin with, the survey found that the extent of garbage collection by private firms had been underestimated in most prior (less comprehensive) surveys. In fact, private firms collect residential refuse in about twice as many cities as municipal agencies do, and they collect commercial and industrial refuse in three times as many cities. It is only because municipal collection tends to be concentrated in larger cities that a greater number of homes is served by municipal collection than by private firms.

But what about the costs of various arrangements? The survey collected cost data from all the cities in the sample and separated them according to whether the service was provided by:

- the city itself (*municipal* collection);
- a single firm hired and paid by the city (*contract* collection);
- several private firms assigned to exclusive sections of the city, and paid by their customers (*franchise* collection); or
- competing private firms, without government involvement, except perhaps minimal licensing (*private* collection).

The results were striking. Contract and franchise service were found to be the least costly possibilities for cities of all sizes. Below about 20,000 population, the differences were relatively small. But above 50,000 population the cost difference was enormous. In those cities it costs the typical municipal agency *68% more* than it costs the average contract firm to provide twice-a-week curbside service. Not only that, many cities do not even know the cost of their municipal garbage service, generally understating it by about 18% in the city budget.

It apparently costs so much more for city agencies to collect garbage because they lack the incentive to be efficient. Their employees are absent about 12% of the time, compared with 7.5% for the contract firms. The municipal agencies use much larger crews (averaging 3.26 versus 2.18), serve fewer households per shift (632 versus 686), and spend more time serving each household per year (4.35 man-hours versus 2.37). Moreover, fewer municipal agencies use labor-incentive systems (80% versus 89%), and they tend to use trucks with smaller carrying capacities (averaging 19.8 cubic yards versus 23.1 cubic yards for private operators). These differences cannot be just coincidences. They clearly reflect the differences between bureaucratic management and profit-oriented management.

It's interesting to note that the Columbia University study found that municipal governments tend to "overproduce" such services as garbage pickup. That is, when given a choice, citizens tend to prefer less-expensive garbage service, even if this means reduced service levels. In cities where a choice is provided, only 33% have twice-a-week collection, whereas over 50% of the cities affording no choice provide twice-a-week service. This finding suggests that cost-conscious city officials may find the public more receptive than they expect to certain reductions in service level—reduced frequency or curbside collection—if these will lead to lower costs.

Although the full extent of the cost difference between government and private garbage collection has not been well known until recently, communities all across the country seem to have been getting the message on their own. Middletown, Ohio, switched from municipal to contract service in 1972, saving $350,000 per year. Camden, New Jersey, which switched in 1974, realized annual savings of $700,000. Among other cities switching to contract service for all or part of their garbage collection are Boston; Oklahoma City; Memphis; Jackson, Mississippi; Gainesville, Florida; Alamogordo, New Mexico; Omaha; Dallas; Charleston, South Carolina; and Utica, New York.

Quite a few large cities have divided up their territory into refuse collection districts, putting some or all of them out to bid. Montreal is divided into 198 districts, 18 operated by the city and 180 contracted out to private firms. The largest contractor serves 68 districts, but some are one-truck outfits that serve a single district. St. Paul, Minnesota, has 40 to 50 companies, Minneapolis has 50, and Wichita has 80. In 1979 New Orleans doubled the number of districts served privately—from 10% to 20% of the total—for an annual saving of $200,000.

The garbage business is not only an opportunity for small entrepreneurs. It is now big business. Its largest firms now operate as chains, with local operations in numerous states. The largest firm is Browning-Ferris Industries (BFI), in Houston. It has grown to giant proportions by acquiring more than 100 local firms in the past decade, and it grossed more than $362 million in 1978. Other industry leaders include Waste Management, Inc., of Oak Brook, Illinois, and Boston's SCA Services, Inc. Like BFI, both have acquired scores of smaller firms, to which they have brought modern $50,000 trucks of labor-saving design and modern management methods. Factors such as these help account for the marked differences in productivity documented by the Columbia University study.

MODERNIZING CITY COLLECTION

If your city already has a municipal garbage collection agency and is unwilling to consider phasing it out in favor of contract service, there are ways of reducing its costs. But to achieve economies like those of private firms, political and bureaucratic obstacles must be overcome.

The biggest potential for saving lies in the area of crew size. A recent survey by the International City Management Association showed that 11% of the thousand cities responding had crews of four or more per truck for backyard pickup, and 2% even had five or more crew members for *curbside* pickup.[2] Yet if more than two people are used for curbside pickup (or more than three for backyard), the amount of time they spend on such nonproductive activities as riding and waiting increases considerably. In contrast to the top-heavy cities, a number of others have been able to switch without difficulty to two-person crews for backyard pickup and one-person crews for curbside pickup. The survey mentioned earlier reported 50 cities using one-person garbage trucks; by now the figure is undoubtedly higher.

The key to making smaller crews effective is redesigned equipment. When Huntington Woods, Michigan, switched to a one-person operation, it replaced old rear-loading trucks with a modern side-loading truck designed for one-man operation. The city achieved annual savings of 28% with no reduction in the level of service.

Some cities have encountered severe labor problems in attempting such a switch. One that did not is Inglewood, California. Over a period of several years it switched entirely to one-person, side-loading trucks, with full support from its employees. Inglewood's approach was to establish a career ladder, whereby refuse collecting is considered an entry-level public works job. The city provides in-service training and subsidizes coursework to improve job-related skills. It also accomplished all reductions in crew size by transfer to other jobs or by attrition (taking advantage of normal turnover and retirement).

Partly mechanized systems, using 80-gallon carts which are rolled to a lifting device on the garbage truck, are in use in Fort Lauderdale, Florida, Shorewood, Wisconsin, and Albemarle, North Carolina. These systems are being used for once-a-week, curbside collection. For collection in alleys, fully mechanized systems that can pick up and empty 300-gallon dumpsters are being used in Odessa and Littlefield, Texas. Smaller mechanized systems, using 90-gallon, roll-out containers, are in use in Phoenix, Arizona, and Alliance, Ohio. Scottsdale, Arizona, is using special polyethylene containers of two different sizes, which can be picked up and emptied automatically.

Another way to economize is to use transfer stations. The number of lengthy trips to the incinerator or landfill site can be reduced by providing close-in locations. Collection trucks dump their loads there and return quickly to their pickup routes. Larger, special-purpose trucks then take the garbage from the transfer station to the disposal site. Neighboring Plano and Richardson, Texas, share a transfer station equipped with multi-load heavy-duty compactors. Each city pays in proportion to the tonnage it delivers. University City, Missouri, and Hamilton, Ohio, are also using transfer stations, as are the two private companies serving San Francisco.

Making the route structure more efficient is yet another important way to save money. The National Commission on Productivity analyzed city garbage-collection routes, finding that most of them are not economically laid out.[3] That means that trucks travel many more miles than necessary each day, wasting time, fuel, and vehicle life. But designing an "optimum" route structure is a complicated mathematical problem, requiring computer analysis.

Fortunately, cities no longer have to rely on their own skills to do this kind of analysis. The Environmental Protection Agency's Office of Solid Waste Management Programs has developed computer programs to do the job. Its Major Technical Assistance Program has now been tried in a number of cities, generally with favorable results. Portland, Maine, for example, used it to redesign its garbage-collection routes to permit an increase in service levels while still saving $23,000 a year. If Portland had kept the service level constant, the saving would have been much greater. The 14 member communities of the Southeast Oakland County, Michigan, Incinerator Authority reduced their average collection costs by 16% in a six-month period by using the MTA program. Little Rock, Arkansas, is saving $367,000 a year, while Wichita Falls, Texas, was able to cut back its collection work force to 1961 levels using computer-designed routes.

Vehicle maintenance is another area for cost saving. According to the National Commission on Productivity, a surprising number of cities do not have regular servicing or preventive-maintenance programs for their garbage trucks. Others choose poor-quality equipment or keep trucks in service well beyond a reasonable life—about five years. And many government repair shops are incompetently managed. Lancaster, Texas, set up a preventive-maintenance program for its garbage trucks that saved $7,900 in its first six months. Victoria, Texas, went to a four-day collection workweek (Monday, Tuesday, Thursday, Friday) that left Wednesday free for preventive maintenance without requiring overtime by the maintenance crews. The four-day week also has led to less commuting time and higher employee morale.

RECYCLING: CASH FOR TRASH

Once the garbage has been collected, the next problem is disposing of it. The two traditional methods, landfill and incinerators, are becoming less and less acceptable. Landfill is winding down because most cities are running out of nearby sites, leading to ever-higher costs for transporting refuse to distant disposal sites. Landfill costs range from $3 to $18 per ton, with more and more cities moving into the upper part of that range. Existing municipal incinerators are increasingly running into trouble from Environmental Protection Agency (EPA) air pollution restrictions, and constructing new ones gets more difficult all the time. Cities find it hard to raise the money, and opposition from potential neighbors has severely restricted possible construction sites.

The Arabs and private industry, an unlikely pair of allies, are coming to the rescue. By substantially raising the price of oil, Arab governments have ended the era of cheap energy. Because of much higher energy prices, it is becoming increasingly feasible to use garbage—plain old everyday residential and commericial refuse—as an energy source. The cost of "resource recovery" from garbage now ranges from $9 to $18 a ton—in many cases rivaling landfill disposal. Private firms, both small innovators and industrial giants, have therefore jumped into the resource-recovery market, developing a variety of processes to extract energy and usable metals and glass from garbage.

In many cases these firms are installing and running the plants, thereby benefiting taxpayers in several ways. First, when waste disposal goes private, its costs are removed from the municipal budget and therefore from the tax burden. Users then pay directly for waste disposal, as part of their garbage-collection fees. As we have seen in previous chapters, user charges are generally far more equitable than taxation. Second, when private industry operates the waste-disposal system, the costs are likely to be less than when government does so, because of the different incentives facing the two types of organizations. In addition, private firms can more readily take advantage of economies of scale in building the plants. Not being confined by municipal boundaries, a company can build a plant to serve several nearby communities, if economies justify it. (There is no inherent reason why cities cannot get together and do the same thing; it's just likely to take a lot longer and involve far more red tape and politics.)

Another advantage is that a private plant remains on the property-tax rolls. Municipal plants, on the other hand, are exempt and increase the tax burden on all other properties. Finally, since a private firm does not possess the power of eminent domain, it must find a plant site by strictly voluntary means. It cannot order unwilling landowners to sell. Thus, private plants are somewhat more likely to be located so as to minimize negative effects on their surrounding environment. (Of course, *all* such plants must meet the same EPA air pollution regulations.)

As of 1979 there were 15 large-scale plants (including five demonstration plants) and seven small plants in operation or under construction. Another six to 18 large plants are being planned, depending on which estimate one accepts. Along the way there have been some notable failures as well as modest successes. Like any new technological venture, garbage power has gone through growing pains, and some companies and cities have gotten burned. But there are enough success stories to demonstrate that both resource recovery and private enterprise operators are here to stay.

There are three principal methods in use today, varying in cost and complexity. The simplest is *bulk burning*—simply burning the refuse in an expensive high-temperature incinerator to produce steam, either for heating or electricity production. Bulk-burning plants are fairly expensive to build but cheap to operate. A newer technique is *refuse-derived fuel*. In this case the garbage is first shredded to separate out glass and heavy metals, which are sold for scrap. The remaining food waste, paper, and plastics can be burned in conventional coal-fired boilers. The capital costs are lower than in bulk burning because an expensive combustion unit isn't needed. But operating costs are higher due to the shredding and separating operation. A third, more costly, process is *pyrolysis*. After shredding and separation, the organic waste is burned with very little oxygen to produce a synthetic oil or gas. Both capital and operating costs are high, and pyrolysis is the most experimental of the three technologies at this time.

Bulk burning has been used for over a quarter of a century in Europe, where more than 150 cities heat buildings with steam derived from refuse. The first such facility became operational in Zurich in 1945 and is producing steam and electricity from 240 tons of refuse per day. Europe's largest plant, processing 2,000 tons per day, is in Amsterdam.

One of America's first bulk-burning operations is the Refuse Energy Systems Co. (Resco) plant in Saugus, Massachusetts. Resco is a joint venture between Wheelabrator-Frye, Inc., an environmental control system manufacturer which has licensed the Zurich technology, and M. DeMatteo Construction Co., which operated a landfill on the site of the new plant. Resco's $50-million plant takes 1,000 tons of garbage each day from Saugus, 12 other towns, and private refuse haulers. The garbage is burned to generate steam, which is sold to General Electric's heavy-equipment plant nearby. Resco's system supplies more than half the energy requirements for the 10,000-employee plant. Thus far, however, the plant has failed to make a profit, losing $10 million in 1978. The company now considers it a "research and development laboratory" in addition to a commercial venture, but is planning to build others.

Another firm getting into the field is UOP, Inc. In 1978 it signed a 20-year contract with Pinellas County, Florida, to develop, operate, and maintain a bulk-burning plant that will generate electricity. The facility will take in 2,000 tons of refuse a day from Tampa Bay communities, burning it to produce steam to drive a 40-MW turbine generator. The electricity will be sold to Florida Power Corporation, the local utility company.

A tale of woe from Tennessee illustrates the potential perils of this new technology—and should serve as a cautionary note to local governments about getting themselves too involved in such matters rather than relying on the expertise of the private sector. In 1972 the city/county government of Nashville/Davidson County, Tennessee, set up a nonprofit corporation, the Nashville Thermal Transfer Corporation. It was designed to utilize all the refuse from the metropolitan area to produce steam for sale to 27 buildings in the downtown area. Unfortunately, technical problems and bureaucratic foul-ups led to a host of difficulties. The emission control equipment failed to meet EPA requirements, the steam pipelines were not completed on schedule, and the tubing on the boilers cracked, forcing use of auxiliary (fossil-fuel) boilers. In its first two years the plant lost $3.6 million and nearly defaulted on its $16.5-million bond issue. The metro government increased its annual subsidy tenfold, to $1.5 million, and raised the dumping fee by $2 a ton. Prices charged for steam were doubled in the first year. As a result, the ten private heating customers found their costs to be higher, not lower, than before.

By contrast, Hempstead, Long Island, elected to put the entire burden on private enterprise. It selected Black Clawson Fibreclaim, Inc., to build and operate a 2,000-ton-per-day plant. Black Clawson set up a subsidiary, Hempstead Resources Recovery Corp. (HRRC), which obtained private financing for the plant. To satisfy its lenders, HRRC obtained long-term contracts with the purchasers of its output: a 17½-year contract to supply Long Island Lighting Company with steam, and other contracts with Alcoa and Reynolds Metal for recovered aluminum and with Glass Container Corporation for color-sorted glass. The company's recycling process is based on hydrapulpers—giant (20-foot-diameter) blender-type vats that pulp and shred incoming refuse and separate out metals and glass. The shredded material is floated off, dried, and compressed into a solid fuel which is burned to make steam for Long Island Lighting Co.

Hempstead officials decided to switch from municipal landfills to private-enterprise recycling for two reasons. The main one was cost: In densely populated Long Island, landfill disposal was costing $18–$19 per ton, whereas Fibreclaim will charge only $15—and rebate $4 of that as proceeds from the sale of steam and salvaged metal and glass. The other reason was expertise: The recycling technology is so complex that municipal officials preferred to rely on the expertise of professionals. Hemptead's only obligation is to supply the contracted amounts of garbage.

Producing solid fuel from refuse has attracted a number of other firms. Nearly half of all garbage-power plants presently in operation or under construction in the United States utilize some variant of this approach. One of the leaders is a relatively small firm, Combustion Equipment Associates. The firm has patented its process for producing what it calls Eco-Fuel II from garbage. The fuel is a fine, dry powder that can be stored without decomposing, burns more efficiently than raw refuse-derived fuel, and can be used in oil- or gas-fired boilers as well as coal-fired ones. The company is pricing it to be competitive with coal and natural gas, and about 20% less than oil. Its first full-scale plant takes in 400 tons of garbage per day in East Bridgewater, Massachusetts. The resulting fuel is then shipped to Waterbury, Connecticut, 160 miles away, where it is sold to a power company for use in oil-fired boilers. It is building a second plant (in a joint venture with Occidental Petroleum) in Bridgeport, Connecticut. This plant, at 1,200 tons per day, will be three times the size of the one in East Bridgewater. A third plant will be constructed in the South Bronx in 1980 under a contract from the New York State Urban Development Corporation. The $100-million plant will be one of the nation's largest, taking in 3,000 tons of garbage per day.

While the latter is under development by the private sector, New York City itself will be developing a plant of the same size on a site at the former Brooklyn Navy Yard. But instead of producing fuel, this 3,000-ton plant will use bulk burning to generate steam for sale to Consolidated Edison. Chicago is already operating a plant that supplies a nearby utility, Commonwealth Edison, but its 1,000-ton-per-day plant produces fuel, by shredding and separation, and pipes it to storage bins at the next-door Edison facility. There it is mixed with coal for burning in the plant.

Milwaukee is another city that has chosen the private sector for disposal. There, the Americology Division of American Can Co. has invested $18 million in a 1,200-ton-per-day fuel-from-refuse plant. The system first shreds the refuse, then separates it by air blower, magnetic separation, and electromechanical sorting. Aluminum, ferrous metals, and glass are all recovered. The remaining 60% is processed into a combustible fiber fuel sold to the Wisconsin Electric Power Co. The power company's Oak Creek plant will save about 75,000 tons of coal per year, thanks to the garbage-based fuel.

Pyrolysis is the third recycling technique. One of the pioneers in pyrolytic conversion was Monsanto's Enviro-Chem Division, which operates a 35-ton-per-day pilot plant in St. Louis. But its attempts to scale up the design for a 1,000-ton plant in Baltimore did not succeed, and the company recommended that the city turn the nearly completed plant into a conventional incinerator. More successful thus far is Occidental Petroleum, whose Garrett Research & Development Corp. subsidiary has a 200-ton-per-day plant in operation in San Diego. The plant produces a synthetic oil which is being sold to San Diego Gas & Electric Co.

San Francisco-based Pacific Gas & Electric Co. (PG&E) hired SRI International in 1974 to study the potential of pyrolysis in the Bay area. The study concluded that the region's daily 10,000 tons of garbage could supply nine pyrolysis plants which could produce enough fuel to supply 10% of the region's electricity. Once oil and gas prices began their steep rise, the feasibility of pyrolysis increased. One local firm, Pyro-Sol, Inc., has set up a pilot plant in Redwood City. It uses the shredded interiors of junked cars to form a clean-burning gas; a third of the gas is used to operate the plant and the other two-thirds to fire a boiler which makes steam to run a 1.65-MW power plant. The electricity is sold to PG&E, which has cooperated with Pyro-Sol in developing the process.

Union Carbide has also entered the pyrolysis business. It has extensively tested its Purox process at a 5-ton-per-day pilot plant in Tarrytown, New York, and a 200-ton demonstration plant in South Charlestown, West Virginia. If the latter plant lives up to expectations, Union Carbide plans commercial plants in the 1,000-ton-per-day range.

About 100 industrial firms around the country have thus far decided to recycle their own wastes via pyrolysis, thereby removing themselves from the community refuse collection and disposal cycle altogether. Their motivation is not conservation; rather, it is protection against fuel supply cutoffs. In the winter 1976/77 natural gas crisis, Rockwell International's truck axle plant in Marysville, Ohio, was nearly closed down, so the company began searching for alternative fuel supplies. Coal-fired boilers proved too expensive and oil supplies were judged too unreliable. But a $500,000 pyrolytic incinerator enables the plant to burn its own and neighboring plants' refuse. Installed in mid-1977, the system is expected to pay for itself in four years, from savings in fuel and refuse-disposal costs.

Another plant reaching the same conclusion is Xerox's educational publications plant in Columbus, Ohio. Its pyrolytic incinerator, installed in 1976, saved $60,000 the first year. The incinerator disposes of the millions of pounds of scrap paper the plant generates each year. "Instead of selling it for $9 a ton," reports engineering manager Nick Masucci, "we get $25 a ton in energy equivalent out of it."

The changing economics of landfill and fuel supplies are making practical a host of new waste-recycling technologies. An old problem (garbage disposal) is becoming a new source of energy. The private sector is pioneering in these efforts, and yet another formerly municipal function is being displaced by the superior expertise of the private sector. Taxpayers and consumers are just beginning to reap the benefits.

8

Leisure and Recreational Services

Cities and counties have traditionally provided a host of leisure-oriented facilities such as parks, golf courses, beaches, marinas, athletic fields, stadiums, auditoriums, museums, and libraries. It is not at all clear *why* provision of such services came to be viewed as the business of local government. Going back to our discussion of public goods versus private goods, it is difficult to consider any of these services as public goods, per se. Each tends to be used by only a minority of the residents of the community. When these facilities are paid for by tax money, nonusers end up helping to pay, so that users can get in "for free." This is hardly equitable. Moreover, in the case of larger cities within a metropolitan area, many of the users of a particular facility are nonresidents, and hence not even among the taxpayers indirectly paying for the facility.

Perhaps it is as a result of such considerations that leisure and recreational services are among those most often subject to user charges by local governments. Yet the extent of user charges varies widely among communities and types of facilities, with no apparent rhyme or reason. Some cities, such as Washington, D.C., impose virtually no charges for any of these services. Others charge for some types (e.g., swimming pools) but not others (e.g., museums). Yet another city may do just the opposite. Even within a single city the user charge philosophy is not always consistent. The whole subject is one that needs a thorough overhaul, with a view toward making these special-interest facilities as nearly as possible self-supporting. Doing so will increase equity and help to reduce the tax burden.

PRIVATE VS. PUBLIC

Municipal recreational services are actually only a small proportion of the total recreational expenditures made by Americans. In 1978 expenditures on recreation totaled $180 billion, compared with only about $4 billion spent by cities and counties. It takes only a little thought to see where the private spending goes: movie theaters, private museums, concert halls, auditoriums, golf courses, bowling alleys, stadiums, campgrounds, and amusement parks (ranging from miniature golf to such giants as Disneyland). The huge market for recreation is being met largely by the private sector.

Tradition may be the immediate explanation for why municipalities are involved at all. But that will not suffice as a justification for continued governmental involvement. And we have already seen that the public-good argument is not valid for this type of service since it is used by only a limited number of readily identifiable beneficiaries. One argument may be that privatization or charging is viewed as impractical.

One reason given why parks, for instance, must be provided by government and made available free of charge is that it would be impractical to restrict admission to paying customers. We can all imagine walling in a city park and stationing a ticket taker at the gate. The change in esthetics and convenience, as well as the high cost of the ticket taker, pretty clearly rules out this approach. But, the argument goes, if we cannot exclude nonpayers and charge users, how can the costs of the park (payments for the land and facilities, and ongoing maintenance) be met— unless, that is, the government owns it and taxes everyone?

There is no single answer to this oversimplified argument. Different cases must be dealt with differently. To begin with, there's a world of difference between a large county park facility offering specific attractions (rides, exhibits, swimming) and small city parks whose principal benefit is to provide esthetic relief in the midst of the city's concrete. The former are already designed in such a way as to facilitate exclusion of nonpayers and generally support enough business (due to their specific attractions) to justify ticket booths or coin-operated turnstiles. So we are left with only city parks that offer merely a pleasant walkway, a place to sit, and a nice view.

An interesting perspective on this case can be gained by asking the following qustion: What if the city suddenly no longer had the funds to maintain such parks? Who would then value their presence enough to come up with the funds to do so? This type of thought experiment helps us to see more clearly who the primary beneficiaries of such parks are. It's unlikely that the entire city's taxpayers would band together to support a park maintenance fund. To be sure, everyone may benefit at least a little from the existence of properly maintained parks, but it is readily apparent that some people benefit far more than others. The people whose homes and businesses are nearest to a park are the primary beneficiaries. They have ready access to it, they can see it every day, and their property value most likely reflects the benefit of having the park nearby. Thus, if any group would band together to maintain a city park, it's the neighborhood nearby, to preserve the park as an asset to their neighborhood (and incidentally, to maintain their property values).

This isn't just wishful thinking. Such a spontaneous demonstration of mutual local self-interest has come into being in Houston. The Houston Anti-Litter Team, Inc. (HALT) was organized in 1976 to clean up and maintain the city's freeway interchanges. When developer Howard Rambin III complained to the state highway department about the "mounting tide of litter" at these intersections, he was told that the state simply did not have the funds. Rambin thereupon decided to get the job done himself by organizing HALT.

The organization's *modus operandi* is as follows. Once an interchange has been targeted for cleanup (litter removal and grass cutting), HALT locates a businessperson near the intersection to serve as a team captain. With the help of HALT literature, the captain then solicits financial support from neighboring businesses—generally from $10 to $30 per month. HALT then contracts with a landscaping or grounds maintenance firm for initial cleanup and regular maintenance, and posts antilittering signs bearing HALT's name. The very first HALT project—the interchange of Interstate 610 and Westheimer Road—got the support of 63 of the 65 nearby owners or proprietors.

Rambin considers keeping the streets and sidewalks near his office building clean to be a normal business expense, and HALT is trying to promote general acceptance of this position. The group has found that initial cleanup of an interchange costs from $1,000 to $2,300, with ongoing maintenance costs of $750–$1,000 per month. HALT's operations have been so successful that it is able to support a full-time director to promote and administer the organization. Thus, we see how even small city parks could be maintained by their principal beneficiaries rather than by all taxpayers.

The same type of thing occurred in Oakland, California, after Proposition 13 was passed. Faced with a large amount of park acreage and serious budget cutbacks (from $19 million down to $13 million), the East Bay Regional Parks District set up an "adopt-a-park" program. The first participant was Kaiser Aluminum & Chemical Corp., based in Oakland, which agreed to adopt 88-acre Roberts Regional Recreation Area. (Kaiser Vice President for Public Affairs Richard Spees lives in the area and jogs in the park every day.) Under the agreement, Kaiser is making regular payments to the district to keep the park properly maintained—and getting a tax deduction in the process. Among other firms helping support park maintenance in California are Clorox Corporation, Atlantic Richfield Co., and *Sunset* Magazine.

National Journal columnist Neal Peirce reports that several nonprofit friends-of-the-parks organizations have been formed in large cities, to help parks departments cope with smaller budgets. The New York City Parks

Council raises private and grant money and mobilizes adult and teenage volunteers to help with park maintenance. In 1977 it built a new waterfront park in Brooklyn's Williamsburg section. Using volunteer labor from local residents and donations of material from local firms, it kept the cost below $10,000.

A park support group is really just an extension of an idea big cities have long been accustomed to: the nonprofit "friends of the zoo" or "friends of the library" or "friends of the art museum." These groups, which traditionally include many leading (and wealthy) members of the community, raise money and provide volunteer services to support their favorite leisure-time facilities. For example, the Los Angeles zoo society provides the funds for all capital expenditures at the city's huge Griffith Park Zoo. The city pays only the operating expenses, one-third of which come from user fees and the balance from taxes. The Oakland zoo society recently signed a contract to take over operation of the zoo from that financially troubled California city.

Another reason why it is argued that cities must operate leisure services is so that poor people won't be denied access to them by lack of money. The same logic is frequently applied to other publicly operated facilities, such as mass-transit systems. Nobody, however, seems to apply it to the fast food restaurants, record stores, or shoe stores used by the poor. But for some reason, when it comes to the services supplied by the public sector, the prime criterion of pricing policy is access for the poor.

This kind of approach is mistaken. Prices serve several valuable functions, which apply to the public sector's services as well as to those of the private sector. Besides producing revenues to pay the costs of the operation (and thereby avoiding unfairly charging nonusers), a price serves to ration demand so as to prevent overcrowding. When the city of Oakland, California, eliminated admission charges at two pools serving partly low-income neighborhoods in 1968, attendance soared—by 29% in one case and by 67% in the other. The pools quickly became overcrowded and unpleasant to use. This is an expected consequence of providing a desired service at a price of zero. Prices also serve to measure people's relative demand for various types of services, thereby giving the providers valuable feedback as to the quantity and quality desired. If, for example, small quantities of lawn chairs, umbrellas, and baby strollers are all made available for rental in a park, their relative popularity—measured by the income received—will tell the park manager which types of equipment are most wanted. They may even experiment with more expensive chairs (at a higher price, of course) to see if there's a demand for such diversity. Were the equipment made available "for free," whatever was there would be used, and most likely abused, and such experimentation would most likely never take place.

Consequently, the decision not to put prices on public services is an implicit decision to produce them inefficiently. The taxpayers are then doubly victimized. They have to pay for services they may not use and they pay more than is necessary to produce the services. If the political process decides that the poor (or the elderly, or any other favored group) must have better access to recreational services, it is far less costly to make this special privilege explicit, by such devices as giving out free or reduced-rate passes to persons meeting certain criteria, or relying on income-supplement programs which let the poor make their own expenditure decisions. That way at least all *other* users will pay a price for the services, and many of the efficiency-promoting benefits of the price system will still be realized.

The *Fees and Charges Handbook* of the Heritage Conservation and Recreation Service[1] suggests a number of ways of reducing the impact of user fees on low-income groups:

- Define differential fee structures.
- Waive fees on an individual basis.
- Have local citizens, businesses, or service clubs provide scholarships or subsidize programs.
- Adjust fee structure according to income level of neighborhood.
- Allow extended payment schedules.
- Provide work exchange ("sweat equity") for admission.
- Allow equipment or supply donations in lieu of fees.

Some agencies are already making use of these ideas. The Fairfax County, Virginia, recreation agency distributes sports complex passes to low-income children identified through the county's school lunch program. The Los Angeles County Art Museum provides free admission one day per month so that senior citizens and others who can't afford the new (post-Proposition 13) $1.50 admission fee can be allowed entry. The San Juan School District in Sacramento, California, arranges for local businesses to give money for "scholarships" for low-income children to attend recreation facilities.

The point of this discussion is that it is not necessary to give up the many benefits of pricing recreational services, simply because some people are poor. Many creative ways can be found to aid the poor—while ensuring that everyone else pays his or her way.

RECREATION USER FEES

There are many types of user fees. The American Institute of Park Executives and the National Recreation and Parks Association classify them as follows:

- *Entrance fees*—to parks, gardens, zoos, beaches, campgrounds, or their parking lots
- *Admission fees*—to enter a specific building or attraction within a recreational area
- *Rental fees*—to use a piece of property or equipment, e.g., a boat, tennis racquets, golf clubs, ice skates, baby stroller
- *Use fees*—to make use of a specific facility or take part in an activity, e.g., an archery range, boat race, reserved picnic area

- *License or permit fees*—to gain seasonal access for hunting, fishing, boating, or similar activity
- *Sales revenues*—derived from proprietors of concession stands, which, in turn, charge their customers
- *Special services fees*

Entrance or admission fees are not usually charged for city parks, playgrounds, and community centers. In contrast, at least nominal fees are often charged for those facilities that are more costly to maintain, more subject to congestion, and easier to fence off. These might include golf courses, pools, tennis courts, and zoos. In some cases, these facilities also charge higher rates during times of high demand, thus shifting some of the demand for the services to off-peak hours and reducing congestion, maintenance, and deterioration.

Several new ideas in park and recreation user charges have been suggested in recent years. One is the annual permit, similar to the Golden Eagle passes one can purchase for access to the National Parks. A 1967 study by the Arthur D. Little consulting firm recommended extending this concept to other recreational facilities, and some cities have been doing just that. Santa Barbara, California, for example, now charges residents $18 a year for a tennis permit that grants preferential admission to the city's popular tennis courts. A permit is not required to play, but permit holders can bump nonholders at any time.

In other cases a permit can be required for access to the facility. To keep administrative costs to a minimum, the permits can be obtainable by mail, and enforcement need not require a tended admission gate. Instead, signs and spot checking can be used to deter use by nonpermit holders.

Another relatively recent development is setting higher user charges for nonresidents because residents already pay for part of the park and recreation program via taxes. Dallas; Fairfax County, Virginia; and Santa Barbara are three of the most recent jurisdictions to introduce a nonresident differential in their recreation pricing. In Santa Barbara the fees for nonresidents are 25% higher in many programs, such as weaving and yoga classes. But for all those that involve the use of major facilities— tennis courts, pools, gymnasiums—nonresidents pay twice as much as residents.

Cincinnati's new pay fountain is one of the most unusual forms of user charges on record. The fountain is part of a $2.8-million structure (including a parking garage) in that city's Yeatman's Cove Park on the banks of the Ohio River. Although water flows in the fountain at all times, insertion of a quarter turns on a spectacular three-minute display. If the fountain is activated only five times an hour, eight hours a day, it will bring in over $4,500 a year, to be used for park (and fountain) maintenance.

There is no reason why leisure and recreational services cannot be made self-supporting by means of user fees. Apart from political obstacles, that is. Private recreational facilities, after all, *have* to be self-supporting or they go out of business. Not only is it *possible* to make these public programs self-supporting—it is actually happening in some communities. The park and recreation agency of Wheeling, West Virginia, is now 98% self-supporting. Its fee programs support nonfee programs to bring overall income nearly into balance with expenses. The famed San Diego zoo is virtually self-supporting from user fees. The recreation programs of Newark and El Cerrito, California, were both made 100% self-supporting in 1979, to cope with Proposition 13 constraints. Santa Barbara's Park Department in 1978 adopted a five-year goal of reaching self-sufficiency. Among the measures being taken are the introduction of parking fees at beaches and expansion of private concessions to provide more revenues. San Diego's Mission Bay Park includes hotels and restaurants as concessionaires; rents from these facilities pay for the public facilities in the rest of the park.

Thus, even if an individual neighborhood park cannot be self-supporting, a city's park and recreation *system* can be, if enough attention is given to finding sources of income and developing appropriate user charges.

PARK CONTRACTING

Regardless of how a park is financed, the cost of operating it can generally be reduced. An increasingly popular way to do this is to turn over park maintenance to a professional landscape-maintenance firm, on a contract basis. All the advantages of private-sector contracting that we have discussed in previous chapters apply equally well to park-maintenance contracting—and the number of potential suppliers is large (in contrast to such services as police and fire protection).[2]

Park-maintenance contracting has caught on rapidly in California over the past several years. Downey reports saving 20% on upkeep of its golf course since the work was contracted out. Ventura County, north of Los Angeles, is also saving 20% by contracting for its park maintenance, with performance incentives written into the contract. Lynwood's first week with contract tree trimming resulted in 500 trees being trimmed. "People around City Hall were stunned," notes administration analyst Gerard Goldhart. "Our city crew did 500 trees in an entire year, literally." The 1979 contract was for $87,000, compared with the previous budget of $125,000 for the city crew it replaced. Reportedly, there are "hundreds" of landscaping firms in California—many of them small, local outfits—that now market their services to local government.

Even before Proposition 13, a number of California cities had begun to contract for some of their park and recreation services. A 1976 survey by the League of California Cities found that seven cities had hired private firms to do their park maintenance; eight, to maintain their street trees and median strips; and eight, to take care of the landscaping around city buildings. Another four used private firms rather than city staff to design and develop new parks. Five cities had private firms running some or all of their recreation programs, and 13 had contracted out their golf course operations.

Since passage of Proposition 13 this trend has accelerated. Alameda, for example, is trying out contract maintenance at its newest park. Rohnert Park has contracted out maintenance of two of its parks, and of the landscaping at city hall and on median strips. San Jose awarded its first two-year contract for maintenance of its downtown parks. Compared with city costs of $12,500 per month, the bids it received ranged from $4,800 to $13,000.

While the operation of parks by private firms is not yet common, golf course operation is a runaway success, especially in Southern California. When Fullerton decided to contract out its golf course in 1974, the winning bidder cut operating costs by 21%—and extended the playing time by five weeks a year. After several years, though, that firm lost out to a competitor which was willing to invest in capital improvements and take over the restaurant and pro shop as well.

Rohnert Park's eight-year-old golf course was losing about $60,000 a year when city officials decided to privatize. The winning bidder, California Golf, signed a 30-year lease contract, rebuilt the course, and guaranteed the city a minimum income of $60,000 a year. Increasingly, like Rohnert Park, cities are turning to long-term leases, under which the contractor takes over the entire operation, leaving the city nothing to do but sit back and collect revenues.

A few California cities are turning other facilities over to private contractors, as well. Fremont and Walnut Creek have contractors operating tennis facilities in city parks. San Joaquin County has contracted out the operation and maintenance of some of its parks, swimming pools, and zoo.

The rapid growth of interest in contracting became evident in April 1979 when California State University at Hayward held a conference on the subject in Oakland. With only minimal advance publicity, more than 100 people attended—park and recreation professionals from all over the state. They eagerly exchanged information on this rapidly growing means of saving money in the operation of park and recreation programs.

PARK EFFICIENCY

Besides using private contracting, officials can make park maintenance more efficient by various analytical and technological improvements. A scheduling technique known as *work measurement* (which is discussed in more detail in Chapter 12) can produce substantial savings by utilizing park-maintenance personnel more efficiently. Wilmington, Delaware, realized an annual saving of 27% thanks to a new work-scheduling system based on this type of analysis. Other cities which have used the technique include Santa Rosa, California; Syracuse, New York; and Honolulu, Hawaii.

Labor-saving equipment can also cut costs, more than paying for itself in subsequent labor-cost savings. For example, a surprising number of cities still rely extensively on hand watering. Automated sprinkler systems offer many benefits. They use only about half as much water as hand watering and they generally increase a park's availability since, unlike gardeners, they work at night. Generally a sprinkler system will pay for itself in labor-cost savings in less than seven years. Other types of equipment can also save time. Chula Vista, California's $10,000 automated swimming pool chemical-treatment system paid for itself in just 13 months due to savings in time, chemicals, and mileage. Winston-Salem, North Carolina, park employees save time applying insecticides by using a centrifugal-force spraying unit. In some applications, instead of cutting and trimming, St. Petersburg, Florida's park crews are using residual herbicides whose effect is much longer lasting; and application of the herbicides takes less time than trimming, thus producing substantial man-hour savings.

Further maintenance savings can be realized by proper design or redesign of the parks themselves. Parks should be planned from the start for automated sprinkler systems. Other time-saving design features include tree-planting configurations that make mowing and trimming easier, avoidance of grass areas that are inaccessible to large mowers, and bordering flower beds with walkways instead of grass. St. Petersburg is an exemplar of such park-design techniques.

LIBRARIES AND MUSEUMS

Libraries and museums can represent large drains on the taxpayers or can be made efficient and self-supporting. Both represent services used mostly by an elite minority of the community which tends to be vocal about "public" (taxpayer) support. Hence, major changes are likely to be slow in coming. But coming they are.

Museums, both public and private, seem to be showing the way. Faced with the decline of wealthy patrons and limitations on what can be drawn from the public purse, museums across the country are deriving increasing revenue from the sale of related products. Former "sales desks" have become full-fledged retail stores and mail order operations offering a considerable assortment of goods, from art prints and statuary to tote bags. New York's Metropolitan Museum of Art, which pioneered museum retailing, took in $12.5 million in 1977, three-fourths of it from catalog mailings to a million households. The Smithsonian Institution sold goods valued at $5.5 million in 1976, New York's Museum of Modern Art $1.5 million, the Los Angeles County Art Museum $800,000. Profits on such sales, which average about 15%, help pay the museums' ongoing expenses.

Most museums are also increasing their admission fees—or beginning to charge them where they never did before. (Some have begun simply by asking for donations—which is better than not charging at all!) Traditionalists have a hard time accepting even modest fees if the museum has been "free" for many years, and some museums report sharp declines in attendance—at first. But after awhile people get used to the idea of pay-as-you-go. A prime success in this regard is the Oregon Museum of Science and Industry in Portland. Rated as one of the four best science centers in the nation, the museum is completely self-supporting. Its $2-million-a-year budget comes entirely from donations, memberships, an annual auction, admission fees, educational program fees, and a periodic fund drive.

Whether or not they sell products, libraries, too, are beginning to charge money. Some now charge a fee for library cards, and a few charge admission. The Los Angeles public libraries charge a daily fee for checking out best sellers, thereby helping to keep these popular books in circulation. They have also doubled their fine for overdue books from 5¢ to 10¢ per day. The public library in Indianapolis is conducting a research project to gauge user reaction to fees for computer searches and interlibrary loans. The Minneapolis Public Library is offering a sophisticated computerized reference service called "Inform." The users, most of which are large firms headquartered in the city, pay $35 an hour for access to the system.

"The user fee idea is cropping up all over," writes Fay Blake: "in public libraries in Minneapolis, in academic libraries for data base services and for interlibrary loans, and in the small freelance operations which provide information for those who can pay." Like quite a few librarians, Blake is opposed to the whole idea, having been schooled in the tradition of "free public libraries." The 1977 convention of the American Library Association witnessed sharp debate on the user-charge issue and ended up passing a resolution in support of "free" libraries—although the organization's governing council had previously defeated a similar resolution.

But the precedent for setting user fees is being solidly established by the growth of computerized information services. In many cases the only way a library can afford to get into these increasingly popular services is to offset the costs via user charges. Several years ago Eugene Garfield, board chairman of the Information Industry Association, told the National Commission on Libraries and Information Science that pay libraries are inevitable. *Library Journal* editor John Berry III, although opposing the trend, seems to agree: "If a city manager is looking for a way to cut the municipal budget, he might look at a library and say, 'Well, if you charge for this (computerized) research, why don't you charge for the story hour for the kids? Why don't you charge for using the catalog?'" Adds Fay Blake, "No hard-pressed city auditor or mayor or council is going to approve a budget for a library's free services once he smells user fees in the offing."

Library administrators also save money for taxpayers by automation. Macon, Georgia, has installed an automated book check-out and check-in system using supermarket-type bar codes on the books and light-wand reading devices. The new system's computer also replaced the huge clerical task of filing and unfiling about a million 3x5 cards each year. It automatically prepares overdue book notices and bills for lost books, maintains reserve book lists, and produces various statistical reports. Library Director Charles J. Schmidt reports that the system has doubled the productivity of his personnel, from an average of 11,000 annual check-outs per staff member to nearly 22,000. The system is now being adapted for the Albany, Georgia, library, as well.

Sunnyvale, California, has automated the process of cataloging new books. Following a study by Public Technology, Inc., library officials there decided to tie into the Ohio College Library Center's automated cataloging system. More than 300 public, university, and federal libraries now participate in the system via time-sharing computer terminals. Previously the library had to wait four to six weeks after a book was received for catalog cards to arrive from the Library of Congress. Now the cards are printed on Sunnyvale Library's printer by the OCLC computer. The system has reduced the cost per card set from 50¢ plus typist's time to a net cost of 21¢. Book processing time has been cut from five weeks to two weeks, and backroom storage space has been reduced 60%. Overall savings work out to $4,000–$6,000 per year.

Like most other public services, libraries and museums provide something of value to identifiable beneficiaries. They can be run well, or poorly, like any service business. Modern management and technological tools can make these institutions efficient, and user charges can begin matching up those who pay with those who benefit. Together, these techniques can eventually remove yet another burden from the backs of the local taxpayer.

9

Transit Systems

The annual deficit of the public transit system is one of the fastest-growing items in many city budgets. From 1971 to 1976 transit deficits increased over 800%. During this period the cost of providing transit service increased at more than twice the rate of inflation, while transit farebox revenues increased at only half the rate of inflation. In the early 1970s, farebox revenues paid for a bit over 90% of operating costs; by 1979, however, revenues were paying only 48% of operating costs. Of the 1979 deficit, about half was made up by local taxes, the balance by federal and state taxes.

Except in a handful of large cities which operate rail lines, mass transit usually means a bus system. Typically, it is the remains of one or more formerly private bus companies that went bankrupt and were consolidated by the city, the county, or a multijurisdictional transit district.

Most of the bankruptcies and takeovers occurred during the 1950s and '60s. During those postwar decades our metropolitan areas underwent a profound transformation. Vast acreage surrounding the central cities was converted to tracts of single-family houses, and automobile ownership soared. These demographic changes spelled economic doom for conventional fixed-route transit systems. The dispersion of homes greatly reduced the ability of a limited number of routes to serve the potential customers. And the proliferation of cars—aided by the cities' construction of expressways and freeways—meant that many fewer people needed to ride the bus.

Bus company managements responded to these changes in rather simplistic fashion. They clung to their fixed routes and attempted to cover rising costs by increasing fares rather than devising new forms of service tailored to the changed market condition. This only served to drive away even more passengers, since transit demand is relatively sensitive to price, and led to bankruptcies.

Political pressure induced many local governments to take over failing bus companies, on the grounds that lower-income people had to have *some* form of public transportation and if the private sector couldn't provide it the public sector would have to. The passage of the Urban Mass Transportation Act of 1964 provided large amounts of federal money to assist cities in buying the failing companies. Originally it was contended that once the cities took over, the financial problems would be solved because (1) the lines would no longer have to pay taxes and (2) they would no longer have to make a profit. (We have encountered this fallacious view of private versus public operations in earlier chapters.) It was even thought that the systems would somehow be able to expand and increase ridership, thereby operating more efficiently.

But none of these fond hopes was realized. The real needs of riders have gone unmet. In most cases service has been reduced, ridership has continued to drop, and costs—especially labor costs—have soared. (In the period 1972-78 labor costs went up 300% in some transit systems!) The federal government is now providing operating subsidies to the systems its original capital-equipment grants were supposed to make self-supporting.

The fundamental flaw, of course, was the failure to realize that a single system of fixed-route buses (or trains) was no longer a suitable response to the changed market conditions of most metropolitan areas. Attempts to force-fit these systems into suburbanized areas will continue to fail and will continue to drain money from the taxpayers. Alternative solutions that can respond to riders' new needs in innovative and cost effective ways are required.

A SOLUTION THAT WON'T WORK

In the past decade, the Urban Mass Transit Administration (UMTA) has been promoting an unworkable solution to large-city transit problems: Build subways. Never mind that a subway is even more of a fixed-route, density-dependent system than a bus line. The idea seems to be that since subways "work" in New York and Montreal and Moscow (where population density is many times that of Atlanta or Denver or Los Angeles), they should work elsewhere. Subways can be made to look modern and technological so people will be dazzled by them, and they *ought* to get people out of their cars and off the streets (hence reducing traffic congestion and air pollution—and everyone's for doing that). Ergo, we'll build subways, and hang the expense!

Unfortunately, hanging the expense is just about what one has to do to consider subways as a transit solution. The showcase modern subways are San Francisco's BART and Washington, D.C.'s Metro. BART was funded by local bonds, being paid off by a special multicounty sales-tax override. It cost over $2 billion, but carries only 130,000 passengers a day. A typical BART commute from suburban Orinda to downtown San Francisco costs

$6.77, including interest on the bonds and "social costs" to neighbors. Figured on a comparable basis, making the same trip in a full-size car costs only $4.49; in a subcompact, $4.05; and on the bus, only $3.21. Excluding the social costs, the average BART ride cost $4.48 in 1975/76. Since the average fare was only 72¢, the taxpayers had to make up $3.76 for every trip—more than five times the fare.[1]

Washington's new Metro is subsidized even more heavily. When completed, the 100-mile system is now expected to cost $7 billion—that's $70 million for every mile of track. During its first nine months of operation, with fares running from 40¢ to 55¢, each ride received a taxpayer subsidy of $10.38—more than 20 times the fare. By 1981 the taxes paid by each household in the Washington metropolitan area to subsidize the Metro will total $1,670—enough to buy a good used car.[2]

Besides costing nonusers a fortune, these new rail systems neither save energy nor reduce traffic congestion. Surveys show that they attract most of their ridership away from buses. Thus, they do very little to reduce the number of cars on the road. And by depriving buses of riders, they serve only to worsen the dismal economics of existing bus systems.

A study by the Congressional Budget Office concluded that "under typical conditions, new rapid rail systems actually waste energy rather than save it . . ."[3] This is because (1) construction of rail lines, especially subways, is particularly energy intensive, (2) rail system riders still drive to and from stations in low-occupancy autos, and (3) the rail systems divert riders from much more energy-efficient buses. Professor Charles A. Lave has calculated that it will take BART 535 years just to break even on the energy costs of building the system.

Despite this overwhelming evidence, UMTA is charging ahead with rail lines as the panacea for big-city transit problems. Atlanta's subway is nearing completion, and other subways are on the drawing boards for Baltimore, Buffalo, Los Angeles, and Miami. UMTA expected to spend $16.4 billion during 1979–82. From what we've seen, cities should avoid this "free money" like the plague. To get stuck with a transit system whose operating costs are five to 20 times higher than what fares will bring in *has* to be a raw deal for the city's taxpayers—especially when there are much better solutions that cost taxpayers little or nothing.

SOLUTIONS THAT WORK

The key to solving America's transit problems lies in devising new forms of service that respond to the actual needs of a widely dispersed population. Those involved in providing transit must find out what these transportation needs are, rather than remain fixated upon moving heaven and earth to get people to use their preconceived idea of what a transit system is supposed to be.

What is needed, in short, is an economic and legal climate that encourages experimentation and risk-taking—a free market, in other words. Unfortunately, in most urban areas there is anything *but* a free market in transportation services. Typically, there is a large municipal rail and/or bus line serving a limited number of fixed routes. There are also one or several taxi companies, in most cases heavily regulated as to the number of cabs, the areas served, and the fares charged. Any efforts to begin other forms of service are usually legally thwarted. They are immediately attacked by the municipal transit line or the taxi companies as draining away passengers ("skimming the cream") and therefore contrary to the public interest.

Should an entrepreneur persist despite these obstacles, he is likely to be classed as a "common carrier" by the state public utilities commission and forced to prove that (a) he is "fit, willing, and able" to provide the proposed service, (b) the operation is necessary for the public's convenience, and (c) the existing carriers are unable to meet the needs the entrepreneur proposes to serve. In some states he must even prove that he will not take any business away from the existing carriers.

These laws, and the public attitudes that support them, have effectively preserved the shared monopoly of municipal bus/rail line and cartelized taxi industry in most communities. And that has left most people with no affordable alternative to the private automobile—despite mounting congestion, worsening smog, and rising fuel prices.

There *are* better ways. Here and there, despite the obstacles, private innovators have developed new forms of transportation service that respond to real needs. These new services are typically grass-roots efforts that require minimal investment and *no* tax funds. They go by the generic name *paratransit*.[4]

Jitneys, gypsy cabs, shared-ride cabs, car pools, and van pools are among the many forms of paratransit. They vary in price, accommodations, and service levels. But they share the common characteristic of *flexibility*, which is very much in keeping with the decentralized nature of today's metropolitan areas. Until recently, they shared a more dubious distinction as well. All of these services (except for car pools in which no money changed hands) were illegal in most cities.

Jitneys

The term *jitney* refers to a small (usually 8- to 12-passenger) vehicle carrying passengers to various destinations, along a relatively fixed route, usually for a flat rate per passenger, but sometimes on a zone-rate fare. Jitneys are typically far less expensive than taxis, often costing little or nothing more than bus fare. Usually the jitney is owner-driven, though the driver may coordinate his operations with other drivers by belonging to an association. Jitneys developed in the 1914–18 period—the heyday of the Model T. In 1915 there were 62,000 of them, in every major American city. So successful were jitneys that they threatened to put the trolley lines out of business. Owners of the latter—generally well connected politically—succeeded in having laws passed in most cities completely outlawing jitneys.

Overseas, however, jitneys often provide a major portion of a large city's transportation. Over half of all daily travelers in Caracas and Buenos Aires ride either jitneys or larger jitney-buses called *colectivos*. Smaller, more conventional jitneys play a major role in Santiago, Chile, and Lima, Peru. "Jeepneys" and free-market taxis provide 25% of all mass transit in Manila, 15% in Seoul. And in Teheran, jitneys and taxis constitute the *entire* mass-transit system.

In the United States only a few jitney services survive, and they are limited to particular areas of a few cities. In Atlantic City, 190 jitneys ply Pacific Avenue, the major thoroughfare serving hotels and restaurants on both sides of the Boardwalk. Two associations operate 117 jitneys along two routes in San Francisco: Mission Street and Third Street. The former serves the major business and commercial district, while the latter extends from the Civic Center to Hunter's Point, a black ghetto. All-black jitneys operate in Baton Rouge, Louisiana, and Miami, Florida. Each runs between a black suburb and the downtown area. All the above are legal jitneys.

Illegal jitneys operate in a number of cities. In Chattanooga, Tennessee, 85 jitneys carry some 20 million riders a year. On a typical route the fare is 35¢, with an extra 10¢ charge for going up to three blocks off the route—a flexibility you'd never find with the city bus line. Though officially denied, an illegal jitney service has operated in the black ghetto of Chicago for many years. Between 50 and 100 unlicensed "private limousines" ply the streets of San Francisco. In New York City the mayor's taxi commission estimated in 1966 that more than a thousand legal liveries (limousines) were operating illegally as jitneys or taxis, both downtown and in black neighborhoods. A St. Louis jitney system comprising 85 vehicles served the city's black neighborhoods from 1917 until it was suddenly put out of business in 1965 by the Bi-State Transit Authority.

In all of these cases—and in many more—jitney service springs up to fill a need for transportation that cannot be met by either buses (too few routes) or taxis (too expensive). In many cases jitneys arise to serve minority areas where bus service is sparse and taxi service nearly nonexistent. In Pittsburgh illegal jitneys, which outnumber the city's legal cabs, operate between downtown and black neighborhoods to the east of the city. Some parallel the bus lines, charging the same 40¢ fare, but for a little extra they will take a passenger home. Others drive what amount to car-pool routes, picking up the same passengers day after day and taking them to and from work. Some wait in front of supermarkets to take shoppers home. Occasionally drivers will extend credit to regular passengers until payday. Besides supplying convenient, low-cost transportation to low-income people, jitneys also provide self-employment to the owner-drivers, with compensation in direct proportion to how hard they work. Jitneys are a perfect example of a form of transportation that fits the changing needs of its riders.

Deregulated Taxis

Studying the taxi industry several years ago, respected transportation economist Martin Wohl of Carnegie Mellon University reached a striking conclusion: "It is my view that changes in taxi regulation, pricing, and operation would markedly improve the availability, usage, and financial viability of cabs *and probably do more than any other transportation improvement to lure commuters out of cars and increase total transit patronage.*"[5] What he was talking about, in particular, was "lifting of barriers" on the number of taxicabs allowed to operate, the places they're allowed to serve, and the fares charged. Political scientist Sandi Rosenbloom studied the effects of regulation on the extent of taxi service in 1970.[6] As Table 3 makes clear, the only three cities with relatively large numbers of cabs (more than about four cabs per 1,000 people) are Washington, D.C., Atlanta, and Honolulu, and they are the only cities that don't restrict either the number of cabs or the number of firms allowed to operate.

Taxi representatives in regulated cities frequently claim that the legal number of cabs is all the market will support and that any larger number

Table 3

TAXI SERVICE IN SELECTED CITIES, 1970

CITY	TYPE OF RESTRICTION	TAXIS IN SERVICE	TAXIS PER 1,000 POP.
New York	Number of cabs	11,722	1.5
Chicago	Number of cabs	4,600	1.4
Los Angeles	Number of firms	885	0.3
Philadelphia	Number of firms	1,480	0.8
Detroit	Number of cabs	1,310	0.9
Houston	Number of firms	473	0.3
Washington, D.C.	None	19,144	10.2
San Francisco	Number of cabs	798	1.2
Boston	Number of cabs	1,525	2.3
Phoenix	Number of firms	99	0.2
Pittsburgh	Number of firms	600	1.2
Atlanta	None	1,900	3.9
Minneapolis	Number of cabs	248	0.8
Miami	Number of cabs	431	1.0
Honolulu	None	1,400	4.3
Birmingham	Number of firms	245	0.8

Source: Sandi Rosenbloom, "Taxis and Jitneys: The Case for Deregulation," *Reason*, February 1972, p. 9.

would simply spread the demand too thin for anyone to make money. This is utter nonsense, as the thriving Washington, D.C., market, with its 10.2 cabs per 1,000 people (compared with New York's 1.5 or Houston's 0.3) demonstrates. Rosenbloom cites a variety of studies to show that there is a large unfilled demand for taxi service in restricted cities. Poor people, housewives, and students all use taxi service in considerable numbers— when sufficient service is available. But in restricted cities, cabs tend to concentrate on business users, serving the downtown, hotels, and the airport, and leaving residential areas greatly undersupplied.

Despite the laws, in many cities illegal gypsy cabs have sprung up to meet part of this unfilled demand. The *New York Times* has estimated the number of gypsy cabs in that city at between 4,000 and 5,000, mostly serving minority neighborhoods. Gypsy cabs cruise the streets openly in Cleveland's black Hough section and Pittsburgh's Hill district. Because they serve such a large market, gypsy cabs are often allowed to operate, so long as they confine their operations to areas poorly served by licensed cabs. But because they operate outside the law, some gypsy cabbies take advantage of unwitting patrons, charging exorbitant fares under threats of violence, or actually robbing them. But for many would-be cab users, it's either risk a gypsy cab or forget about taxi service altogether.

The last few years have seen the beginning of a trend toward deregulation of taxi service. Major monopoly or near-monopoly cab companies have gone bankrupt in Los Angeles, San Diego, Philadelphia, and elsewhere, leading the first two cities to ease restrictions on entry. In Los Angeles, the area formerly served exclusively by bankrupt Yellow Cab was opened to competition. Now a new Yellow Cab Co. competes with two associations of independent cab owners. In 1979 the City Council removed all restrictions on the number of cabs allowed to operate in Los Angeles. San Diego, faced with a similar bankruptcy situation, began licensing individual owner/operators to compete with cab companies. A year later (1979) the City Council doubled the number of new cab licenses to be issued each month and raised maximum fare levels far above market levels, to promote competitive pricing. Eugene, Oregon, deregulated taxi fares in 1978, as did Seattle. In each case, deregulation is leading to more service and lower fare levels.

Shared-ride Cabs

Somewhere between conventional taxis and jitneys is the shared-ride cab. Like a regular taxi, this service uses a conventional sedan and provides personalized, door-to-door service. Like the jitney, however, it carries several passengers making *different* trips at the same time. Consequently, fare levels are a good deal lower than in regular taxis—although more than bus or jitney fares.

Unfortunately, most city governments—other than Washington, D.C.— ban shared-ride service. Two that don't, however, are Davenport, Iowa, and Hicksville, New York. In both cities private cab companies provide low-cost, high-volume, shared-ride taxi service that appeals to many of the same people who ride bus lines.

Davenport's Royal Cab Company increased its ridership by 179% in five years, while the patronage of the local bus system dropped by half. Royal Cab now carries nearly as many passengers per year as the bus system. Many users prefer the shared-ride cabs, because they provide door-to-door service at an average fare of only $1.05 and, even with stops, take less time than the bus. The time savings are particularly important to the Hicksville riders of the Orange and White Cab Company, most of whom are commuters racing to catch the Long Island Railroad.

Professor Kenneth Heathington of the University of Tennessee's Transportation Center has made an extensive study of the Davenport and Hicksville companies.[7] He found that their operating costs are much lower than those of the highly touted Dial-a-Ride systems funded by the federal government—systems that provide a similar kind of service, but with a heavy subsidy.* But the Davenport and Hicksville companies are private, profit-making concerns that don't receive a cent of tax money. They have simply found a ready market for this type of intermediate transit service. Partly due to Heathington's research, both Knoxville, Tennessee, and Los Angeles have recently legalized shared-ride service.

Car Pooling and Van Pooling

Transportation planners have recently discovered car pooling—a form of paratransit with significant potential for reducing congestion, air pollution, and energy use. But any large-scale use of car pooling requires that people who are otherwise strangers find each other and work out a suitable sharing arrangement. One of the smoothest ways to do this is for one person to be the driver and the others to pay to be driven. Unfortunately, in many states *any* such exchange of money is construed by the public utility commission as offering transportation service for hire— making the driver a common carrier subject to incredible regulations. Thus, the success of car pooling depends considerably on whether such absurdities of the law can be removed.

A pioneer in doing just that was Mrs. Garlene Zapitelli. Several years ago, fed up with rush-hour congestion and concerned about the energy crisis, she bought a Dodge van and began carrying fellow commuters to work, for a small fee. In short order, she was hauled before the California Public Utilities Commission and charged with operating an illegal bus line that unfairly competed with existing bus companies. Several appeals and many thousands of dollars later, the legislature voted to exempt for-hire car pools and van pools from state jurisdiction, provided the driver was also a commuter.

With that decision, California became one of a handful of states—

*Dial-a-Ride systems feature small vans dispatched by radio in response to phone calls from users; some utilize sophisticated computer systems to assign vans to origins and destinations.

including Minnesota, Tennessee, Virginia, and Connecticut—to legalize car and van pooling. Commuters especially like van pooling because, compared with bus service, it offers door-to-door transportation and a semblance of privacy. And compared with driving your own car, the van offers a chance to stretch out and relax, sometimes in airliner-type seats with stereo music, at real dollar savings. A 12-passenger van, in fact, is more energy efficient than the New York subway, providing more than 110 passenger miles per gallon of gas.

The biggest growth in van pooling is occurring in the corporate arena. This approach was originated by Robert Owens of the 3M Company in Minneapolis. Under his plan, the company provides—and insures—12-seat vans to volunteer employee drivers. The first eight passengers pay the company a monthly charge that covers all operating costs. The driver can add up to three more passengers to earn an income and can take the van home on weekends for a small mileage charge.

"The beauty of (corporate) van pooling is that everybody wins," says Owens. The company saves on parking expenses, commuters save $150–$750 per year in commuting costs, and the general public saves in terms of reduced congestion and pollution—as well as reduced demand for tax-funded mass transit systems.

Corporate van pooling is rapidly gaining converts; about 150 large corporations are now involved in such projects. Atlantic Richfield (ARCO) has helped sponsor the Commuter Computer Vanpool Project in Los Angeles. Led by ARCO and the Crocker Bank, the project operates 133 10-passenger luxury vans and 13 economy 15-passenger vans in five Southern California counties. The vans and all operating costs are paid for by participating employers and employees. In 1979 the State of California got into the act, purchasing 1,000 12-passenger vans for lease to individual pool drivers.

The Tennessee Valley Authority is perhaps the most enthusiastic employer to back pooling. In 1976 TVA officials in Knoxville decided to construct two new office complexes to house 3,400 people. Instead of building parking garages in the congested downtown area, it decided to try to change employee transit patterns. It surveyed the employees and actively helped set up numerous car pools, 100 van pools, and 30 "bus pools" using subscription buses (see below). Prior to the program, 68% of the 2,800 employees came to work in single-occupancy cars. Today only 16% of the larger 3,400-member work force arrives in that manner.

SALVAGING BUS SERVICE

Subscription Buses

Bus service is not dead, despite the earlier comments about changes in demand due to changes in demographics. There are still roles that buses can play, as part of an overall transit/paratransit system. But the sensible role for buses is no longer to be *the* transit system. As we have seen, the many forms of paratransit can do a convenient, efficient job of serving the low-density portion of the transit market. Where buses still make sense is on heavily traveled commuter routes. And it is on these routes that bus service can pay its own way. It can even be turned back to the private sector.

Exactly that is beginning to happen in a number of metropolitan areas, with the phenomenon known as *subscription bus service*.[8] The basic concept is simple. Employees in a large office or industrial complex who live in the same suburb band together and rent a deluxe, highway-type bus (reclining seats, air conditioning, music) from a private charter bus company. In some cases one employee obtains a bus driver's license and serves as the regular driver, perhaps with another employee as back-up. In other cases, the bus company provides the driver as part of the deal. In still other cases, the employer hires the bus, complete with driver.

Subscription bus service is especially prevalent in sprawling Southern California. Many large firms, especially aerospace companies, draw employees from up to 100 miles away. Lockheed Aircraft, for example, has hired buses to bring groups of employees to its plant in Palmdale where L-1011 jumbo jets are built. One bus makes the rounds of the San Fernando Valley, where many of the employees—who used to work at Lockheed's Burbank plant—still live, 50 to 75 miles from Palmdale. Another Lockheed bus comes from Ontario, racking up 172 miles each day on the round trip.

When General Telephone centralized many operations in Santa Monica, a group of employees who were transferred from Pomona organized their own "Rural Transit District" and hired a bus to take them from Pomona to Santa Monica each day—100 miles round trip. After the system was set up in 1973, an official of the Southern California Rapid Transit District (SCRTD) offered to provide the same service at $65 per passenger per month—more than double the $32 the private bus company was charging. For several years SCRTD attempted to discourage the growth of subscription buses, complaining that they would "dilute" the district's revenues and its ability to provide such services. (Eventually, under pressure from environmentalists and foes of highway congestion, the SCRTD set up its own subscription buses—subsidized by the taxpayers.) There are estimated to be several hundred private subscription buses today in Southern California.

One of the largest of these operations is COM-BUS, based in Huntington Beach. It began in 1967 when some McDonnell-Douglas employees were transferred to that city from the firm's Santa Monica plant. Employee Ron Hoffman hired a bus and learned the ropes of getting Public Utilities Commission (PUC) approval. As more employees were transferred (the Santa Monica plant was being phased out), more buses were added, until COM-BUS became a service business, developing and managing commuter bus routes for employee groups at a number of Southern California firms. It conducts employee demand surveys; establishes routes and schedules; hires late-model, luxury buses with professional drivers; selects a route coordinator from among the employees for each route to collect fares and manage its operations; assures that the necessary Certificates of Convenience and Necessity are obtained from the PUC; and handles complaints and miscellaneous business matters. Essentially, COM-BUS serves as the link between a number of charter bus companies and a growing number of employee groups. As of 1978 there were 28 COM-BUS routes in operation, using 35 buses.

Twelve subscription bus companies serve the United Airlines base at the San Francisco airport, carrying 1,295 of its 8,500 employees. All the companies complain about the onerous regulations imposed on their small firms by the state Public Utilities Commission—regulations intended for giants like Greyhound and Trailways.

Among the other successful subscription bus firms are the Colonial Transit Company of Fredericksburg, Virginia, and the Reston Express, of Reston, Virginia. Both provide commuter service between Washington, D.C., and its northern Virginia suburbs. And in the St. Louis area the Specialty Transit Company hauls mostly blue-collar workers from 14 communities to the huge McDonnell-Douglas plant.

A public agency in San Francisco—the Golden Gate Bridge, Highway, and Transportation District—is also operating a subscription bus service. Beginning in 1971, it has set up a number of "commute clubs" among white-collar workers of large San Francisco employers who live in Marin and Sonoma counties. Each club determines the schedule and pickup points, collects dues, and makes a monthly subscription payment to the District. It, in turn, hires buses from charter bus companies via competitive bidding. As a public agency, however, the District does not charge a high enough price to fully cover the costs of the operation; taxpayers therefore end up subsidizing it a cost of several hundred dollars per bus per month.

Like car pools and van pools, subscription bus service succeeds where conventional transit fails. It gets commuters out of their cars and into an efficient, less-polluting alternative. A ridership survey on the Reston Express in 1971 showed that 21% of the passengers had actually reduced the number of automobiles they *owned* as a direct result of the subscription bus service. And another 8.4% said they would probably do so in the future. But its greatest advantage—except where operated by government transit districts—is that subscription bus service costs the taxpayer nothing.

A variant on subscription bus service has turned up in New York City. Some 75,000 commuters pay three times the city transit fare to ride privately owned express buses—making the 12 companies involved the joint equivalent of the fifth largest mass transit service in the United States. The city government franchises the companies, limiting them to specific routes. Despite having to pay city, state, and federal taxes; pay for the buses themselves (no UMTA funds); and build their own depots; the private lines make money. By charging three times the regular 50¢ fare and operating on high-volume commuter runs, they can cover all their costs and still make a profit.

What attracts riders? High-quality service seems to be the key. New York

Bus Line, for example, provides high-back reclining seats, individual reading lights, heating and air-conditioning that work, a seat for every rider, cleanliness, safety, and customer-oriented service—attributes similar to those of subscription buses and van pools. (The main difference between the express bus and a subscription bus is that the former makes a number of stops and accepts occasional passengers, instead of limiting itself to regular subscribers.)

Improving City Bus Service

Private contracting can help make regular bus service viable. A number of cities or districts are hiring private firms to operate their bus systems. A survey by the International City Management Association found that such contracting was occurring in only 18 cities as of 1973. But by 1978, the Urban Institute estimated that about *half* of the 1,023 public transit systems are now being operated by private contractors. The generally poor level of management competence in most municipal transit systems is a prime reason for hiring a contractor. ATE Management and Service Co., one of the largest such firms, finds that providing an on-site manager backed up by specialists makes a major difference in the operations of the 41 transit systems it manages.

There is no guarantee that contract operation will bring cost savings. If the city or district insists on maintaining service on low-density routes, refuses to permit the hiring of part-time drivers to cover peak-load periods, and keeps fares at below-cost levels, the best of private firms will still be operating a money-losing system. The more that operational and cost decisions can be placed in the contractor's hands, the greater the likelihood of reduced costs.

One idea with some merit is to build performance incentives into the contract. The Minneapolis-St. Paul area's Seven County Regional Agency contracts with a large private transit contractor. The contract calls for a negotiated monthly fee, payments of $3 per 1,000 passengers carried over and above 50 million per year, and another $3 for every 1,000 more above 65 million. In contrast to this contract, in most of the other 20 cities it serves, the firm is paid simply a percentage of gross operating revenues. But note that paying for higher ridership does not necessarily benefit the taxpayers. It would do so only if the added ridership generated enough extra revenue to put the entire operation in the black, taking it entirely off taxpayer subsidy.

There *are* examples of private contractors who save money. The ServiCar Company in 1976 was hired by San Mateo County, California, to take over the operation of 35 buses owned by several of that county's cities. Through better utilization of its (union) labor, the firm is able to achieve a cost per vehicle hour well below that of most publicly operated systems.

Fairfax, Virginia, has had a similar experience. In 1978 it opted out of its bus service arrangement with the Washington Area Metropolitan Area Transit Authority (Metrobus). Despite the city's attempts to get Metrobus to adopt cost-cutting methods and drop lightly traveled routes, the agency remained unmoved—but announced a cost increase for 1979, from $82,600 per year to $287,000! Instead of Metrobus, Fairfax hired Gray Line to do the job for a sliding fee ranging from $46,800 to $93,500, depending on occupancy rates. Fares on the Fairfax City Express were cut from $1.20 to $1.10, saving each commuter about $50 a year.

A major cost-cutting reform is the use of part-time drivers during rush hours, instead of paying a full day's wages to all the drivers needed to cover those three or four hours. Typically, only *half* as many buses are needed at midday as at rush hour. Seattle in 1978 became the first major city to negotiate a union contract permitting part-time bus drivers. Under the hard-won agreement, Metro may let the number of full-timers decline from 1,176 to 900 by attrition and may hire up to 700 part-timers. All must join the union and work either the morning or evening rush hours, Monday through Friday, and receive no fringe benefits. As of 1979 part-time drivers had also been accepted by the transit systems of Baltimore, Washington, Charlotte, and Los Angeles.

Another way of cutting costs is to lop off the uneconomical tail ends of bus routes that generate very few passengers. One way to do this—and still provide transportation—is to replace them with paratransit. Knoxville, Tennessee, is surveying bus riders in such areas and telling them about the recent legalization of shared-ride taxi service. City transit planners hope to develop shared-ride cabs as a "collector service" to feed into heavily traveled bus routes. This would make the bus service more economical (by cutting out the uneconomical routes) while providing additional business to the cab companies.

One much-touted idea for improving bus service is to attract more riders by all-weather bus shelters at many of the bus stops. A whole new industry has arisen in the last few years producing these shelters, and federal grants to install them are being urged on transit districts. But there are two, quite distinct, ways to go on bus shelters. One *costs* taxpayers a bundle, while the other generates ongoing savings.

The costly way is the way promoted by federal grants. It calls for the agency (city, district, or whatever) to buy and install the shelters and maintain them. For a large-city system, such as the 2,000 shelters proposed for Houston, even with 80% federal funding, the initial cost to local taxpayers would still be $1.4 million (at a price of $3,500 per aluminum-and-plexiglass shelter). But that's only the beginning. Maintenance of each shelter averages $900 a year—to remove graffiti, repair broken panes, and keep them clean. For 2,000 shelters, that's $1.8 million a year—with no federal grants available. Total system cost for ten years: $19.4 million.

But there *is* an alternative. A number of private firms are now in the business of installing, owning, and operating bus shelters. They will do the whole job at no charge—in fact, they will *pay* the transit agency for the privilege. Why? So they can sell advertising space on a portion of the shelters

—just as the transit agency already does on its buses. Typically, such firms will pay 5% of all their ad revenues, while taking full responsibility for the shelters, including all maintenance. For a 2,000-shelter system, that 5%'s yield of $20 per shelter per month would yield $480,000 per year. In other words, instead of *spending* $19.4 million over ten years, the transit agency would be *receiving* $4.8 million. That's a considerable saving to the taxpayers.

Yet private bus shelters have turned out to be controversial in some cities. Chicago has refused to allow them on grounds that the advertising is an eyesore. Houston and Los Angeles officials reluctantly agreed to permit both public and private shelters to be built on a trial basis, to see how terrible the ads would really be.

All the while, cities like New York, Louisville, and St. Louis have accepted private shelters with equanimity. Bustop Shelters, Inc.—the firm that pioneered the concept in New York and has installed 500 there—has representatives marketing the idea in about 25 other cities. Competitor Transit Shelter Advertising has signed up more than a dozen of Chicago's suburbs for its larger private shelters, each of which generates a royalty of about $40 a month to the city.

Thumbing its nose at such advertising revenue—when its own buses carry advertising—is the height of hypocrisy for a transit agency. Instead of "protecting" the public from private shelters, such agencies should be doing everything in their power to seek ways of generating revenues and cutting costs. Substituting private for public bus shelters is an excellent way to do both.

PUTTING IT ALL TOGETHER

Developing a free and responsive market in transit services is the key to ending the drain of tax money into uneconomical bus or rail networks. Frequently, however, both local and state laws and regulations are major barriers to the development of such a market. Knoxville, Tennessee's Department of Public Transportation Services (DOPTS) provides a good example of how a city can cut through such barriers. The innovative concept involves seeking and encouraging diverse forms of transportation, then helping match up riders with services.[9]

The idea had its genesis at the University of Tennessee's Transportation Center. Dr. Frank Davis of the Center had long contended that the traditional hostility of public transit operators to competition from the private sector was a major obstacle to improving urban mobility. Davis's view was that public and private operators must work together to expand the market for all forms of transit. Instead of throwing up barriers, public officials must work to remove them.

This unconventional view got a chance to prove itself in 1975. That year city officials met with Center personnel to devise a way out of their public transit mess. The local bus line, taken over by the city in 1967 and operated by contractor Knoxville Transit Corporation (KTC), was losing over $1 million a year because of continually declining ridership and doubled operating costs. Even at rush hour, only half the seats on the buses were filled.

The Center and the city put together a proposal to set up an agency to act as a "ride-sharing broker" that would try to match supply and demand. Rather than focusing on convincing more people to ride the fixed-route bus system, it would begin with individual consumer needs and seek whatever forms of paratransit would best meet them.

One of the new agency's first steps was to make an inventory of all potential transportation suppliers in Knoxville. The results surprised nearly everyone. Including charter bus and school bus companies, taxis, limousines, and church buses, there were 770 vehicles (only 80 of which belonged to the public bus line) with 27,671 seats (only 3,600 of them on city buses). Clearly, Knoxville had considerable untapped transit potential.

The next step was to defuse the fears of existing transit operators that the project would shift riders away from *their* services to other forms of transportation. The project's potential to expand *total* ridership (by luring more people out of their cars) was stressed, and most operators proved willing to give it a try.

Once under way in 1976, DOPTS moved quickly to stimulate the introduction of subscription buses and van pools. The city's role as broker became especially valuable in clearing away barriers to these services. DOPTS and the University successfully lobbied the state legislature to exempt private car and van pools from common carrier licensing and regulation. They also lobbied the insurance companies so that van-pool drivers would not have to bear liability for all passengers. Finally, they convinced local lenders to treat van-pool loans to would-be drivers as *business* rather than personal loans, to enable 100% financing.

What has the Knoxville experiment accomplished? In its first 21 months, DOPTS stimulated the creation of car pools carrying 1,000 people and van pools carrying another 600. Another 1,200 people were using new KTC and private-subscription bus service. Several of the private bus firms have expanded, one going from two to 13 buses. DOPTS has also persuaded the city to legalize ride-sharing in taxis, and is experimenting with shared-ride cabs as a feeder to the KTC bus line.

The Transportation Center estimates that as a result of these activities, about 2,000 cars have been removed from Knoxville's streets, thus reducing both congestion and pollution. Ridership in subscription buses and van pools already totals one-fourth that of the city bus line (which has also increased its ridership).

The Knoxville experience is being duplicated in Southern California by Commuter Computer. This organization promotes private car pooling by computer-matching potential ride-sharers, and has aggressively promoted van pooling, as mentioned earlier. Recently it also helped the Los Angeles taxi industry introduce shared-ride service—despite a city ordinance prohibiting cab companies from "forming taxi pools." Commuter Computer pointed out that the law didn't prohibit riders from *joining* a taxi pool. So it has now launched "Come Together" ride-sharing, in which it is helping riders form taxi pools.

The transit brokerage concept is a low-cost, effective way to improve urban transportation. By stimulating the private market, it expands the supply of unsubsidized transit. Moreover, unlike the case of costly new subways like BART which attract mostly bus riders, these new paratransit options succeed in luring commuters from their cars. Thus, besides giving taxpayers a break, they accomplish the elusive goals of reducing both congestion and pollution.

10

Social Services and Health Care

Taking care of those in need with taxpayers' money has become a $340-billion-a-year business, as of fiscal year 1978. According to the Joint Economic Committee of Congress, there are more than 90 separate social welfare programs that transfer cash and services to those judged as needy.

Reviewing all of these programs is far beyond the scope of this chapter. Many of them are operated completely at the federal level and do not affect local government at all. Social Security, Medicare, and federal unemployment and disability insurance are of this nature. These, together with state unemployment and disability programs, are not truly "welfare" programs, in that the recipients have made at least some sort of "contribution" into the programs' operating funds.

True welfare programs involve the granting of cash and services to poor people who have made no contribution to the funds from which the benefits come. Included in this category are such major programs as Aid to Families with Dependent Children (AFDC), Food Stamps, Medicaid, Social Services (Title XX), and CETA (Comprehensive Employment and Training Act). Although funded largely by the federal government, these programs are administered *locally*. In administering them, local officials have considerable discretion in interpreting such matters as eligibility—and therefore can markedly influence the total level of spending.

In addition, most local governments operate some form of "general assistance" program—cash and services to indigents who do not qualify for the various federal welfare programs. For the most part, general assistance is funded locally and is therefore totally within the discretionary control of local officials.

These local officials are often disposed to claim that they have no way of affecting the cost of welfare programs. All they can do, they say, is carry out what is ordained by Washington or the state capitol. But this facile argument neglects the necessary element of discretion—the gray areas— inherent in administering these programs. How efficiently caseworkers operate, how eligibility standards are interpreted, what kinds of controls on fraud are maintained—all these issues directly affect costs. And all of these are subject to local control.

Keeping a tight control over such matters has a high priority at some welfare agencies while others seem almost not to care. Washington, D.C., for instance, has a 35% rate of fraud and error, compared with less than 3% in Los Angeles! New York City officials will not even release their fraud/error figures. But New York State overall has a 12.1% rate, compared with an 8.5% national average and only 3.6% in California.

This chapter explores some of the avenues for cutting costs in public welfare and health-care programs. Public hospitals are considered separately because, as large, fixed facilities, their problems differ considerably from the service-oriented elements of the welfare system.

WELFARE CONTRACTING

As we have seen in earlier chapters, private contracting generally leads to lower costs. Although studies documenting cost saving are relatively few in the field of social services, a recent review by the Urban Institute found a number of examples in which lower cost was one of the reasons local governments contracted out social services.[1] Other reasons included:

- taking advantage of unique, innovative services developed by highly motivated nonprofit organizations;
- providing services needed only at certain hours of the day;
- gaining access to specialized skills that might not be available within local government (or that might be too costly to provide on a small scale); and
- retaining maximum flexibility in the face of fluctuating federal funding.

The Institute found that contracting for social services is now "fairly common" and has been growing rapidly in recent years, especially since passage of the Title IV-A (1967) and Title XX (1975) amendments to the Social Security Act. Both specifically permit local governments to contract for social services. As a result, many organizations have entered the field, ranging from traditional nonprofit entities like Goodwill Industries to subsidiaries of large profit-making firms such as the Homemakers International division of Upjohn Pharmaceuticals.

Day care is the service most frequently contracted for. A 1970 three-state survey by Booz, Allen and Hamilton found that more than 80% of the contracting funds were spent on day care. The second-largest amount, 6%, went for family counseling services. Other contracted services included halfway houses, vocational rehabilitation, institutional care, children's protective services, meals-on-wheels, and homemaker services.

Perhaps because profit-making firms tend to predominate in the latter category, homemaker services are one of the few in which hard cost-comparison data are available. In 1972 Minnesota's largest county—Hennepin County, home of the Twin Cities—requested competitive bids on homemaker services. After eliminating one extremely low bid that they could not believe, county officials estimated what it would cost the county to provide the services itself. On the average, the cost of county provision came out 29% higher than the average of the second- and third-lowest bidders. Interestingly, when the county asked all the suppliers if they would match the "unrealistic" lowest bid, three of the other six said they would.

Hennepin County was subsequently prodded into further contracting by a unique nonprofit organization that acted as a broker of services: Public Services Options (PSO). Set up in 1974, PSO worked to encourage public agencies in the Twin Cities to consider contracting, for reasons of cost and flexibility. In 1976 PSO helped persuade county officials not to build a major food preparation service plant as part of its new Metropolitan Medical Center. Instead, they built a much smaller center, relying largely on commercially prepared food and run by a management contractor. The net savings was over $1 million per year.

Dade County, Florida (the Greater Miami area), provides several other examples of contracting with profit-making firms. Most public day care in Dade County is provided by private firms, paid by the county on a per-child, per-week basis. The contract spells out specific requirements for staff (number, qualifications), food quality, and hours of service, and requires periodic reports. In addition, most publicly supported nursing care in Dade County is provided by private, for-profit firms, under similar contractual arrangements. Fees are negotiated with each company.

In Santa Barbara County, California, after the large Homemakers International/Upjohn firm had held the contract for homemaker services to the blind, aged, and disabled for a year and a half, county officials opened the contract to competitive bidding for fiscal year 1978/79 and received three bids. By choosing the "lowest responsible bid," that of the Olsten Corporation of Long Island, the county's Board of Supervisors saved 5.5% over the high bid of the incumbent contractor. Interestingly, the winning bidder offered to hire any and all local employees who would otherwise lose their jobs due to loss of the contract.

In Los Angeles County, a county-operated alcoholism outpatient program cost $62 per hour for individuals and $14.50 for group treatment. By switching to a private contractor, these costs were cut to $22 for individuals and $6.70 for group treatment—very substantial savings.

As local officials gain more experience in specifying service standards and performance measures, we can expect contracting of services to become a more common way to save on costs. And while it is still difficult to specify social services in objectively comparable ways, competitive bidding is gaining increasing acceptance.

A VOUCHER SYSTEM (Welfare User Fees)

It may seem contradictory to speak of "user fees" in relation to welfare services. After all, the basic idea of welfare is to transfer wealth from those with money to those without. To expect the clients of welfare programs to pay for them is ludicrous—or is it?

In his classic 1962 book *Capitalism and Freedom*, Milton Friedman proposed the idea of vouchers as a replacement for state-provided schools, job-placement training, and other social services for the disadvantaged.[2] Instead of spending $X on the program itself, the government would set aside the same amount of money to redeem vouchers—entitlements to a specific quantity of the service, cashable at *any* institution providing the service. The vouchers would be issued to poor people to "spend" as they see fit, choosing among competing suppliers of the services. Each supplier, on receiving a voucher in payment, could cash it in with the government for its dollar value.

From the client's standpoint, a voucher system for social services would give each person considerably more choice than exists at present. No longer restricted to dealing with an impersonal bureaucracy, he or she would be free to shop around seeking the most responsive organizations. Surely *that* would be an improvement over being regimented and regulated by today's frequently impersonal, uncaring welfare bureaucracies.

From the taxpayer's standpoint, recall our discussion from earlier chapters on the benefits of privatization and user charges. A voucher system would mean privatization of welfare service providers; we'd have competition among numerous providers, instead of municipal monopolies. Other things being equal, that should result in lower costs of providing the services, as we've seen. And by *pricing* various services, providers would be experimenting to see what specific kinds and amounts of services (homemaking, meals, day care) people really wanted and which ones they could do without. Again—the usual benefits of pricing. So overall, we could expect a reduction in waste and an increase in efficiency from a welfare voucher system. And that would mean a long-term decline in costs.

A small example of a social service agency funded by fees rather than taxes is the Colorado Economic Development Association (CEDA).[3] Unlike most minority business development agencies (which are funded by federal and state grants), CEDA is funded mostly by service fees from the banks and small businesses it serves as clients. Thus, the better CEDA performs, the greater its revenues. If its effectiveness in developing businesses falls off, so will its revenues. In its first six years of operation, CEDA helped start nearly 1,000 businesses, the largest of which employs over 1,500 people. That's quite a fine record.

THINKING SMARTER ABOUT WELFARE

As noted earlier, local officials possess considerable discretion in administering the principal welfare programs, both federally funded and mandated ones (like AFDC) and locally operated general assistance. Yet measures to improve welfare administration so as to hold down costs are far from universal. Variations in the rates of error and fraud among counties and states are quite large.

Studying one aspect of this problem, administrative errors, the Urban Institute found that nearly one out of every four welfare cases involves some kind of error, such as paying money to someone who is ineligible or paying incorrect amounts.[4] The tab for these errors is $1 billion a year!

A study team from the Institute made a statistical analysis of the administrative practices of welfare agencies in all 50 states, to identify which management techniques seem to be most effective in lowering error rates in AFDC programs. They found five especially worthwhile methods:

1. *Keep case files up to date.* Many AFDC clients frequently change addresses, jobs, living arrangements, and family composition. Federal rules require that continued eligibility for AFDC be reviewed every six months. But many states are far behind in doing so. It would cost only $6 million a year nationwide to keep eligibility records up to date, to ensure that only those still eligible are receiving benefits. Doing so would eliminate about $80 million in payment errors, for a net saving to taxpayers of $74 million.

2. *Make the forms readable.* Although 75% of welfare recipients can read at no more than an eighth-grade level, only one in ten welfare forms—which clients are expected to fill out—is readable at that level. Over one-third require college-level reading skills. Naturally, lack of comprehension of the forms leads to incomplete and inaccurate information being given to caseworkers. If the forms were revised to eighth-grade levels and oral interviews were substituted for some written questions, more than $100 million in payment errors could be eliminated.

3. *Increase caseworker skills.* All too often, AFDC caseworkers are hired with little or no formal training. Besides working inefficiently, these untrained workers don't remain on the job very long. Turnover often exceeds 50% per year. If better staff-development programs (like the one used in Florida) were introduced nationwide, more than $100 million could be saved through reduced payment errors and increased worker efficiency.

4. *Simplify eligibility rules.* Many local eligibility formulas and benefit computation rules are cumbersome and hard to administer. Some states have adopted extremely simple rules (e.g., a flat grant of $250 to any family of four). If all states adopted the most streamlined rules, say the researchers, $150 million worth of administrative errors would be avoided.

5. *Use advanced computer techniques.* Modern computer procedures for keeping case records up to date, checking for errors, and allocating extra staff resources to cases identified as error prone can be very cost effective. Such systems are in operation in West Virginia, parts of California, and some other states. If all states adopted such systems, about $80 million in payment errors would be eliminated.

California is one of the most advanced states in reducing welfare costs.

Its highly publicized 1971 welfare reforms actually *cut* the total caseload by 350,000 persons in three and one-half years, reversing what had been an upward trend of 40,000 additions per *month*. Key elements of the plan included tougher enforcement of child-support laws, enforcing work requirements for the able bodied, and cracking down on fraud and errors.

Los Angeles County provides an excellent example of how these reductions were made. In 1973 the county's fraud/error rate was 12%. And its staff was increasing rapidly to keep pace with a growing caseload. Keith Comrie, head of the Department of Public Social Services, decided the time had come to act. So he put into effect a work-measurement program (see Chapter 12) and began development of full-scale computerization of AFDC case files.

The results are impressive. By 1976 the fraud/error rate was down to 4.4%. And by 1977, when the welfare case management information system (WCMIS) became fully operational, it had dropped still further, to 2.67%. Since each 1% cut in fraud and error means a corresponding 1% cut in the department's $700-million budget, the total saving amounted to some $65 million.

Comrie's reforms also streamlined operations to the point where nearly 2,000 fewer employees (out of about 13,000) are on the department's payroll today than in 1976. The net result (after inflation and other factors) is a saving of another $10 million a year in administrative costs.

The computer doesn't perform any feats of magic to produce such savings. Essentially, it just makes numerous checks and cross-checks more quickly and accurately. For example, in just three seconds, caseworkers can now check to see whether an applicant has applied for or received welfare at any of the department's 26 major district offices. This makes it harder for someone to receive multiple benefits by signing up at several offices.

The computer also makes it easier to perform cross-checks against various records of employment. Although it is not illegal for welfare recipients to work, it is illegal for them to conceal or under-report their earnings. The Los Angeles system automatically cross-checks the files of state disability payments, unemployment offices, and federal, state, and local government employees. When the cross-checking program went into effect it turned up 2,000 county and city employees on the welfare rolls — about 200 of whom were not reporting their incomes.

Another example of major savings took place in San Francisco. Years of very lax welfare administration had led to such situations as 24-year-old "children" receiving AFDC benefits and numerous welfare recipients with hidden assets. The 1976 error rate was 48% and the total caseload was 18,000. After implementing reforms in eligibility checking devised by consultant Robert Carlson, the caseload was cut to 15,600 and the error rate to 11% — in just one year. San Francisco taxpayers are saving over $10 million a year.

Yet another example of thinking smarter occurred in Denver County,

Colorado. An experimental program required all AFDC recipients to report their economic status every month, instead of every three or six months. Because more frequent reporting permits more rapid discontinuance of payments to those no longer eligible, the Denver procedure cut costs by 6%.

Thus, we have seen that our three reforms—contracting with the private sector, user charges (in this case via vouchers), and thinking smarter—can be applied by local governments to welfare and social service programs. The fact that most such programs originate in Washington is no excuse for wasting money at the local level. Local officials have a number of options for cutting costs—and providing better service for those truly in need.

CURING CITY HOSPITALS

Health care is one of the most expensive social welfare services. Everyone is aware that hospital costs have soared in the past decade. Charges of $150 to $200 a day are common; in big cities like New York, they are more like between $200 and $300 a day. Despite these record-high charges, New York City municipal hospitals had a combined deficit of $74 million in 1976—losses that the city's hard-pressed taxpayers had to make up. This hospital problem is not simply one of "public versus private" because most nonprofit "voluntary" hospitals, though private, are just about as badly off as municipal (government-run) hospitals.

The problem goes deeper, having its roots in a misguided philosophy. Somewhere along the line the idea developed that providing intensive medical care services isn't really a business and that therefore each institution in the field must focus solely on "doing good." It should be all things to all people, regardless of the cost.

As a result, virtually every hospital in a city seeks to provide every conceivable service—emergency room, maternity ward, intensive-care unit, CAT scanner, etc. Never mind that nearby hospitals may be doing the same, and that specialized people and equipment at each stand idle a good deal of the time. The important thing is to provide the service—and hang the expense! Our system of public and private insurance reimbursement has only added to the problem. It tends to reimburse whatever costs hospitals manage to incur without questioning whether they are really necessary.

With traditions like this, it's no wonder hospital costs have soared—especially when the federal government greatly stimulated demand by enacting Medicare and Medicaid a decade ago. But here and there around the country, innovative private companies are challenging this swollen concept of hospitals. In doing so, they are bailing out the municipal and voluntary hospitals of a growing number of communities.

There is a trend for cities and hospital societies to contract out hospital management to private firms. The typical management contract costs a nonprofit hospital from 3% to 8% of its annual revenues. But the savings generally run three to five times as much as the cost of the contract.

Hospital Affiliates, the largest such firm (with 93 contracts), finds that it can typically cut staff costs 15% and purchasing costs by 10% the first year. Other important management firms include HCA Management Co. and American Medical Care International. As of 1979 about 300 American hospitals were managed by for-profit firms—three times the number in 1975.

But an even more promising trend is for private firms to take over the hospitals. In the past decade private hospital chains have come into being that do more than just bring in modern management and cost controls. They have begun to rethink the idea of the hospital as all things to all people.

The 21-member Intermountain Health Care (IHC) chain in Utah provides a good example. Taking over a number of hospitals within a region, it is able to cut costs by eliminating duplication between nearby facilities. IHC's hospitals in Salt Lake City and Provo, for example, share a $150,000 simulator device used in cancer treatment. The blood bank at IHC's LDS Hospital serves two other hospitals as well, and IHC is considering making it into a blood distribution center for the whole chain.

Having a number of facilities serving a large population gives IHC the opportunity to experiment. The firm has tried out various combinations of registered nurses and aides, with the hospitals comparing notes on how well each combination worked and how much it cost. IHC also monitors performance. Each physician and every hospital service is audited continually, with performance compared to standards established for each facility. That way unusual occurrences of complications and increased lengths of stay can be spotted readily.

IHC's patients pay 28% less per admission than the national average, and remain hospitalized an average of 5.1 days compared with a national average of 7.4. The firm gets high marks from community leaders—especially from those in smaller towns whose affiliated clinics or hospitals now have access to a broader range of medical personnel, facilities, and equipment.

Nashville's Hospital Corporation of America began in 1968 with a single hospital. It now has nearly 100 and revenues approaching $1 billion a year. Its hospitals all operate as businesses, paying their own way, paying taxes, and earning a profit for the company's shareholders. And if numbers are any indication, hospital chains are the wave of the future. There are now 31 major hospital chains, owning nearly 1,000 hospitals with 108,000 of the nation's 1.4 million beds. Revenues of investor-owned hospital firms grew from $2.6 billion in 1972 to $10 billion in 1978.

The hospital firms achieve important cost savings thanks to central management systems and economies of scale. (American Medical Care International, for example, operates mobile CAT scanners, to serve more than one hospital.) They also hold down the number of full-time employees on each hospital's payroll, relying more on specialists to go where needed. As a result, investor-owned hospitals average 2.8 full-time employees per patient, compared with the national average of 3.2. And as chains, the hospital firms are able to obtain supplies in bulk, at substantial discounts.

The chains are not just "skimming the cream," taking only the easy business. Most provide the full range of hospital services—though not necessarily all in the same building (as we saw with Intermountain). Thus, they can often end up with a large portion of the business. In Louisville, Humana, Inc., has only one of ten hospitals but takes in 25% of all patients—and does it for only 19% of the total hospital expenditures in Louisville. (Nationwide, Humana's average patient charge in 1977 was $1,073, compared with a national average of $1,447 for nonprofit hospitals.)

Another private-sector innovation is advertising—to improve hospital utilization. Las Vegas's Sunrise Hospital, part of the Humana chain, has solved its problem of low weekend utilization by advertising a 5.25% discount for weekend admissions and holding drawings to award holiday cruises to patients admitted on weekends. These promotion methods paid off in a 50% growth in weekend occupancy in 1978, since many people rescheduled elective surgery in response to the ads. Reducing sharp fluctuations in occupancy greatly eases personnel-utilization problems, usually resulting in lower costs.

Private, profit-making hospitals aren't limited to large corporate chain operations. Some individual doctors and entrepreneurs are setting up efficient, responsive hospitals—and making money doing so. A good example is low-cost Prospect Hospital in New York's South Bronx.

Located in one of the most blighted of the city's slums, Prospect provides high-quality care to its mostly Spanish-speaking community. It keeps costs low and utilization high by concentrating on routine medical procedures— the things that constitute 95% of a hospital's normal workload. Owner-operator Dr. Jacob Freeman calls Prospect a "general consumer hospital." It has no maternity ward, for example, because there isn't enough demand to keep one utilized enough of the time to pay for itself. Nor are there intensive-care units or CAT scanners. Freedman leaves these to the many other hospitals in the area.

As a result, Prospect's costs remain low, although its quality of care is high. It has no trouble attracting doctors, all of whom could earn more elsewhere but prefer this kind of community-based practice. And because of its efforts to reach out to the surrounding ghetto community, Prospect has become the hospital of choice for area residents. Hence, its high occupancy rate of 91% at a time when many city hospitals are having trouble keeping 70% of their beds filled.

Another low-cost specialist is Oklahoma City's AM-PM Minor Emergency Care Clinic, a free-standing emergency room for the most frequent kinds of medical emergencies: dog bites, puncture wounds, cuts and scrapes. By avoiding the use of costly equipment, Dr. Sam Collins's clinic can charge less than half what full-service emergency rooms have to charge. The clinic is housed in a 2,300-square-foot frame building with a reception area and six examining rooms. It began operation in 1978 on an 8 A.M.-to-11 P.M. schedule but plans to go 24-hours-a-day in the future; also on tap is expansion of the idea to other Sunbelt states.

Although most of our success stories come from the private sector, some municipal and voluntary hospitals *are* making progress in learning to think like businesses. Some have joined together to make purchases of supplies at quantity discounts. The Dallas Hospital Council unites 45 hospitals. By aggressively seeking discounts on large-volume purchases, the council saved $743,000 in 1977 and more than $1 million in 1978. When it began in the early 1970s, the council's purchases were limited mainly to laundry, soft drinks, and paper products. But now it operates a central microfilming center and a pharmaceutical supply house for member hospitals.

Other hospitals are getting serious about their bad-debt problems, often a notorious source of red ink at public hospitals. The General Hospital of Santa Barbara County installed a modern accounting and bill-collecting system in 1977. Turned loose on a large backlog of bad debts from prior years, it collected more than $1 million—about $700,000 more than expected. The 600-member Texas Hospital Association hired a professional debt-collection agency to tackle an accumulation of "hopeless" debts. Instead of a complete write-off, the hospitals are now receiving 20% of these "uncollectible" monies.

We can learn a lot from all this. It's becoming clear that taxpayers can no longer afford to support city hospitals that operate as if cost were no object. Private individuals and large corporate chains alike are demonstrating that hospital services can be provided economically. We must no longer insist that each and every hospital try to do everything. Instead, hospitals must start running more like businesses.

By allowing hospitals to specialize, like other businesses, we can halt the cost spiral of recent years. Using private firms, either to run city hospitals or to replace them, can make hospitals into self-supporting operations. As such, they will no longer be a burden on the taxpayers. And new, innovative approaches to health care will often be part of the bargain.

11

Planning and Zoning

Planning and zoning is one of the newer functions of many local governments. Attempting large-scale control over a community's land usage goes back only 60 years or so. In 1916 New York City enacted the first comprehensive municipal zoning code, which became the model for most subsequent zoning ordinances. Most large cities adopted zoning prior to World War II, and the practice was extended to many smaller cities and counties in the postwar period. That period also saw the rise of the profession of urban planning, and the creation of professional planning departments in many cities and counties. Their principal functions are:

- to determine the city's goals and objectives;
- to study the city's physical features, resources, population, and its past, present, and ongoing trends;
- to develop a master plan for land use in the city, based on the above considerations (the "general plan");
- to develop specific elements of the general plan for such areas as transportation and housing; and
- to develop specific ordinances defining permissible land uses in each area, consistent with the general plan.

Although most planning departments carry out activities corresponding to each of these functions, much of this work bears little relationship to the day-to-day reality of how and why the city grows and changes. Zoning ordinances, for example, are frequently quite inconsistent with the general plan, the latter reflecting the planners' utopian vision of what they'd like to see, the former representing the result of market forces setting property values—which in turn influence the political process and yield variances, general plan changes, and "legal nonconforming uses."

IS ZONING NECESSARY?

A growing minority of urban experts find great fault with zoning, in particular, regarding it as a poor means of preventing land-use conflicts, a force for exclusion of those with less social, economic, and political influence, and a violation of traditional American concepts of property rights. One of the earliest critics of zoning was Jane Jacobs, who in her book *The Death and Life of Great American Cities*[1] pointed out zoning's tendency to impose a monotonous uniformity on cities, thereby contributing to their decay.

The planning and zoning function accounts for only a small percentage of a typical municipal budget. Nevertheless, it is of major economic consequence, because zoning decisions can affect millions of dollars in land value. For example, a planning commission decision to "downzone" land from commercial to residential use may cut its value in half. Yet cities may frequently be caught between harsh actions of this kind and a general plan that bears little relation to reality.

In this era of revolt against big government, there has been surprisingly little questioning of local government's control over citizens' use of their own land. Few people even realize that in one major American city there is a completely different approach to protecting land values, one that avoids arbitrary controls over private property. And interestingly, it turns out that this approach costs taxpayers substantially less than conventional planning and zoning methods.

The city is Houston, Texas. Of the 20 largest American cities, only Houston lacks a traditional system of zoning, though like the others it has a planning department. Data on planning department expenditures for these cities (excluding New York, Washington, and Detroit, which did not respond) collected by the International City Management Association revealed per capita costs ranging from 26¢ in Houston to $2.41 in Columbus (Table 4). And Houston's figure is *by far* the lowest, being just a bit more than half as much as the second-lowest expenditure, Philadelphia's 48¢ per person. The *average* city in this group of 20 spent $1.09 per person on planning and zoning.

Although Houston is the only *major* city without zoning, it is not unique, by any means. Surrounding Harris County has no zoning ordinance, nor do eight of its other cities besides Houston, including Pasadena (100,000 pop.) and Baytown (45,000). Neither does Wichita Falls (100,000), Beaumont (114,000), or Laredo (70,000). And many rural towns and counties across the country don't have zoning ordinances, either.

Houston has attracted the attention of economists and land-use specialists precisely because of its anomolous distinction. The definitive work on the subject is Bernard H. Siegan's *Land Use Without Zoning*, published in 1972.[2] Professor Siegan spent two years as a University of Chicago Law School research fellow, examining land usage in Houston in minute detail and comparing it with land use in zoned cities like Chicago and Dallas.

Actually land is used in Houston very much as in other cities that developed in the automobile era. Houston is widely spread out, with many major thoroughfares and freeways and a low population density of 2,500 persons per square mile. The Houston City Planning Department identifies seven specific types of land use:

1. *Mixed uses in older areas.* Most of these areas consist predominantly of smaller single-family homes. On major streets there are commercial developments, and within the residential areas there are small service businesses that serve the neighborhood. Some industrial areas are close to these residential areas, and, according to the Planning Department, "provide job opportunities for low to moderate income groups conveniently located near their homes."

2. *Strip commercial development.* Many major thoroughfares are lined with typical commercial strips, similar to those of other cities.

3. *Single-family suburban pattern.* Large single-family tracts comprising three-fourths of the built-up area have been developed since World

Table 4

LARGE CITY PLANNING EXPENDITURES

CITY	1970 POPULA- TION (000)	1970 PLANNING BUDGET (000)	BUDGET RANK	SPENDING PER CAPITA
Chicago	3,367	$1,600	3	$0.475
Los Angeles	2,816	3,185	1	1.131
Philadelphia	1,949	929	7	.477
Houston	1,233	318	18	.258
Baltimore	906	1,168	5	1.289
Dallas	844	2,004	2	2.374
Cleveland	751	396	17	.527
Indianapolis	745	593	11	.796
Milwaukee	717	549	12	.766
San Diego	697	1,014	6	1.459
San Antonio	654	478	15	.731
Memphis	624	370	16	.593
New Orleans	593	314	19	.530
Phoenix	582	656	10	1.127
Columbus	540	1,300	4	2.407
Seattle	531	548	13	1.032
Jacksonville	529	898	8	1.698
Pittsburgh	520	546	14	1.050
Denver	515	312	20	.606
Kansas City, Mo.	507	837	9	1.651

Source: 1972 *Municipal Yearbook*

War II. Developers concentrated their shopping areas, leaving the residential areas uniformly single-family, as in other big cities.

4. *Apartment development.* These areas occur throughout the city, with mostly one- to three-story garden apartments and a few high-rise buildings.

5. *Townhouses, cluster housing, and planned unit development.* These newer types of development are found throughout the city. According to Planning Director Roscoe H. Jones, "Without zoning Houston has seen innovation and new approaches to housing development which would have been impossible, or at least many years in coming to fulfillment, under the application of traditional zoning procedures."

6. *Scatteration of industries.* Industrial facilities occur throughout the city and are not limited to one or two massive industrial areas. But their location is not haphazard. Most require access to a major thoroughfare, a rail siding, a port, natural resource, or product pipeline. So, in fact, their locations are relatively predictable and concentrated, not spread out at random. Many suburban areas are adjoined by "attractive industries and industrial park subdivisions which provide job opportunities closer to home."

7. *Scatteration of low-income and minority groups.* Without any overall large-lot zoning, anti-apartment zoning, or other exclusionary devices, these groups have been free to move into all sections of the city. Houston's actual "ghetto" areas represent a relatively small fraction of the total land area.

It should be clear from this brief description that Houston's land uses are not "uncontrolled." Economic forces provide a potent controlling factor. Siegan points out that oil companies planning gas stations have a free choice between $50,000 lots on major thoroughfares and $5,000 lots *within* residential areas. They invariably choose the major thoroughfares, because that's where the business is. Likewise, a boiler factory will not be built in the midst of tract homes but will be sited close to a highway or railroad siding.

But economics isn't the only factor controlling Houston's land use. Private deed restrictions, also known as restrictive convenants, are a major factor. For those who wish tight control over land use, deed restrictions provide a way that is in many respects *better* than zoning. On the one hand, deed restrictions cannot be changed by the political process—as everyone knows happens regularly with zoning (variances, general revisions, upzoning, downzoning). On the other hand, the deed restrictions generally run for 20 to 30 years, at which time they are renewable *if* the area's residents agree to renew them. If, however, the area has changed character significantly over the years, the residents are no longer bound by the covenants and may make changes (e.g., converting a single-family house to a duplex to take advantage of higher land values and increased apartment demand).

About two-thirds of Houston is covered by some 10,000 separate deed-restriction agreements. The widespread use of this private form of land-use control has given the majority of Houston's suburbs an appearance indistinguishable from those of other large (zoned) cities. Since 1965 the city government has assisted property owners in developing and using deed restrictions. And they are enforceable in court.

So what does the City Planning Department do? Director Jones expresses its philosophy this way:

> Too often city planners approached the preparation of a city plan from a utopian view that results in a plan more contoured to daydreams than honest recognition of the democratic context of the American city. . . . Too often planners have attempted to create a land use pattern which from their middle class value system might be termed "well-ordered" and "good," but often these have frustrated the achievement of other social and economic goals. . . . Perhaps, rather than proposing a rigid plan enforced by a rigid land use control system, the planner can gain more by forecasting the future of his urban area and preparing plans for public facilities and services to meet this change.[3]

And *that*, essentially, is what the Department does. It attempts to *forecast*, not plan, the city's future in order to develop the *public* facilities—streets, water and sewer lines, libraries, and parks—needed to accommodate it. It leaves control of *private* land largely in private hands.

Specifically, the Planning Department divides its activities into large-scale (macro) and small-scale (micro), as follows. The macro-scale efforts include:

- *Major Thoroughfare and Freeway Plan* for the entire 2,000-square-mile metropolitan area.
- *General Study Plan for 1990.* Not really a "plan," this document consists of generalized forecasts of future growth, to assist those who plan private projects as well as the city in its public facilities planning.
- *Capital Improvements* providing information to identify the need for new airports, water systems, waste-water treatment plans, flood control, and other area-wide public facilities.
- *Urban Data*—collecting and disseminating useful statistical data about the city to the private sector, for use in residential, commercial, and industrial decision-making.
- *Jurisdiction Surveillance.* By law, the city has certain jurisdictional functions extending five miles beyond its borders. The Planning Department monitors development in this region.

The micro-scale activities include the following:

- *Subdivision Controls* provide for street standards, building setbacks, and minimum lot sizes in residential subdivisions.
- *Private Street Ordinance* ensures that large apartment developments have adequate internal streets.
- *Off-Street Parking Ordinance* requires that residential developments provide off-street parking, based on the number of bedrooms.
- *Capital Improvement Program* coordinates the timing of construction

of individual public facilities (e.g., parks and sewers) with the pace of private development.

- *Private Deed Restrictions and Civic Clubs* assist private citizens and developers, on request, in establishing and using deed restrictions. There are some 150 civic clubs (neighborhood associations) in Houston concerned with maintaining their deed restrictions and improving their neighborhoods.

Though these sets of functions are a far cry from *laissez-faire*, they are far less extensive (and hence far less *expensive*) than the functions of a typical city planning department. And Houston taxpayers realize savings from more than just a smaller planning department. Marie Ristroph, head of the Comprehensive Planning Division, points out that there are no costly, time-consuming zoning hearings or appeals in Houston. Hence, costs are lower for the City Attorney's office, City Council staff, and the Planning Commission. Moreover, without the possibility of zoning variances—since there are none to grant—the city is spared the possibility of payoffs to officials to gain favorable rulings, an all-too-common practice in many other cities.

Houstonians benefit in other ways, too. Professor Siegan spent a good deal of time comparing housing conditions in Houston and Dallas. While finding the cities almost identical in many characteristics, he discovered that Houston has a much greater supply of apartments—not surprising, since zoning usually restricts apartment construction. The result of this more abundant supply in Houston is lower rents—10% to 20% lower than in Dallas.

Former Houston planner Dick Bjornseth pointed out some other benefits in an article in *Reason*.[4] Without zoning, much of the land in Houston is free to adapt to changing conditions—such as the energy crisis. Now that gasoline has more than tripled in price, many people don't wish to commute long distances. In Houston all sorts of new housing has sprung up downtown, and new light industries have located near the suburbs in response to these changed conditions. Likewise, run-down old neighborhoods (where deed restrictions have expired or never existed) are being privately "recycled" into thriving new mixed commercial/residential areas. This has been happening all over Houston's "inner city"—particularly in the formerly run-down Montrose section, where deed restrictions have expired.

Zoning laws were originally intended to prevent conflicts between land uses. They don't, of course. And in the case of Houston, the absence of zoning does not encourage or exacerbate conflicts. Some conflicts do occur, of course, according to a recent study. But there are far fewer conflicts than might be expected. Some involve violations of the deed restrictions; these can be resolved in the courts, if need be. Interestingly, the study found that "Many examples of land use arrangements . . . should theoretically conflict but do not."[5]

It turns out that in many cases small commercial operations or clean, quiet light industries can coexist peacefully with housing. It is only when a facility generates noise, odors, vermin, or excessive traffic that a "conflict" exists. And if public nuisance laws are enforced, these cases are "relatively easy to minimize, without adding to the spiraling cost of government or infringing on property rights."

REPEALING ZONING

Nonzoning works in Houston. And perhaps it can work equally well in other cities or counties which, like Houston, have never been zoned. But can a city with an existing structure of zoning repeal it, without creating chaos? It turns out that some communities have already repealed zoning ordinances. Four Missouri counties have voted to repeal their zoning ordinances—Grundy, Lafayette, and Phelps in 1968 and Jefferson in 1970. But in each of these cases, although the ordinance had been enacted some years earlier, it had not actually been put into effect.

In *Land Use Without Zoning* Siegan addresses the problem of repealing a functioning zoning system and concludes that it should not really pose much difficulty, once the costs and benefits of zoning and its alternatives are understood. To begin with, the problem of sudden changes in land values—which might be occasioned by repeal of zoning—already occurs whenever there is a major revision of the zoning ordinance. Every time a new general plan is introduced in a zoned city, a major revision of the existing zoning map is required, to bring usage into conformity with the plan. The effect of repealing the ordinance would be no different in principle; only the specific impacts might differ.

Repeal would not necessarily replace zoning with a vacuum. Siegan suggests measures to protect property owners: a temporary moratorium on use changes, government assistance in setting up deed restrictions, and introduction of specific ordinances aimed at controlling true land-use conflicts (e.g., noise, odor, or traffic impingements). He separates the effects of repeal on three different categories of homeowner:

- Those in affluent subdivisions have both the knowledge and the desire to set up deed restrictions, probably stricter than the former zoning. They will thus see themselves better off after repeal.
- Middle-income homeowners would more likely need assistance in drafting deed restrictions and would probably make them less restrictive than the first group's and possibly less restrictive than the former zoning provisions.
- Those in the lower economic brackets would probably experience little harm from repeal. (In Houston and Baytown it is lower-income and minority groups that most strongly oppose zoning.) There is evidence that up to 5% of the structures on local streets would in time be converted to commercial uses, most of them providing services to local residents. Since lower-income people often have restricted mobility, this

would be a net benefit. In addition, property values in blighted areas would increase, once the properties were free to be converted to more intensive use.

Hence, once fears of the unknown were overcome, most residents would find that they would benefit from repeal of zoning. And the benefits include much more than the accompanying tax savings, as we've seen.

Repeal of zoning ordinances has not yet become a burning public issue. Here and there, however, those who have studied zoning objectively have begun making public the case for repeal. David J. Mandel, a former Hudson Institute consultant, concluded a 1971 article on zoning's failure in New York City with a call for outright repeal. Siegan repeated this message in his 1972 book. So did John M. Ross in a 1972 *Southern California Law Review* article. It was not until 1977, however, that the case against zoning received mass-media airing. After attending a conference on city revitalization in Houston, *National Journal* columnist Neal R. Peirce devoted an entire syndicated column to the role of nonzoning in redeveloping Houston. "The Houston success story is strong enough to suggest that zoning may be the land-use dinosaur of the '70s," he concluded.

BUILDING CODES

The enactment and enforcement of building codes are other aspects of local government's control over property. Ostensibly to protect people from shoddy workmanship and dangers to life and limb, building codes have increasingly come under fire for inflating housing costs, ruling out design innovation, discriminating against the poor, discouraging rehabilitation, inviting bribery, and discriminating against nonunion contractors.

That's quite an indictment, to be sure, but each of these charges is discussed in the 1979 report of the National Commission on Neighborhoods, which concluded that the entire American building code system should be drastically reformed, particularly if the rehabilitation of older neighborhoods was to have much chance of taking place.[6]

Actually, it's not surprising that the Commission reached this conclusion. A previous group, the National Commission on Urban Problems, made essentially the same finding in 1968. And numerous studies and articles over the past decade have pointed out the many defects of today's rigid building codes.

Because many different codes are in use across the country, for instance, manufacturers cannot market standardized components for nationwide sale. Instead they have to concentrate on those localities where their products are legal, or build many different versions. Either way, costs are higher. And many cost-cutting innovations (e.g., plastic pipe, prefabricated plumbing cores) are altogether prohibited by many city codes.

The problem really becomes serious in decaying older neighborhoods. Many older houses and apartment buildings could be rehabilitated into safe, comfortable dwellings—if it weren't for rigid code requirements. A few of these provisions work to ensure safety (e.g., fire exits), but most simply add endlessly to the cost of refurbishment, so that the building can comply with someone's arbitrary idea of "suitable" housing. All too often, rehabilitators either resort to bribery to get around the codes, or do the work in secret, using semiskilled labor, or give up the project altogether because it has become too expensive.

Everyone suffers as a result. Besides paying taxes to support an army of building inspectors, we all—whether owner or renter—pay higher prices for housing. The National Commission on Neighborhoods conservatively estimated that building codes add 10% to the cost of rehabilitation. It's impossible to estimate how many building rehab projects are never even undertaken, because of expected hassles from city building departments.

Yet few would deny that the original impetus for building codes was a good one: to protect housing consumers from shoddy construction. The question we must ask is whether there's a better way to accomplish this end. Looking overseas, the Commission thinks it has found that better way.

It turns out that France has never had an equivalent of the U.S. code-enforcement system, except for fire-safety regulations in public-access buildings. It *does* have a variety of codes and standards, but adherence to them is voluntary. The key factor protecting the public is that French law imposes strict civil liability on builders for the quality of construction. For major structural systems (roofs, walls, foundations), the builder is liable for ten years; for secondary components like windows, he is liable for two years.

This liability is "enforced" in the marketplace. To protect themselves against claims, builders purchase warranty insurance. The insurance companies, in turn, hire private inspection firms (there are four such nationwide firms in France) to inspect buildings under construction. Banks and other mortgage lenders generally will not make loans to builders who do not carry warranty insurance. And French casualty insurers won't insure such buildings, either. As a result, virtually all French builders are covered by warranty insurance.

Comparing the French system with our own building-code enforcement, we can see some important differences. Except for the fire-safety aspect, the French system is flexible, not rigid. It leaves rehabilitators free to use their ingenuity to come up with cost-effective ways of salvaging old buildings, so long as basic safety conditions are met. In addition, the French system does not prohibit totally noncode construction. An innovator can build whatever he likes, a back-to-nature hippie can build a one-room cabin, or an architect with revolutionary ideas can put them into physical form. Thus, nonconformists and innovators can have their day, as well.

The ability to choose among inspection firms is also important. A city building-inspection department is a monopoly and tends to operate as such: You play the game their way or you don't play at all. With competition among firms, service to the customer (rather than bureaucratic procedure) becomes the norm. Thus, privatization again provides a better deal for the citizen-taxpayer.

INSPECTIONS

Until we can privatize building codes, city governments will retain the inspection function. Most cities make a variety of inspections, ranging from fire prevention to a number of types of building-code (for new structures) and housing-code (for existing structures) inspections. Usually, each type of inspection is performed by a separate individual. Each, therefore, requires a separate trip, separate paperwork, and its own overhead costs.

Several cities are cutting costs by consolidating the inspection functions. Raleigh, North Carolina, and Phoenix, Arizona, have cross-trained their building inspectors to handle all types of building and construction permits. Consequently, it is unnecessary for several inspectors to visit a single construction site. The saving—estimated at $750,000 a year in Phoenix—includes reduced personnel expenses per building project and reduced vehicle usage. In addition, the morale of both the employees and builders has improved.

Chula Vista, California, has instituted a single-permit system under which a general contractor or owner can take out all the permits needed for a job in a single visit. In a similar move, Salem, Oregon, has set up a Permit Application Center, centralizing all permit applications in a single location, using a single application form. This change has cut the annual cost of issuing permits from $74,000 to $56,000.

Several cities have gone further in consolidating inspections. In Dallas, Texas, inspectors from all of the following departments are cross-trained: litter control, fire, health, zoning, urban rehabilitation, plumbing, electrical, building, and action center. As a result, a single inspector can handle all of these functions, identifying and reporting common multicode violations. Over 80% of the violations now being reported are brought into compliance by the originating inspector, without involving personnel from the other departments. Normal, Illinois, has combined all its inspection functions into a single Inspection Department, while Plainfield, New Jersey, has consolidated all inspection activities into its fire department. Springfield, Illinois, is gradually consolidating fire inspections with other types of inspections. During an eight-year transition period, inspections are being made by two-person teams consisting of a fire-safety inspector and a building inspector. Eventually, the fire department will take over this role altogether.

The Institute for Local Self Government has studied the Phoenix and Springfield programs and has devised a model fire-safety and code-enforcement-inspection program.[7] Under this plan all building, housing, and safety inspections would be carried out by cross-trained firefighters as part of their fire-prevention duties. This would better utilize the 98% of firefighters' time spent on nonemergency activities and would completely eliminate the need for most other inspectors. Only a few specialists in the particular code areas would remain. They would be available for special referrals by the generalist inspectors and for the relatively few highly technical inspections.

We have seen in this chapter that much of the city's efforts aimed at protecting property—planning, zoning, and inspections—can be privatized. Planning can be confined to forecasting the city's needs for infrastructure development: roads, water and sewer lines, fire stations, etc. Land-use conflicts can be prevented at low cost and with desirable flexibility by a system of private deed restrictions rather than by zoning. And by further developing new-construction insurance, the inspection function, too, can be privatized. Each of these changes not only cuts taxes but also leaves people freer to pursue creative, new solutions to building and housing problems, without imposing on their neighbors.

12

Public Works

The term "public works" refers to those physical facilities that provide basic services—the physical infrastructure of the city. Streets, bridges, water systems, sewer systems, city buildings, gas and electricity systems (where city-owned), and airports and harbors are the facilities generally included under this heading. All are characterized by large-scale capital investments. Except for streets and city buildings, the services provided by these facilities are relatively easy to charge for. Because of this, they are not always provided by government, and private examples of each are known (and in the case of gas and electricity, predominate).

PUBLIC OR PRIVATE?

Local government provides for most of these services, but there is no inherent reason for that to be the case. Franchised private firms can provide water and sewer systems as they now provide telephone, electricity, and gas systems. In point of fact, a 1963 U.S. Public Health Service survey of water facilities found that 29% of all city water systems were privately owned, especially in smaller communities. (Three-fourths of the private water companies were in cities of under 5,000 population.)

The feasibility of large-scale private airports is demonstrated by the existence of the Hollywood-Burbank Airport, owned and operated for 40 years by a subsidiary of Lockheed Aircraft Corporation. This major commercial airport serves more than 2 million passengers a year via several major airlines. By the mid 1970s, however, a variety of discriminatory government policies reduced Lockheed's profit on airport operation to only 2%, leading it to sell the airport for $51 million to the cities of Burbank, Glendale, and Pasadena. In 1979, one year after this sale, the Federal Aviation Administration proposed a change in the eligibility requirements for Airport and Airway Improvement Act funding, to allow privately owned airports to receive such grants for the first time. The need to pay for all capital improvements from its own funds had put the Lockheed airport at a significant competitive disadvantage compared with government-owned airports. The new policy may lead to a resurgence of private airports.

Bridges, too, are sometimes privately owned, self-supported by tolls. One of the largest is the Ambassador Bridge linking Detroit, Michigan, and Windsor, Ontario. When the bridge's owners recently offered it for sale, four firms eagerly submitted bids. The bridge earned a 27.5% return on equity in 1976. Another major suspension bridge is Lion's Gate Bridge linking Vancouver and West Vancouver, British Columbia. Built as a private venture in 1938 for $5.7 million, the bridge was operated on a profit-making basis by the First Narrows Bridge Company until 1955. At that point the province's socialist government turned down the firm's proposal to build a second span and purchased the bridge itself. To date, the government has widened the approach roads and main span but has yet to build the needed second bridge. Smaller private toll bridges include the Dingman's Ferry Bridge across the Delaware River, a bridge linking West Virginia and Maryland across the upper Potomac River, and a bridge crossing the Tug River linking Kentucky and West Virginia. The Port Authority of New York and New Jersey, which owns and operates the major bridges, tunnels, airports, and harbor facilities of the New York metropolitan area, though nominally a government agency, in effect operates as a multibillion-dollar corporation, funded from charges on its users.

Private streets and roads are also more common than most people realize. Many upper-middle- and upper-income suburbs have private road systems, maintained by a local homeowner's association to which all homeowners belong as a condition of buying into the community. The association may have a full-time maintenance crew or may hire outside contractors only when needed. But this pattern also exists in some large cities. In St. Louis, for example, purely residential streets are sometimes organized as "private" streets (though legally remaining city streets). The local neighborhood association simply assumes responsibility for regulating their use and providing for their maintenance.

New York City boasts true private streets in all five of its boroughs. Best known of them all is Rockefeller Plaza, a 600-foot-long thoroughfare owned by Columbia University and leased to Rockefeller Center. Once a year it is closed to all traffic to legally maintain its private character. Maintenance and legal liability rest with the Rockefeller Center management. Most of the other private streets are residential. They are maintained by local block associations made up of homeowners fronting the streets. Parking spaces belong to the owners and through traffic is not permitted. The owners must arrange for private contractors to pick up their garbage and remove winter snow.

Yet another example shows how commercial-area roads can be provided privately. In this case the "roads" are underground, beneath Houston, Texas. An extensive, fully private network of tunnels links 30 major buildings and parking facilities—and provides access to a thriving complex of subterranean shops and service business. Since property owners in Houston retain ownership of land to the center of the street (granting only easements to the city for road use), they retain full subsurface and air rights. As a result, downtown owners have cooperated to develop and maintain the tunnel system, providing climate control, maintenance, and private security as amenities to attract shops and customers. The result is a thriving mini-city beneath Houston's (also thriving) central business district.

The point of these examples is to illustrate that "public works" do not necessarily have to be owned and operated by government. Here and there entrepreneurs and groups of individuals have found it advantageous to provide these facilities, developing user-pays methods of funding instead of taxes. Those incorporating new communities should not automatically assume that public works *must* be provided by government. The benefits of privatization—user-pays funding, cost-conscious (non-bureaucratic) management and operation, keeping the facility on the tax rolls—may make it an attractive option for harbors, airports, bridges, water and sewer systems, and perhaps even roads.

There may also be a case for privatizing existing government-owned public works. Urban observers around the country report that the "capital infrastructure" of our cities is decaying badly. Needed maintenance has been put off for years. And now, just when the situation is becoming critical, along comes the tax revolt, restricting even further the cities' ability to do the work. George Peterson, director of a HUD-financed study of the problem for the Urban Institute, reports that in Cleveland, Pittsburgh, and many other large cities numerous bridges urgently need upgrading or replacement. Newark is under court order to replace its water and sewer system—at a debt cost four times the present legal limit. New York City is repairing its streets on a 200-year cycle, instead of on a prudent 20- to 25-year basis. Its water and sewer mains are on a 300-year cycle, instead of the recommended 100 years. A nonprofit agency—The Road Information Program (TRIP)—has identified the ten states with the largest numbers of unsafe and obsolete bridges: Iowa heads the list with 14,000, followed by Oklahoma with 5,945, Pennsylvania with 5,939, and New York with 5,750.

Privatization as a solution to capital shortages and obsolete facilities has already begun. In 1972 Cleveland sold its sewer system to a regional authority for $32 million. Detroit sold its sewers to a similar authority for $15 million in the early 1960s and is considering doing the same with its mass-transit system. Boston has created a water and sewer commission to take over these functions from the city. And in 1978 two Urban Institute researchers proposed that New York City sell its aging water system to a newly created public authority.

To be sure, none of these buyer agencies is, in fact, a private entity. Each is semipublic, much as the New York Port Authority is. But such sales illustrate the benefits of transferring capital assets from a political entity to a professional, businesslike entity:

- The city receives an immediate cash benefit from the proceeds of the sale, to relieve other obligations or refund to the taxpayers.
- The new owner issues revenue bonds to pay for both the purchase and for needed capital improvements.
- Funding shifts from taxes to 100% user payments, with the usual gains in efficiency.
- Professional, businesslike management is required by the bondholders, further ensuring an efficient operation.

Actual sale of a water system to a private firm was considered in 1978 by Garden Grove, California, as a way of offsetting revenue losses from Proposition 13. It was thought that interest on the $35 million to be received from the sale could replace the lost revenue. Although further analysis made the sale look less attractive, City Manager Dick Powers still considers the concept sound, even though not adopted by Garden Grove.

PUBLIC WORKS CONSTRUCTION

Roads, water lines, sewers, airports, and government buildings are nearly always built by private firms, on contract to the responsible local government agency. (The exceptions are certain residential subdivisions, where the developer will construct the basic facilities within the tract, as part of the cost of developing it.) It is rare to find a local government itself getting into the construction business. Although cities typically have engineering departments, the actual design of most public works projects is also contracted out. The city's engineering function is there mainly to ensure that the city has the necessary technical expertise to deal competently with outside architects, designers, and contractors.

There are several methods of financing the construction of public works projects. Most of these projects, being long-term capital improvements, are financed by issuance of municipal bonds. There are two main types of municipal bonds: general obligation bonds and revenue bonds. A general obligation bond bases its repayment on the general taxing power of the municipality; that is, it is a long-term claim upon future tax revenues. Many smaller cities have tended to avoid general obligation bonds on the grounds that it is unjust to obligate future taxpayers to pay for today's projects. Revenue bonds, by contrast, do not depend on taxation for repayment. Rather, they are based on the projected future revenues of the project in question—revenues to be paid by the project's users. Airports, harbors, and toll bridges are usually financed with revenue bonds, as are many water and sewer systems.

Clearly, from the standpoint of the taxpayer, revenue bonds are the preferable alternative. Most public works (except streets and government offices) generate revenues. There is thus no inherent reason why *all* revenue-producing public works cannot be financed with revenue bonds, thereby ensuring that the construction costs are paid for only by the users, in proportion to their use, rather than by all the taxpayers. And in fact this seems to be the emerging trend, helped along by the tax revolt. Since 1970 the volume of revenue bonds issued by local governments has grown more than 300%, from $6 billion to $26 billion in 1978. California's Proposition 13 effectively prohibits issuance of new general obligation bonds (unless approved by a two-thirds vote of the citizenry), so revenue bonds have become virtually the only kind issued in California since 1978.

Who should pay for additional streets and sewers in new suburbs has become a highly political issue in some communities in the last few years. Foes of "urban sprawl" have suggested that these costs are being subsidized by taxpayers in already developed sections of the city. Developers and advocates of growth tend to see this as an attack on free enterprise. But such issues are worth posing. Although solid empirical data are not readily available (and may vary widely from area to area, depending on the extent and nature of user charge versus tax financing), it seems likely that some subsidization of new development *is* occurring, especially in cases of "leap-frog" development (where a new subdivision is built some distance from existing developed areas).

This type of thinking lies behind a number of "phased growth" measures adopted in recent years by the San Diego, California, city council. Before planning officials issue permits for new development, a cost-revenue analysis must be completed, showing the impact on public works needs. If the costs to existing taxpayers are excessive, the permits are not issued. Since the option of having the developer pay the additional costs has not been provided, the program has caused considerable controversy. But its underlying aim of avoiding taxpayer subsidies to new development is commendable.

Several communities have gone one step further by imposing a "systems-development charge" on new development. It is an up-front tax or fee designed to cover a percentage of the city's cost of installing arterial streets and trunk water and sewer lines. Although builders' organizations claim such fees will raise the price and reduce the supply of new homes, the experience of Corvallis, Oregon—one of the first to adopt such charges— has been only a modest increase in new-home prices and no reduction in building activity. It is to be expected that the price of houses will go up, for that is precisely the point of the systems-development charge. The beneficiary—the new-home buyer—is the one who should bear the cost of new public works, not the taxpayers who are already well served by existing facilities. Existing taxpayers should not be forced to subsidize new construction.

Systems-development charges have spread from Corvallis to other Oregon cities, among them Cottage Grove, Eugene, Junction City, and Lake Oswego. And following passage of Proposition 13, the idea moved into California, as well. Both Irvine and San Juan Capistrano began imposing a systems-development charge of 1% of a building's value in order to finance public facilities. Other cities adopted annexation fees, new-school-impact fees, or new-water/sewer-hookup fees designed to accomplish the same thing (although a school-construction fee was ruled unconstitutional by the California attorney general in May 1979).

Perhaps the most sophisticated (and fairest) of these efforts is the Urban Growth Management (UGM) program in Fresno, California.[1] Instead of charging a fixed fee, city staff subjects each proposed development to a service-delivery review. A special committee analyzes the need for fire protection, water, sewers, and streets and estimates both the capital and operating costs of these facilities. Five-year costs for other city services are also estimated. Next, all revenues expected from the development over the next five years are also computed. Costs and revenues are then compared, leading to one of three possible outcomes:

- If revenues exceed both capital and operating costs over the five-year period, the project is approved with no fee.
- If revenues exceed only the operating costs, this surplus is compared to the capital requirements. The difference is charged to the developer as a fee.
- If five-year revenues do not even cover five-year operating costs, the proposal is returned to the developer for modification. In certain cases such projects may still be approved, e.g., if the project provides badly needed low-cost housing.

After UGM's first 18 months of operation, a review by the International City Management Association found that it had markedly shifted construction from outlying areas to areas within or directly adjacent to the city. It appeared *not* to have reduced the level of construction activity, although it had increased housing prices (the city estimated the average increase at $350). UGM also seemed to have spurred the growth of apartments, at the expense of single-family houses. Another interesting effect was the formation of an eight-developer consortium to share in the costs of public facilities construction in a large geographical area of the city.

Thus, the costs of new development *can* be charged to the users instead of being subsidized by all taxpayers. It is taking some time to develop equitable mechanisms, but Fresno's example points clearly in the right direction.

PUBLIC WORKS OPERATIONS

A large percentage of the operational costs of public works is already met via user charges. Utility operations, especially electric and gas utilities, are operated on a businesslike basis, usually making a profit which is turned over to the city's general fund. Airports and harbors more often than not cover their costs out of revenues. Water and sewer systems, however, are often partly financed out of general taxes instead of being completely user-paid. There is no apparent rationale, other than tradition, for this practice, and a worthwhile reform would be to put water and sewer systems on a fully user-supported basis.

To do this requires elimination of the tax component and increasing the user-charge component of the water or sewer system budget. But existing water or sewer rates should not simply be raised across the board. Most existing water and sewer systems price their services in ways that lead to unintended side effects. They generally charge the same rates throughout the area they serve—no matter how much the cost of service may vary. Likewise, they charge the same rates in summer as in winter, despite huge variations in demand. Economists point out that this type of pricing policy leads to uneconomical expansion of the water system.

Professor Steve Hanke of Johns Hopkins University has studied the economics of municipal water systems.[2] He points out that the present "average-cost" pricing and "fair-return on invested capital" policies lead to large overinvestment in facilities, mostly at the expense of those who live in high-density urban centers. These policies lead to the urban poor subsidizing the water supply of affluent suburbanites. They also encourage "premature development of land at the urban-rural fringe"—that is, urban sprawl. Hanke also notes that the waste of resources is potentially very great, because studies have shown that the quantity of water demanded is quite sensitive to changes in price.

Especially now that many parts of the country are experiencing water shortages, water-pricing policies must be revised. Charging more in the summer months, when lawn sprinkling normally causes huge peaks in demand, would promote conservation during those months, thereby reducing peak-load demand on the system. This will reduce the needed capacity of the system in any given year, thereby keeping both operating costs and expansion below what they otherwise might be.

In the past decade a new development in public works operations has occurred: private contract operation of municipal public works facilities. One of the most important inroads for privatization has been in municipal sewage-treatment plants. New requirements from the EPA have left many municipalities severely short of adequately skilled plant operators. In 1979 the EPA reported that one-third of all sewage-treatment plants were in serious violation of its standards. Private enterprise has rushed to fill the gap. Typically, a private firm (usually a spin-off of a pollution-control manufacturer) offers the city a long-term operation and maintenance (O&M) contract. Supplying equipment, managers, and sometimes other personnel, the firm *guarantees* compliance with EPA requirements—and generally cost savings, as well.

The leading contractor in the field is Envirotech Systems, Inc., of Belmont, California. The company's first O&M contract, with Burlingame, California, rescued that city from a threatened shutdown of its plant. Envirotech quickly achieved a 51% improvement in biological oxygen demand, a 27% improvement in suspended solids, and an 89% reduction in effluent coliform count. The company hired most of the city plant employees and put them under the direction of a 17-year veteran of treatment-plant operations. This field team was then backed up by a home-office group making use of computerized data analysis to schedule preventive maintenance and keep tighter control of daily operations. The Burlingame contract has been renewed several times. Envirotech has gone on to land similar contracts in Cambridge, Maryland, Great Falls, Montana, and California's Fairfield-Suisun Subregional Wastewater Treatment Plant. An East Coast competitor, Cleveland-based ES Environmental Sciences, Inc., offers a similarly guaranteed service.

Although relatively new, contract operation offers cities with existing government-owned facilities a less-radical alternative than selling them to private investors. At relatively little risk, they can contract the operation and maintenance of facilities to experienced professionals and hold them accountable for meeting high performance standards. The same approach that works for waste-water treatment can also be applied to water systems, airports, marinas, and other public works.

One further example of privatization comes to us from England, and concerns a service originated by the private sector. Several dozen British communities now have illuminated directional signs at major intersections, provided by a private firm at no cost to the taxpayers. In fact, each sign yields about $200 a year in revenue to the city coffers. The key to the operation (as we saw with private bus shelters) is advertising. On top of each signpost there is an illuminated box with four advertising panels for local businesses. The box revolves three times per minute. The company, Silux U.K., Ltd., pays all costs, including electricity and maintenance. All signs are produced in accordance with Environment Department specifications. As of mid-1979 Silux was negotiating for a U.S. distributor. If the controversy surrounding bus shelter advertising is any indication, selling the idea to local bureaucrats may not be easy. Yet it's another clear winner for local taxpayers.

MAINTENANCE

Keeping various public works in good repair is one of the major day-to-day tasks of local government. Public works departments generally rely on large field crews to carry out such operations as repairing water-line breaks, trimming trees, and patching pavements. To get the crews to the job, a fleet of radio-equipped vehicles is also required. Regardless of the specialty of a particular crew, the general problem of managing the field operations is pretty much the same. A variety of techniques has been developed to manage field forces more efficiently.

Contracting

According to the American Public Works Association, more than half of all cities contract out part or all of their building and equipment maintenance. A small number contract out maintenance of utilities, water lines, sewer lines, and related public works. A study by the Phoenix,

Arizona, Management and Budget Department found that the cost per square foot of building space cleaned would be substantially lower if the work were contracted out. But a study of ground-maintenance operations at the city's Sky Harbor Airport found little cost difference between city and private maintenance. (Perhaps that is because the airport is already run essentially as a business, more or less independent of city government, and turns a profit each year.) In any event, after what we've already seen of the comparative cost effectiveness of private contracting, it would not be surprising to encounter cost-saving potential in many areas where private contracting could be used.

A city that is saving money in this area is Lafayette, California. In 1977 it hired RJA Maintenance Contractors to take over all public works maintenance: patching streets, replacing traffic signs, maintaining drainage ways, etc. Costs for these operations had been increasing at 10% per year. After the first year of contract operation, costs actually dropped 15%—$370,000 instead of $438,850. The firm keeps costs low by controlling its overhead. Since work needs fluctuate considerably, its resident manager leases or rents most of the vehicles and equipment needed and relies largely on contract labor instead of on a full-time staff (which would have to be paid even when there wasn't much work to do). Thus far, support from both local officials and the public has been enthusiastic.

As noted earlier in this book, contract operation does not guarantee efficiency. New York City, for example, has for many years contracted out street-light maintenance at a cost of about $13 million per year. A 1978 audit of the program by the comptroller's office found that the same two firms had shared the business for more than 25 years, without real competitive bidding. As a result of lax bidding procedures and poor contract supervision, service levels were poor and the firms were estimated to be making profits of between 24% and 30%. The audit recommended a number of changes, including revised bidding procedures and dividing the service area into a number of smaller areas to promote competition. Savings of up to $5 million a year were projected from these changes.

Thinking Smarter

A variety of techniques known as work measurement will also make public works maintenance more efficient. Work measurement refers to the systematic analysis of job functions, their redesign for greater efficiency, and the implementation of a continuous performance measurement system.[3] A well-designed work-measurement system can be used for program planning and budgeting, staffing analysis, route balancing, daily work scheduling, performance reporting, evaluating alternatives, and maintenance planning and control.

Work measurement improves productivity because the jobs we're discussing are often poorly designed, or not really designed at all. Often, no priorities exist among tasks, skills are used inefficiently, personnel switch back and forth between unrelated tasks, and too many or too few people are assigned to specific jobs. The tasks may be improperly sequenced or badly coordinated, and obsolete procedures may still be in effect. The equipment available may be inappropriate for the work at hand, and the forms used to document and control the work may be inadequate. By correcting such deficiencies and setting up efficient procedures, a work-measurement program can usually result in savings of 20% or more in just the first year—enough to pay for the one-time costs of developing the program.

Quite a few cities have begun to adopt work-measurement techniques and programs. One of the most extensive programs applies to about 40% of the municipal work force of Phoenix, Arizona, where it is saving about $12 million per year. Other programs, more limited in scope, are under way in Anaheim, California, Kansas City, Missouri, King County, Washington, and Witchita Falls, Texas. All except Anaheim have inventoried all streets and their characteristics, in order to schedule street maintenance on the basis of predicted need—and then developed work standards for their crews.

Another form of thinking smarter to improve productivity is to adjust the days and hours worked. As part of their work-measurement analysis, Fairfax County, Virginia, public works officials concluded that a four-day work week for its parks and maintenance crews would reduce travel time and increase equipment utilization. This is true, typically, because large amounts of job time are lost each day in traveling from the city yard to the day's job site and returning again to the yard at the end of the day. A four-day week reduces this lost time by 20%.

Springfield, Missouri, instituted a four-day week for its street-maintenance crews. As a result, the crews spend less time each week waiting for asphalt patching material to warm up, since each crew's equipment is switched on only four days a week instead of five. To keep streets clean throughout the week, half the division works Monday through Thursday while the other half works Tuesday through Friday. The plan has had the added benefits of increasing the number of miles of streets cleaned and reducing the total fuel consumption.

Newark, Delaware, found a different way to cut unproductive time. Its public works crews used to work from 8 A.M. to 5 P.M., with an unpaid hour for lunch plus two 15-minute breaks. Besides the official break time, crews would generally leave about 15 minutes early and return late. The city was able to work out a new labor agreement whereby the work day was reduced to 8 A.M. to 4 P.M., with a 30-minute paid lunch break and only one 15-minute break. The workers also agreed to take the break on the job site. The net result was a saving of 75 minutes of extra productive time per employee per day.

Yet another way to reduce wasted time, at least in large cities, is to decentralize the city yard. This puts crews closer to their probable job sites at the beginning of the work day, reducing unproductive travel time. Phoenix, Arizona, public works crews now operate from four service centers located in the four quadrants of the city rather than from a single city yard. Equipping all field vehicles with radios also helps ensure they are at the right place at the right time.

Reducing overtime can also be a source of savings. In order to provide round-the-clock emergency-response capability (e.g., to deal with water-line breaks), many public works departments pay specialists from every division—parks, streets, water, sewers, electrical maintenance—to be on call during night and weekend hours. Santa Barbara, California, formerly paid such standby specialists for two hours' work for every eight hours they agreed to be on call. Several years ago the city decided to replace this system with a small Emergency Services Crew. It cross-trained three employees in all of the repair skills and assigned them to night and weekend duty. When not responding to emergencies, they are assigned to repair water meters. The city estimates net savings of $50,000–$60,000 per year.

Scottsdale, Arizona, now contracts with the (private) fire department to provide after-hours emergency service, using off-duty firemen. The contract cost is $415 per month, compared with an average of $1,000 per month that the city had been paying in overtime to regular city employees. On-duty Scottsdale firefighters utilize spare time repairing broken water meters and assembling refuse containers for the city's mechanized refuse-collection system. These tasks are carried out at no charge to the city, providing additional public works cost savings.

In this chapter we've seen that even those most basic physical components of a city—its infrastructure of streets, bridges, ports, water and sewer lines—are amenable to privatization, user charges, and thinking smarter. And because of the large amounts of capital tied up in these facilities—and the critical shortage of taxpayer-derived capital in the years ahead—the case for privatization of these facilities is even stronger.

13

City Management

In all the previous chapters we've talked about services that local government delivers to the citizenry. We've explored many ways in which these services can be provided more efficiently—by turning them over to the private sector altogether, by farming them out to private contractors under city supervision, by changing the supply/demand relationship through the introduction of user charges, or by applying sound thinking and businesslike methods where they haven't been applied before.

But there remain local government operations that we haven't yet covered: the internal, "housekeeping" functions that keep the city or county government in operation as an organization. Included are such routine functions as operating the city vehicle fleet, buildings, and computers; carrying out architectural, engineering, and legal services; and managing the city's money and its people. Although citizens seldom observe these functions of government, they, too, can be a source of waste—or an area for creative cost-cutting. We'll discuss each of these areas in turn.

VEHICLES

Police, public works, parks, and other city departments typically operate large numbers of vehicles, ranging from sedans to costly, sophisticated special-purpose trucks. Over the past five years a number of cities have taken a hard look at the number of vehicles actually required and have developed useful ways to economize. One of the most important is the in-city rental concept.

Under this approach, one city department "owns" all the vehicles and rents them to the other departments. The goals of the program are to decrease the total number of vehicles, utilize them more efficiently, eliminate high-cost single-function vehicles, and control losses that may be incurred by poor vehicle selection or untimely replacement. This is accomplished by providing dollars-and-cents incentives for operating managers to justify their vehicle needs.

One of the cities making use of in-city rentals is Fort Lauderdale, Florida. Virtually all of the city's vehicles—police cars, trucks, street sweepers, and backhoes—are owned by the Vehicle Maintenance Division of Public Works and rented to the user agencies. The rental rates are set high enough to cover not only maintenance costs but also replacement costs and a contingency fund. Thus, like a private business, the city is charging depreciation on its vehicles, rather than waiting until they wear out and fighting to have replacements authorized as capital expenditures, as is the practice in most cities.

By putting vehicle operations on a businesslike basis, the system produces substantial cost savings. First, the total number of city vehicles has been reduced. Many types of vehicles, ranging from sedans to 3/4-ton trucks, can be shared among a number of departments, none of which needs all of them full time. Accordingly, the vehicles are utilized more efficiently. Cars and trucks sit idle a smaller percentage of the time.

In addition, high-cost units are gradually being weeded out and replaced by more economical vehicles. The police department has shifted from full-size to intermediate sedans, and most other city cars are now subcompact Pintos rather than gas-guzzling LTDs. Economical diesel trucks are being phased in to replace gasoline-powered ones. New vacuum-type street sweepers have cut operating costs in half by doing the job twice as fast.

Further, the rental concept promotes replacement at the optimum point in a vehicle's life cycle. Hal Sherron, the city's central garage superintendent, points out that in 1971, when the program started, more than half the city's truck fleet was more than ten years old and about 40% of the sedans were more than six years old. Maintenance costs were climbing rapidly. Today, the city's cars and trucks are replaced before they start to deteriorate, thanks to the depreciation charges built into the rental structure.

The in-city rental idea is not really very new. Keene, New Hampshire, has been using it successfully since 1948. Assistant Public Works Director John Ranagan reports that department managers clearly prefer letting Public Works have all the headaches of maintaining and replacing vehicles. Springfield, Massachusetts, Santa Barbara, California, and Whatcom County, Washington, have also joined the trend to in-city rental.

Private contracting can assist cities with their vehicle fleet, as well. We noted in Chapter 3 that some police departments are contracting out maintenance of their patrol cars—frequently one of a city's largest fleets of vehicles. The same rationale applies to all the other city vehicles. Once a centralized fleet approach has been adopted, it is that much easier to turn the whole maintenance burden (facilities, equipment, personnel, parts, inventory) over to a private contractor. Gainesville, Florida, did just that in

1978, hiring ARA Fleet Services, a division of $2-billion-a-year ARA Services, one of America's largest service firms. Under the contract, ARA assumed responsibility for all aspects of maintenance, hiring the city's former workers but putting in its own managers and methods.

A way of minimizing the need for costly special-purpose vehicles is being tested in Scottsdale, Arizona. That city's public works department has constructed five modular trucks that are completely interchangeable. The trucks consist of an all-purpose chassis with interchangeable bodies, cabs, running gear, and other components. For example, the refuse truck modules can be removed and the street-patching modules installed in less than an hour. Vehicles with such features are starting to appear on the market. Fort Lauderdale's new street sweepers combine both a vacuum and a brush. Seattle's lawn mowers can be equipped with attachments for cleaning reservoirs.

Finally, as an outgrowth of higher fuel prices, several cities have discovered the advantages of bicycles for short trips between in-town offices. Sacramento, California, and St. Petersburg, Florida, have set up bicycle pools for employees. The bikes are used for making interoffice deliveries and for attending meetings. The cost, of course, is far less than that of operating automobiles.

BUILDINGS

Maintaining city buildings can be costly, especially if the city invests in specialized equipment and personnel. As mentioned in Chapter 12, savings can often be realized by contracting out janitorial services. A 1969 survey by the American Public Works Association showed that 37% of the cities surveyed were contracting for "building maintenance" and 62.5% for "janitorial maintenance."

Des Moines, Iowa, and Fort Lauderdale, Florida, are using outside companies to clean the windows of public buildings. The Des Moines city manager says flatly, "Contracting is cheaper." Tampa, Florida, contracts for library custodial services, with requirements that certain items (e.g., drinking fountains and carpets) be cleaned daily and others (e.g., book shelves) weekly. All building maintenance in Rochester, New York, has been contracted out for the past several years.

In most cases, cutting costs is the principal reason for contracting with outside firms. Some smaller cities, like Newington, Connecticut, and Ashland, Oregon, have gone to contractors because their small size didn't provide enough work for a full-time janitorial staff. Others, like Coronado, California, and Phoenix, Arizona, have simply found that private firms operate more efficiently, accomplishing the same work for less money.

Other ways to save money on city facilities involve "recycling" old buildings. A number of cities have been able to turn obsolete public buildings into "new" facilities for another purpose, at less cost than starting from scratch. Greece, New York, converted its sewage-treatment plant to a new police headquarters, at a cost of only $200,000. The cost of constructing a new facility had been estimated at over $1 million. Thornton, Colorado, converted two abandoned waste-water treatment tanks into a new shop complex. One tank became the vehicle-maintenance garage and the other the meter-repair shop. The concrete facilities required roofing over, cutting of doors and windows, and addition of heating and air conditioning, but the cost still was less than starting from scratch. Newington, Connecticut, converted an unneeded high school into a new town hall. Total cost was $1.95 million, compared with an estimated $2.2 million for a new facility with much less room. Lumberton, New Jersey, converted an abandoned Nike missile base—bought from the federal government for only $60,000—into a police headquarters and city offices. The renovations were carried out by the voluntary labor of police officers and other city employees.

When a city has no further need for new buildings but still finds itself with surplus facilities, it makes sense to sell or lease them to the private sector. A number of school districts have sold or leased excess classroom spaces to private schools, day-care centers, or nonprofit social-service groups. This is especially possible now that the student population is shrinking and schools are going unused.

COMPUTERS

The age of the computer caught many city governments unprepared. Although the greatest fiascos caused by technically naive managers are now history, many cities are still operating costly, inefficient computer systems, often "captives" of a single supplier. A city administrator lacking computer training may be hard pressed to determine whether the electronic data-processing (EDP) department is operating with obsolete equipment or software, or whether it is vainly seeking the newest in sophisticated systems for the pure joy of having the latest model.

A 1974 audit of Newark, New Jersey's computer operations found that the system had been designed without standards and necessary guidelines, had no clear priorities or management control, and showed little regard for user-agency needs. More recently, a survey of city data-processing managers, conducted by the University of California–Irvine, found that the highest priority of most city EDP managers was expanding the size of their operations. Near the bottom of the list was meeting the real needs of city agencies.

One way a city can avoid creating a computerized white elephant is illustrated by Orange County, California's second-largest county. In August 1973 it signed a seven-year, fixed-price contract with Computer Sciences Corporation (CSC), under the terms of which the firm assumed responsibility for all of the county's data-processing operations, including hiring and firing of personnel and ownership of the equipment.

The price of $26.6 million was almost one-third less than the county's own EDP department had planned to spend over the next seven years. The company offered jobs to all the former county employees, and over 98%

accepted. It brought in only two of its own people—a director and a quality-assurance manager. But their management knowhow made quite a difference.

Private firms such as CSC can operate at lower cost for several reasons. Years of operating in a profit-and-loss environment enable the firm to carry out government data processing in a truly businesslike manner. Decisions can be made and carried out, rather than endlessly passed back and forth among layers of bureaucracy. For example, two months after the start of the Orange County contract CSC decided that the data-input equipment was obsolete. It naturally went ahead and placed an order for modern key-to-disk units. The county had been studying this problem for nearly three years without reaching a decision.

Because a private firm serves many customers, it can develop specialized computer programs for one city and adapt them to many others, instead of developing them from scratch each time as most cities have to do. As Dr. Mario Montana of CSC explains, "What we look for is commonality in applications. Whereas a government agency is under pressure to create its own programs, our motivation is exactly the opposite. We act as a catalyst for resource sharing between the agencies."

Yet another source of savings is found with personnel. While a city is generally limited to its in-house EDP personnel, the company is free to draw upon its entire professional staff, not just those normally assigned to a particular city's EDP operations. And the firm can usually do the job with fewer people. Although CSC made the transition in Orange County without any layoffs, over time it reduced labor costs. After two years, only 72% of the original employees were still at work on the county's operations. Some had left CSC through normal attrition, but others transferred laterally or upward to other jobs in the company. The availability of whole new career paths, encouraged by company training programs and career guidance, has been a key factor in boosting employee morale.

The success of Orange County's experience has not gone unnoticed. Since landing that contract in 1973, CSC has made similar arrangements with Cleveland, Ohio, Torrance, California, Newark, New Jersey, and Pierce County, Washington. Other firms have entered the field, among them Boeing Computer Services, Electronic Data Systems, and System Development Corporation. One market research firm put the total "facilities management" market for government and industry at $481 million in 1976, and expected it to reach $820 million by 1980.

At present, the major computer services contractors hesitate to work with cities of less than 150,000 people. But for smaller cities, the service bureau option exists. Firms such as Xerox Computer Services and Optimum Systems now offer computer services to local governments on a shared-use basis—a single computer center serves a number of users. More than 600 banks also provide data-processing services for cities, handling such routine tasks as payroll, bookkeeping, and issuing utility and tax bills. As computer costs continue to come down, more and more small cities will find it economical to utilize service bureaus for some or all of their data-processing needs.

PROFESSIONAL SERVICES

At one time or another, most local governments consult with architects, engineers, or attorneys. Some cities are contracting entirely for such services, instead of providing them in-house with full-time personnel. A 1970 ICMA-Advisory Commission on Intergovernmental Relations survey found that some 10% of the 2,248 responding cities obtained their engineering services in this way, 8% their legal services, and 4% their planning services.

The most likely users of full-time contract-engineering services for instance, are cities of 10,000 to 15,000 people. Often these cities do not have a public works department either, and they rely on private firms for the design, construction, and maintenance of streets and other public facilities. Sometimes the contracting is with a nearby, larger unit of government. A number of smaller cities in the Los Angeles area contract with the county's engineering department, instead of having a city engineer. But even though less costly than having its own department, contracting with a large bureaucracy can be costly and troublesome. The city of Lawndale, for example, several years ago canceled its engineering contract with Los Angeles County when it found it could hire a private consulting engineer at less cost.

Smaller communities are also most likely to contract for legal services. The Urban Institute reports that 30% of towns of under 15,000 population contract for legal services on a part-time, retainer basis. They simply do not have enough legal work to require a full-time legal staff. Medium-size cities may hire a law firm on a full-time basis. About half of these firms also continue to serve private clients.

Because the outputs of these services are difficult to measure or specify in contracts, it is not always clear whether contracting for them saves money. Because few of these contracts are awarded on the basis of competitive bidding, cost comparisons are all the more difficult. But contracting clearly does save money when the volume of work is less than enough to justify employment of a full-time professional. It may do so generally in other cases, as well, because of the general efficiency of private versus public operations, but studies documenting such savings have not yet been done.

ADMINISTRATIVE SERVICES

The 1970 ICMA-ACIR survey that showed the extent of contracting for professional services also turned up a surprising variety of miscellaneous administrative services that were being provided to cities by private firms. Of the 2,248 cities responding, 99 contracted for utility billing, 60 for payroll, 41 for microfilming, 31 for tax assessing, 23 for tax collection, 14 for treasury functions, 8 for records maintenance, 7 for election administration, and even 2 for voter registration.

In contrast to professional services, these services are much easier to specify in precise, output-oriented language, and they can then be obtained via competitive bidding. Contracting for these technical services permits a city to take advantage of the latest technology in both equipment (hardware) and procedures (software). And as we've seen in other cases, a contracting firm can frequently offer lower unit costs because it serves more than one customer with the same equipment.

Property-tax assessment provides a good example of the use of contracting. A 1970 survey by the International Association of Assessing Officers (IAAO) found that "mass appraisal" firms existed in more than half of the 50 states and had an annual volume of over $25 million. The IAAO estimates that appraisal firms do over 10% of all property-tax assessment. Although some states forbid cities or counties to contract for this service, Ohio actually requires contracting.

Most of the assessment firms consist of a core staff of managers and trainers, who hire and train people to be used on specific jobs. This structure is dictated by the fluctuations in demand for appraisal services. Most appraisal firms are hired to supplement a municipal assessor's office staff when the latter decides to do a complete reassessment in a short period of time (rather than the more usual partial reassessment each year). Hence, the firms must be able to gear up for a large workload on relatively short notice. As a result, some appraisal firms have gotten into trouble due to insufficiently good training programs or underestimating the time needed to do a job.

Despite this caveat, which applies only to firms using part-time help, private appraisal still looks promising, especially as a full-time replacement for a city assessor. Several years ago, for instance, an independent evaluation was carried out, comparing property-tax assessment in Ohio with that of other states.[1] It found that on the standard measure of assessment quality (a comparison of assessed value and actual sales prices for single-family homes), Ohio—which contracts—came out best. And the cost of assessment in Ohio is only *half* the average for other states. These results seem to indicate that contracting as an alternative to in-house tax assessment is highly cost effective. The case for supplemental-tax assessment contracting is not so clear-cut, with no studies providing evidence one way or the other.

THE CITY MANAGEMENT APPROACH
The city or county manager form of government is not universally accepted, perhaps because many cities distrust professional managers as proponents of expanding bureaucracy. Nevertheless, a good city manager can make all the difference in determining whether a municipality implements money-saving measures of the kind discussed in this book. If he or she encourages department managers to be innovative and try out new ideas, there's much more likelihood of cost-cutting success. If, on the

other hand, the city manager implicitly or explicitly encourages the status quo, significant change is unlikely.

"The thing that sets Scottsdale [Arizona] apart," says City Manager Frank Aleshire, "is a willingness to take risks." That willingness includes a recognition that some proposals are bound to fail, but that fact should not be an excuse for not trying them. Scottsdale's meter readers tried out electric golf carts, for example, but found them uneconomical. So the experiment was ended, and no heads rolled. Failures like that are offset by successes like the city's semi-automated, one-person garbage trucks, which save more than $200,000 a year.

Many of Scottsdale's innovations—like its contract with a private company for fire protection—were the brainchildren of William Donaldson, its first city manager. After a successful career there, Donaldson moved on to Tacoma, Washington, where he fostered the same kind of climate of innovation. In 1975 he was hired to bail out Cincinnati—one of the costliest city governments in America. In the three years he served there, budget increases were held to about one-half the inflation rate (meaning true spending went down) and the permanent work force was cut from 9,200 to 7,200, mostly by attrition. Donaldson simply told the citizens they'd have to do more things for themselves, instead of running to city hall with every problem. And he involved employees in developing means of improving productivity.

There's more to good city management than just an entrepreneurial city manager, however. Besides having a chief executive committed to efficiency, the management team must have the tools to enable it to get meaningful information about what the city departments are doing and what their operations are costing. Several specific techniques have been developed to do this.

One of these is the concept of *program budgeting*. Although not a money-saver in and of itself, it can be an important means of identifying "where the money goes" and making it more visible. Because of this, it can be a tool for cost savings. Program budgeting identifies expenditures according to the specific function or program area in question, rather than by line item. A well-designed, detailed program budget can provide ready answers to questions like "How much are we spending to enforce laws against victimless crimes?" or "How much of the public works budget goes for street sweeping?" A conventional line-item city budget usually cannot provide the answers to such questions—it is simply a list of all the resources expended by each department: salaries, fringe benefits, equipment, etc. Program budgeting is being used in a few large cities such as Phoenix, Arizona, and San Diego, California; a few medium-size cities like Sunnyvale, California, and Boulder, Colorado; and a few small cities like Newport, Rhode Island, and Loon Rapids, Minnesota.

Another important tool is the idea of *measures of effectiveness*. It is not enough simply to ask how much a particular program *costs*, either in absolute terms or relative to last year. There must also be meaningful measures of what it has accomplished. There are many ways to measure the results of government services. On the one hand there are relatively simple *process* measures—for example, the number of miles driven by police cars on patrol and the number of hours devoted to street patching. Although these are useful for some purposes, the more important measures for evaluation are *outcome* measures—for example, the rate of apprehension of burglars or the percentage of pot-holes patched within three days of a complaint. When outcome measures are related back to program costs, we can develop evaluations based on *cost effectiveness* and begin to answer questions like "Is it better to spend another $20,000 staking out liquor stores or adding equipment in the crime lab?" Cost-effectiveness measures make it possible to give department heads specific goals to meet within a given budget. Among the cities using cost-effectiveness measures are Lakewood, Colorado, and Palo Alto, California.

Another technique is known as *impact analysis*. Before deciding on any new program or activity, some cities insist on an estimate of the effect the proposed service would have on the budgets of the other departments. Frequently, without such a check, an important source of "surprise" cost increases is an increase in one department's workload caused by an unexpected new program of another department. Walnut Creek, California, now requires all city departments to prepare a maintenance-impact statement for each new program or capital project. The department must analyze the total cost of the program, including maintenance, and allow the city's maintenance staff to propose modifications that would reduce maintenance costs. Phoenix's uniform reporting system requires that all staff reports in favor of new programs or capital projects include a financial impact statement, delineating the program's city-wide cost impact. In Lakewood, Colorado, each capital budget request must also include an operating budget impact statement that lays out the total requirements for personnel, operating and maintenance supplies, and other charges and services.

MONEY MANAGEMENT

The behind-the-scenes details of how a city manages its money can make a big difference. One need only recall the sorry state of the financial management of New York, Cleveland, and other near-bankrupts to realize the importance of sound financial practices. In fact, it was not until the plight of New York City came to the fore several years ago that people began to realize just how slipshod many cities' financial management practices really are.

In 1976 two of America's largest public accounting firms, Arthur Andersen & Co. and Coopers & Lybrand, issued reports critical of the fiscal management and reporting practices of American cities in general.[2,3] They recommend that cities follow the practice of private businesses by issuing a single, consistent set of financial statements that clearly set forth the sources and uses of funds, changes in city equity, and overall financial position. The latter firm also recommended that city taxpayers and buyers of municipal bonds be protected by financial disclosure laws as stringent as those applied to the private sector by the Securities and Exchange Commission.

Since those reports were written, several changes have taken place. A 1977 provision of federal revenue-sharing legislation required that by 1980 all municipalities receiving more than $25,000 a year of revenue-sharing money would have to have an "independent" audit done on their financial situation. According to a Treasury Department official, the provision required 11,000 municipalities to have outside audits, many of which had *never* had one before. Some cities are now hiring CPA firms to do outside audits, as bond underwriters, more cautious since the New York debacle, have demanded more complete accounting data.

The preliminary results of these audits began to appear as this book was completed. In Boston, a Coopers & Lybrand audit found comingling of funds between special-purpose enterprises and the general fund. Careful study revealed the existence of substantial operating deficits. In Cleveland, Price Waterhouse gave up its attempt, declaring the city's books unauditable. A second firm found that $40 million in bond proceeds had been used illegally to pay operating expenses. Peat, Marwick & Mitchell's audit of New York City totaled up $17 billion in legal claims against the city of which the city had failed to keep adequate records. According to Peter F. Rousmaniere of the Council on Municipal Performance, "These findings are just the beginning."

In 1978 Coopers & Lybrand published a set of model financial reports and standards for municipal governments, in an attempt to "close the communications gap" between cities and both taxpayers and bond buyers.[4] The Financial Accounting Standards Board is developing new municipal accounting standards. Both the American Institute of Certified Public Accountants and the Council of State Governments have task forces working on the problem. "The accounting principles for municipalities have to be changed," says Kenneth Johnson of Coopers & Lybrand. "We have to ask ourselves, what should the financial statement reflect, does it give a true picture of the financial condition of the municipality?"

One of the worst financial problem areas is *municipal pensions*. For many years the majority of local governments have followed unsound practices in operating their employee pension systems. The basic flaw is their failure to set aside enough money out of current budgets to meet expected future outlays. This fundamentally dishonest practice makes promises to employees today, but leaves paying these promises to future politicians and taxpayers. Moreover, the actuarial calculations on which pension-fund contributions are based usually have either neglected, or have vastly underestimated, the effects of inflation.

As a result, the "unfunded liability"—the extent of future liabilities for which no money has been set aside—totals $24 billion for California's public employees, between $7 billion and $13 billion in Massachusetts, $5.7 billion in Illinois, and $5.3 billion in New Jersey. "I don't think voters any place realize what they have gotten themselves into," says Dan Mattrocce, general manager of San Francisco's employee retirement system. "Politicians use retirement systems as a means of placating employees because it's a pay-later system. . . . It's easy to give away something that you don't have to pay for right now. It's reached a point now where the community just can't afford them."

The congressional task force on municipal pensions found that, as of mid-1978, more than half of all municipal pension funds hadn't had an actuarial evaluation in five years—and 25% of them have *never* had one. This is an important first step for many cities.

Once a particular pension fund *has* been actuarily evaluated, the painful next step is to restore its soundness, so as to prevent a future bankruptcy. This means future revenues must be increased to match future benefit payments. Frequently that has meant increasing the tax money allocated to pension funds (though it *could* also mean increasing the amount deducted from employees' pay for this purpose). Courts have prohibited cities from cutting back benefits for current employees, viewing these as contractual obligations that must be met. Hence, the only alternatives to massive future tax increases are (1) increasing employee pension deductions (without granting corresponding increases in total paychecks), (2) sharply reducing benefits for *future* employees, or (3) sharply decreasing the *number* of future retirees. Los Angeles County supervisors adopted the second idea, voting to cut benefits by 45% for workers hired after September 1, 1978. San Francisco voters cut future pension benefits by 20% in 1976.

But the third method—reducing the number of future retirees—has recently focused new attention on private contracting. When a city shifts from in-house to contracted data processing, for instance, the employees go to work for the contractor. They thereby *leave* the municipal pension system and enter the *contractor's* retirement system instead. Thus, yet another benefit of privatization of city services is relief from the potential bankruptcy of unsound pension systems.

How the city manages its cash is another nuts-and-bolts item. Cities tend to be inept at doing this compared with private firms. Yet businesslike *cash management* is just as significant a money-saver in the public sector, and local governments should be held accountable in this area. The State of North Carolina assists local citizens in monitoring their cities' cash-management practices by publishing comparative cash-management performance data on local governments each year. This kind of exposure gives lagging local officials an incentive to make changes.

When Baltimore County, Maryland, sought competitive bids for its banking services, it was able to consolidate its accounts from 51 to 10 and significantly reduce its average daily balance. The county is earning an additional $50,000-$100,000 on its money, thanks to shopping around.

Small cities can also experience savings by smart cash-management practices. Tiny (pop. 2,500) California City, California, recently put into effect a businesslike cash-management system based on three principles: (1) accelerate receipts, (2) delay disbursements, and (3) pay careful attention to the investment portfolio. Implementation of these principles increased the city's rate of return by 2.3 whole percentage points, earning an extra $300,000 in one year ($120 per capita!).

A number of California cities are getting up to 1.5% more interest by taking part in the Pool Money Investment Account. This is a cash pool set up jointly with the state government. By pooling their funds, they can shop more effectively for high interest rates. As of 1977 the cities and towns had put $1.3 billion into the pool, where it was added to $6.5 billion of the state's own short-term funds. Larkspur, California's treasurer figures that her city is earning about 25% more on its cash, thanks to the pool. The city of Milpitas estimates $52,000 in extra income.

California is not the only state that permits local jurisdictions to pool their cash. The concept got its start in Connecticut in 1972. Other states that allow pooling include Massachusetts, Wisconsin, Illinois, and New Jersey.

MANAGING PEOPLE

One of the keys to doing more with less in local government is to use personnel more efficiently—that is, to do more work with the existing number of people, or to do the same amount of work with *fewer* people. Except where cities are growing rapidly, increasing productivity and efficiency inevitably means the latter alternative. Yet the idea of reducing (or even not increasing) the work force often leads to fear and resistance on the part of employees. And today most city employees belong to unions. Being able to communicate and negotiate with employees and their unions can be a key factor in making cost-cutting changes successfully.

There are many ways in which confrontations with unions over productivity and cost-cutting can be avoided or defused. *Involving workers* in the productivity improvement process can foster a spirit of cooperation, especially if incentives for increasing productivity are provided. Nassau County, New York, has developed a Productivity Benefit Increase Plan, whereby a portion of all dollars saved from productivity improvement is deposited into a deferred-compensation trust fund, the proceeds of which are made available to participating employees when they leave the job. Detroit, Michigan, added a provision to its sanitation workers' contract whereby savings resulting from the use of larger garbage trucks are shared with employees. In the first year of the contract, the city saved $300,000 and each worker received a productivity bonus of $300. Cincinnati's William Donaldson stressed the key role played by a public works labor-management committee in working out productivity improvements that included new work schedules, labor-saving trucks, and personnel cutbacks.

In many such cases, the other key to making the productivity improvements work is the avoidance of layoffs by making use of *attrition*. The idea is to take advantage of the natural turnover rate (often 5% to 10% per year) by not replacing employees who quit or retire. The savings permitted by the productivity improvements may not be realized quite as rapidly that way, but they will occur much more peaceably. Los Angeles County cut its work force from 83,815 to less than 76,000 in three years, by simply not filling vacancies. Cincinnati's cut from 9,200 to 7,200 over three years was also accomplished by attrition.

Keeping employees involved and satisfied should be an important goal for most cities. In unionized cities, this should help to engender a cooperative attitude toward productivity improvements. And in cities without unions, it may help to prevent the unions from gaining a foothold. This may well be a plus—not because unions are dysfunctional in principle, but simply because there is a strong tendency for unions to be supporters of the status quo and opponents of flexibility in work assignments and productivity improvements. The best defense against that sort of unionism is a motivated, satisfied work force. Workers who are given responsibility and a degree of autonomy, who participate in redesigning jobs for greater efficiency, and who are rewarded for increases in productivity, are not prime candidates for unionization.

One way to give workers greater autonomy is called *flextime*. Local governments tend to have higher than average levels of sick leave and other absentee problems compared with private firms, all of which ends up increasing the costs to taxpayers. The level of absenteeism is generally an indication of employee morale, which tends to be poor in many civil service jobs. Under flextime, employees are given flexibility in setting their working hours. They must be on the job during core hours but are allowed freedom to set their own starting and quitting times, provided they put in the required total number of hours. Firms using flextime report up to a 25% reduction in days lost due to absenteeism, and tardiness virtually disappears. Workers tend to become task-oriented, instead of watching the clock, and take more responsibility for their work.

One of the cities which pioneered in the concept is Inglewood, California. Using flextime, the city was able to keep city hall open from 7:30 A.M. to 6 P.M. This afforded better service to the public without adding personnel and resulted in an annual saving of $20,000 in overtime. Other cities using flextime include Torrance, California, Baltimore, Maryland, and the city and county of Honolulu, Hawaii.

Despite all their efforts to deal responsibly and creatively with employees, city officials may still find themselves involved in difficult labor negotiations. Too often, the mayor or city administrator leads the city's bargaining, even though he or she may have no experience in labor negotiations. Instead, cities should follow the advice of the mayor of San Jose, California, Ronald James: "Pay for negotiating experience and back it—come hell or high water." A growing number of large cities, including Boston, Detroit, and New York, employ full-time *labor relations profes-*

sionals. Cities lacking the need for a full-time person can utilize on-call consultants, recommends Sam Zagoria, head of the Washington-based Labor-Management Relations Service (LMRS). LMRS provides training to local officials on how to deal constructively with employees.

Cities can also improve their bargaining positions by making themselves less vulnerable to strikes, thereby safeguarding themselves from being stampeded into excessive wage settlements for fear of chaos. This can be done by avoiding arrangements that make a city overly dependent on a single large work force (e.g., not merging all area police departments into one metropolitan force). Retaining small and medium-size departments (with at least the possibility of separate unions) and resisting city-county mergers are elements in such a strategy. So is the use of private contractors, as discussed in earlier chapters. Cities should develop detailed, written contingency plans for dealing with strikes in vital public services—police, fire, garbage collection, and so forth—drawing on alternative sources of supply and making use of civilian volunteers (such as police or fire reserve forces) whenever possible.

14

Schools

In most cases school systems are not part of the local government itself although they typically consume 50% to 60% of local property tax revenues. They tend to be independent school districts, whose governance and funding are completely separate from the city and county governments, per se.

Moreover, public schools are not truly *local* public services, like police or fire protection. In every state, the public school system is actually a state/local hybrid. A significant amount of both control (curriculum, programs, policies) and funding resides with a state education department, and a small but growing degree of control and funding comes from the federal government. In fact, *local* revenues provide more than half the public school budget in only 18 of the 50 states.

For these reasons, the public school system is really a secondary consideration for this book, directed as it is toward showing local taxpayers how they can cut the costs of their local government. Nevertheless, the local property tax has been the principal focus of the tax revolt, and since a large proportion of the monies raised from this tax go to support public schools, this chapter is necessary.

As everyone knows, the public schools have serious problems. There is, encouragingly, much that can be done on a local level to cut rising costs and improve the quality of our educational system.

WHAT'S WRONG WITH PUBLIC SCHOOLS?
America's public schools are spending more and more to turn out students who can do less and less, and they are doing so in an atmosphere increasingly characterized by violence. Although these facts have been

pointed out in numerous forums, it is useful to review just a few points, to appreciate the true dimensions of the school system's failure.

High Costs

To begin with, the cost of public schooling has escalated at an almost unbelievable pace. In 1950 there were 25.1 million pupils enrolled in American public schools (excluding colleges). Total expenditures were $5.88 billion, for an annual cost of $234 per pupil. By 1976 enrollment was at 44.2 million, but costs had leaped to $67.3 billion. Hence, per-pupil expenditure had grown to $1,523.

Of course, the dollar in 1950 was worth more than the dollar in 1976—in fact, it was worth 2.36 times as much, according to the government's Consumer Price Index statistics. So if we multiply the 1950 per-pupil expenditure by 2.36 we have an equivalent of $553 in 1976 dollars. Thus, in *real* terms, per-pupil spending increased from $553 in 1950 to $1,523 in 1976—2.75 times as high.

A large portion of this tremendous increase has gone into higher salaries. In *real* dollar terms (i.e., adjusted for inflation), average teacher salaries in 1974 were 1.9 times those of 1950. In other words, teaching as an occupation nearly doubled in real compensation over this time period.

Another important factor is the decline in average class size. From 1950 to 1974 the average number of pupils per teacher in public elementary and secondary schools dropped from 27.5 to 21.5—a 22% decrease. That meant the number of teachers required to teach 1,000 students, for example, went up from 36 to 47—boosting school budgets still further.

A third factor in increased budgets is the proliferation of nonteaching personnel on school-system payrolls. Besides teachers, the typical public school system includes principals, assistant principals, program administrators, consultants, supervisors, counselors, psychologists, coaches, librarians, aides, and paraprofessionals. As Table 5 shows, in big-city school systems nonteaching personnel can account for 50% to 60% of the total budget. The tendency to spend more on nonteaching personnel seems to be greater the larger the total budget of the school system. The top nine cities in total spending average 45.6% of their expenditures on nonteaching personnel, compared with 39.7% for the bottom nine cities. And these figures apply all across the country. A recent study by HEW's National Center for Education Statistics showed that four out of every 10 public school employees are engaged in nonteaching activities.

Declining Effectiveness

But as we've seen elsewhere in this book one can't just look at costs—one also has to look at performance. The truly shocking fact is that schools are doing not even as well as in 1950 but *much worse* at their basic task: educating students.

Dr. Norvell Northcutt of the University of Texas headed a team that conducted a nationwide survey on literacy over a five-year period, 1971 to

1976.[1] Northcutt's researchers found that one in five adult Americans is not competent to perform basic daily chores requiring reading, writing, and arithmetic. They found that among those who completed school in the period 1952–61 (ages 30 to 39 when surveyed), 11% were functionally illiterate. But among those who completed school in 1962–73, when school spending was at least twice as high, 16% were functionally illiterate. Not only that, but public schools have failed utterly to educate minorities, one of the sacred rationales for public schools. While "only" 16% of whites were found to be illiterate, the figures were 44% for blacks and 56% for Spanish-surnamed people.

The unparalleled drop in scores on standardized tests over the past decade is another indication of the decline in educational effectiveness. Of course, a growing number of educators have rightly pointed out the limitations of standardized tests as the sole indicator of educational quality. Nevertheless, standardized tests are *one* important measure of an

Table 5

SCHOOL SYSTEM PER-PUPIL EXPENDITURES, 1976

CITY	TOTAL SPENDING PER PUPIL	DIRECT INSTRUC-TION PER PUPIL	PERCENT DIRECT	PERCENT NON-TEACHING
Columbus	$2,425	$ 915	37.7	62.3
Philadelphia	2,301	1,531	66.5	33.5
New York	2,283	934	40.9	59.1
Denver	2,272	1,590	70.0	30.0
St. Paul	2,240	N/A	–	–
Detroit	1,918	1,113	58.0	42.0
San Jose	1,892	851	45.0	55.0
Boston	1,759	1,311	74.5	25.5
Newark	1,745	807	46.2	53.8
Cleveland	1,727	880	51.0	49.0
San Diego	1,717	821	47.8	52.2
Baltimore	1,708	1,056	61.8	38.2
Dallas	1,679	1,047	62.4	37.6
Buffalo	1,574	997	63.3	36.7
Milwaukee	1,496	N/A	–	–
Fort Worth	1,466	819	55.9	44.1
Indianapolis	1,353	859	63.5	36.5
St. Louis	1,325	828	62.5	37.5
Memphis	1,284	868	67.6	32.4
Jacksonville	1,142	661	57.9	42.1
Average	$1,765	$ 993	56.3	43.7

Source: Citizens Public Expenditure Survey of New York State
N/A = not available

educational system's performance, for two principal reasons. First, they do measure an important aspect of educational attainment that is, in fact, related to subsequent success in college and jobs: mathematical and verbal reasoning, mastery of grammar, and arithmetical operations. Second, because they are *standardized*, they measure the *same* thing year after year, permitting an objective comparison of how well a school system was doing at different times at getting across those abilities that the tests can measure.

During the past decade, scores on standardized tests across the nation have plummeted. A 1976 investigation by *Los Angeles Times* education writers Jack McCurdey and Don Speich covered the Scholastic Aptitude Test (SAT) and American College Testing Program (ACT) taken by high school seniors, as well as primary and secondary school achievement tests in 24 states and the District of Columbia. "In nearly all cases," they wrote, "the scores on tests measuring reading, writing, and mathematical ability rose steadily or held constant until the mid-1960s . . . and then dropped, signalling the beginning of a year-by-year decline that continues to this day."[2] The decline spans all ethnic groups, all economic classes, and all regions of the country.

From 1963/64 to 1974/75 the average SAT verbal score dropped 38 points, the math score 25 points. From 1965/66 to 1976/77, the fraction of students scoring above 600 on the SAT verbal test declined 36%, above 700 by 48%. For the math portion, the corresponding declines are 11% and 15%. The Hudson Institute's Frank Armbruster and Paul Bracken documented similar declines on state achievement tests from Iowa, New York, Hawaii, and California.[3]

College professors and administrators across the country have acknowledged that today's entering students are far less able to cope, academically, than those of a decade ago. "They don't read as much, they haven't been given enough practice in thinking and composition," says Stoddard Melarky, associate liberal arts dean at the University of Oregon. Adds Johns Hopkins President Steven Muller of entering freshman, "The[ir] ability to read and write . . . [is] significantly worse than three to five years ago, and they tend . . . to know less history."

Violence

Since 1970 the public schools have been experiencing an epidemic of violence. In 1974 the National Institute of Education (NIE) was asked by Congress to document the extent of the problem. Its 1978 report, *Violent Schools—Safe Schools,*[4] provided these horrifying figures:

- Fully 25% of American public schools suffer from moderately serious to serious problems of vandalism, theft, and personal attack.
- In a typical month, one out of every nine secondary school pupils will have something stolen from him or her, as will one out of every eight teachers.
- One out of every 80 secondary school pupils will be attacked each month, as will about 5,200 teachers.

These figures probably understate the extent of the problem, since it is known that schools report only a small proportion of violent offenses to the police (e.g., only one-sixth of the attacks that result in a personal injury).

Pupils are also destroying school property. Vandalism is costing the public schools $600 million a year. Violence and vandalism are not confined to urban ghettos. Although the problem is most severe in those areas, school violence is spreading to the suburbs and even to rural schools, says the NIE report.

Thus, we have a public school system that doesn't work: horrendously costly, decreasingly effective, and physically dangerous to pupil and teacher alike.

There are things that can be done to produce affordable and safe schools that work. And they turn out to be the same techniques that make it possible to provide other public services of higher quality for less money: privatization, user charges, and thinking smarter.

Public schooling is yet another example of a supposed public good that is really a private good—that is, a service that has very specific, identifiable beneficiaries: the students. To be sure, we all *do* benefit from living in a society where most people are educated, but it is far from clear that we need a public school system to achieve that result. In late 18th and early 19th century Boston, for example, without compulsory attendance laws and with mostly private schools, over 90% of the children attended school.[5] The displacement of early America's thriving private school industry occurred largely for ideological (Unitarian versus Calvinist) reasons, rather than because of any failure of private schooling to do the job.

Later on in this chapter we'll look at the trends toward privatization of schools and charging users rather than all the taxpayers. But because public schooling is so deeply ingrained in America's thinking, we'll look first at the kinds of thinking smarter that can increase the cost effectiveness of any school, private or public.

INCREASING COST EFFECTIVENESS

There are many ways of making schools more effective, often while simultaneously reducing costs. Few of them have been tried in the public schools, however, because they run counter to the prevailing orthodoxy. Much as we found in the case of police and criminal justice, however, these superficially "obvious" points often are *not* based on fact. We'll look at a number of such points in this section.

Classrooms That Work

It was an article of faith until recently that smaller class sizes were a key to increased educational quality. But a major statistical study by two educational researchers has shattered that assumption. Harvard's Christopher Jencks and UCLA's Marsha Brown analyzed data from 98 public high schools.[6] Comparing the schools on a variety of measures of educational effectiveness—including the students' later success in careers—they found that *larger* classes, not smaller ones, were correlated with both educational and occupational achievement. They also found no correlation between per-pupil expenditure and any measure of educational or occupational attainment.

These results—massively documented and not refuted since they were published in 1975—demolish the usual arguments for smaller classes and higher budgets. They strongly suggest that pupil/teacher ratios, at least in high schools (which is all they studied), could be safely increased back to the levels that prevailed two decades ago—about 27 to 28 per teacher instead of 19 or 20—without harming (and perhaps even helping) student achievement. If this were done, the number of teachers needed would be only 78% of the present number. Thus, savings of about 22% of the teaching budget should be possible with no loss in effectiveness.

One of the most effective ways to enlarge class size while actually *increasing* the extent of individualized instruction goes by the name of *peer tutoring* or *cross-age tutoring*. The basic idea is to have students tutor each other, under carefully supervised conditions, as part of the educational program.

One of the first educators to popularize this idea was 19th-century English private schoolmaster Joseph Lancaster. Concerned about the problems of the poor, Lancaster sought ways of teaching large numbers of children at low cost. He called his solution the "monitor" system. Lancaster or his headmaster began by teaching the fundamentals to a few of the most promising older children. Once a child attained the required degree of proficiency in a subject, he or she became a monitor for that subject, and a portion of his or her day was then spent in tutoring a group of ten younger children. There were separate monitors for each subject: reading, writing, spelling, arithmetic, etc. Besides tutoring, the monitors took roll, gave exams, and generally managed the education of their younger charges. The school was ungraded, with children advancing at their own pace in each subject. Lancaster's school was so economical—since it needed so few paid teachers—that the poorest children were admitted at no charge. (This, remember, was before the establishment of public schools.)

Lancaster established more than 100 schools in England and later in the United States. For about three decades, from 1818 to around 1850, Lancaster's system flourished in America. But as education grew to be more and more the responsibility of government, as state normal schools began turning out teachers imbued with a strong sense of professionalism, the use of student tutors came under attack as undignified and unprofessional. The New York City Education Department, a bastion of the new professionalism, went so far as to ban the monitor system outright in 1846.

After more than a century of disinterest, though, the monitor system began attracting adherents in the 1970s, under the names peer tutoring or cross-age tutoring.[7,8] Teachers began to see in it a way to provide badly needed individualized instruction, without huge increases in budgets. From a few beginnings in New York antipoverty programs and Ann Arbor, Michigan, classrooms, student-tutoring programs have been rediscovered and implemented in selected schools across the country.

One of the most successful of these programs was developed by Dwaine McCleary, a principal in the public schools of Palo Alto, California. Begun in 1974 in Loma Vista Elementary School, the program has achieved impressive results. Third grade reading achievement, for instance, improved from the 70th percentile to the 99th percentile. The program pairs up students for as little as 20 minutes a day. They alternate as tutor and tutee, taking turns reading aloud and checking one another's speed and accuracy. "You can easily have 40 teams of students supervised by one teacher," says McCleary.

Unfortunately, today's student-tutoring programs generally fail to take advantage of the economies inherent in them, to reduce the number of teachers or aides needed in the classroom. As would be expected, teachers' unions strongly oppose any such move, and so far they have prevailed. Yet Lancaster's system in its original form worked well, educating students at a fraction of the cost of conventional methods. It could certainly accomplish the modest goal of returning pupil/teacher ratios to the levels of the 1950s.

All too often the least competent teachers in today's public schools are also among the most highly paid. Because of both tenure and union contracts, it is almost unheard of for an experienced teacher to be fired, even if he or she is incompetent. Once tenured, a teacher is virtually guaranteed a secure job, with annual salary increases based on longevity and the cost of living. Should cutbacks be necessary, those with the least seniority are the ones laid off, regardless of competence. Over a period of years, the result can be that the most costly and least effective teachers are retained.

Some schools have found ways to substitute part-time teachers for full-time teachers who quit or are laid off. This will both improve teaching quality *and* reduce costs. Cynthia Parsons, education editor of the *Christian Science Monitor*, reports the experience of a school district that hired two half-time teachers for one class. They found "there was never a need to hire a substitute for that class; they also discovered that each 'half-time' teacher gave at least three-fourths time to working with the students." Neither received any fringe benefits—they cost the district no retirement funds or insurance. The Leeds, South Dakota, school system makes a policy of hiring part-time teachers whenever possible, and estimates its savings from this policy at $50,000 a year.

Most private schools and some public schools rely on the use of volunteers as classroom aides. Many parents are glad to volunteer, if approached in the right way. Retirees can bring to the classroom the diversity of their lifetime experiences, broadening the education of the children and reaping psychological rewards by becoming more valuable members of the community.

Cutting Overhead

We noted earlier that some 40% of all public school employees have nothing to do with teaching—and in some districts as many as 60%. This is an obvious area for cutbacks that can save money without impairing educational effectiveness. Many parochial and other private schools operate with less than 10% nonteaching personnel. Without getting into arguments about *which* nonteaching positions are least valuable, we should realize that quality education *can* be provided without a large supporting cast.

One way to minimize overhead is to contract out support services. "We use outside services for every possible activity, so the burden of responsibility falls upon others," says James McGowan, business manager of the private South Boston Heights Academy. "The payroll is done by the bank while a CPA does the accounting." To minimize the need for costly special facilities, the school relies on the nearby Boy's Club for its gym and on the public library. In addition, selected teachers do double duty, serving as part-time administrators in addition to their teaching responsibilities.

Some schools are saving money by contracting for cafeteria services. Philadelphia's public schools now purchase about half of their food from a private supplier and—because of good service and lower cost—are gradually increasing the percentage. The school systems of Buffalo / Rochester, New York; Madison and Racine, Wisconsin; and Chicago, Illinois, are likewise now contracting for food service. One of the most publicized contracts is that of Denton, Arkansas. That school district has hired McDonald's, the fast-food chain. The firm's food is much more popular with the students and the contract is saving the district about $130,000 per year.

As we have seen in earlier chapters, maintenance of both the school buildings and the grounds can be contracted to private firms, generally at savings over what an in-house staff would cost. Public schools could also emulate private schools and consider having the children carry out some of the maintenance tasks. "Cleaning, varnishing, painting, trash disposal, carpentry repairs, and grounds upkeep all are chores that youngsters can and should be taught to do," notes Cynthia Parsons. Students who attend to such tasks for an average of half an hour a day bring down school operating expenses and are much less likely to vandalize property at off-hours.

Another aspect of "overhead" is the waste involved in unused classrooms and school buildings. There are few good reasons for most schools to shut down for three months every summer (except perhaps in primarily agricultural areas comprising about 5% of the population). About 100 schools in California are now operating on a year-round basis, including six elementary schools in the San Diego Unified School District. Those schools operate on the "45-15" plan, wherein pupils are assigned to one of four attendance groups, each of which attends school for nine weeks (45 days), followed by three weeks (15 days) of vacation. The four groups are staggered so that at least one is away on vacation at any given time, thereby requiring 25% less classroom space for the same total enrollment. By this method a district can increase its classroom capacity without building new facilities. San Diego, for example, saved $355,000 because of not having to build an additional elementary school. In areas where there is no need for new buildings, however, operating schools year-round may actually increase costs and should therefore be avoided.

Another way to cut classroom costs is to permit students who no longer need to be in school to leave, thereby cutting down on the need for teachers and classroom space. In 1976 California legislators ordered the state education system to give proficiency tests each year. Students scoring high enough qualify for early graduation, regardless of how much time they "officially" have left to serve. In the first two years 18,000 students qualified and chose to graduate early, saving taxpayers $4.7 million.

School districts tend to be inefficient property managers. In most cases, classrooms stand empty from 3 to 10 P.M., as well as all weekends and all summers. Some districts even have surplus classrooms or entire schools, because of declining enrollments. Few private organizations would invest so heavily in facilities and then underutilize them to this extent.

Schools should make more of an effort to rent out facilities that are not in use, charging realistic rates for the space. In the past, when outside groups used school facilities, schools tended to charge nothing at all or only a token charge for janitorial services. In the wake of Proposition 13, however, California schools began charging much higher fees for the use of auditoriums, tennis courts, ball fields, and classrooms. In New Jersey more school districts are now renting school buildings to churches and synagogues for evening and weekend use, thanks to a state Supreme Court ruling upholding the practice. Rentals of this sort were found to be constitutional so long as they are on a temporary (up to five-year) basis and the rental fees cover the costs of services provided (which they should, anyway).

School districts also tend to underutilize their extensive stocks of educational materials. Some districts operate huge central materials centers, stocking films, tapes, craft supplies, teaching machines, and many other materials that are made available upon request to individual teachers. Meanwhile, private schools in the community are often unable to afford any of these materials. The districts could raise revenue by making these materials available to private schools on a rental basis, with priorities so that their own classroom uses were not interfered with. The same type of arrangement could be worked out with school libraries, permitting access by private school pupils on a user-fee basis.

Questionable Special Programs

The proliferation of specialized federal programs is one of the principal reasons for the huge size of public school administrations. Although generally looked on as "free money," because their direct per-pupil costs are paid for by federal funds, nearly all such programs carry with them such a burden of accounting and report writing that they add considerably to the need for administrative personnel. They are more costly than they seem, especially in light of recent studies questioning their effectiveness.

Rand Corporation researchers Paul Berman and M. W. McLaughlin studied a whole range of federal educational programs and found that overall they have not improved educational quality.[9] Here and there a particular program accomplished good results, but not because of federal funding; the same program failed in many other districts. The only places they succeeded were where they were put into effect by committed, dedicated, creative teachers and administrators, who would be effective even without these programs.

Other studies have faulted particular programs as failures. Title I of the Elementary and Secondary Education Act of 1965 has pumped $23 billion into providing special education for poor children. But a number of studies indicate that the program has been little or no help to those it is supposed to benefit. And some, such as Professor Gene V. Glass of the University of Colorado, argue that it has actually harmed poor children. That is because, in the majority of cases, school districts have found it easier and cheaper to "pull out" those pupils targeted for Title I help into special remedial classes part of the day. Glass argues that this tends to unfairly label those children, reduce their opportunities for peer tutoring and role modeling, and segregate them racially—since a high percentage of the disadvantaged children are members of ethnic minority groups. One study of the Emergency School Aid Act showed that the more time a pupil spent in a "pulled-out" setting, the lower he or she scored on reading and math tests.[10] A 1975 study by the General Accounting Office indicated that progress gained from such remedial situations is not sustained from one school year to the next.[11]

Special education programs have, indeed, presented schools with a dilemma. While the "pull-out" procedure has been less costly, it seems to be either harmful or at best of no real help. The alternative—"mainstreaming" the children with special needs in the regular classrooms—is difficult for the schools to cope with administratively. Moreover, it relies on extensive retraining of all regular classroom teachers—a process not only costly but also resented and feared by many of these teachers.

Rather than attempt to recycle the regular teachers into special-education teachers, it would be more cost effective to set up self-contained areas within the school in which instruction was contracted to special-education consulting teachers. Children in these classes would still be able to make use of the school's common areas (playground, cafeteria, etc.) and would not be stigmatized by having to go to "special" schools. Since they would not be in regular classes, however, schools could avoid the large expense of retraining all their teachers to serve double duty as special-education teachers. Specialists would be relied on, instead, for those children who actually need such help.

Doubts have also been raised about mandated bilingual programs. A study of such programs in 150 schools conducted by the American Institutes for Research[12] reached a number of negative conclusions:

- Fewer than one-third of those participating were actually limited in their ability to speak English.
- Those in bilingual programs started—and remained—at a lower level in English than pupils from similar backgrounds who were not enrolled in such programs.
- Achievement gains in mathematics and English reading skills were about the same, whether or not the pupil was in a bilingual program.

All of which is not to say that bilingual programs are of no value. There may be valid cultural and psychological reasons for teaching children certain basic skills in their native language first. But it appears as if bilingual programs produce minimal gains in academic skills, per se. And it also looks as if they are being used for many students who already speak English sufficiently well to be taught in it.

Overall, then, most of the federal programs introduced in the past 15 years have been of little real value in improving education. And they have contributed markedly to the growth of school districts' administrative bureaucracies. In many cases, school districts might be better off without the "free" federal money and its attendant costs and controls.

Ending Free Babysitting

Summer school is a costly item in many districts' budgets. Although some students do benefit from summer programs designed for remedial instruction, many summer-school programs are basically a form of babysitting. After Californians passed Proposition 13 and school districts were forced to set spending priorities, one of the first items cut out was summer school. Officials conceded that no one could demonstrate that any serious academic loss would result from the cancellation. And most have concluded that "the big, come-one-come-all summer programs of the past" are gone forever, with only remedial programs remaining. California taxpayers are saving $107 million a year thanks to this decision.

But some California parents really do want summer schools—and they're now willing to pay for them. The first year, school districts were very cautious, because of a provision of the California constitution which says that public school classes may not charge tuition. That led to various efforts to lease classrooms to other groups—many of which hired regular public school teachers. But this kind of ploy may no longer be needed, according to Thomas Griffin, chief legal counsel of the state education department. Since the summer programs are supplemental, not mandated by law, schools are simply making their facilities more available to the community for a fee. They've been doing so for years by letting service clubs rent the auditoriums, and by offering adult-education programs and lectures, sometimes charging fees.

Testing the limits of this approach is the South Bay Union High School District in the Los Angeles area. Under authority of the State Community Services Act (under which it has previously offered adult programs for a fee), the district in 1979 offered summer classes in driver education, math, physical fitness, band, typing, and other supplemental subjects. It charged $30 per course for six weeks of two-hour-daily course work—and Griffin's office thinks it's legal.

The California Teachers Association (union) sued the Glendale School District for contracting with the University of LaVerne for summer classes. But to no avail. Superior Court Judge Jerry Pacht ruled in July 1979 that there is no mandatory duty for public schools to provide free summer schools. Hence, summer school does not fall within the state constitution's ban on tuition charges.

Besides the University of LaVerne, several other colleges and one private firm operated summer programs under contract to California public schools in 1979. The private firm was American Learning Corporation (ALC), which had contracts to operate summer programs in 25 public elementary schools in 12 districts around the state. ALC's programs covered kindergarten through eighth grade and lasted four hours a day for five weeks. For each tuition-paying class (of 24 to 32 students) the company offered a free scholarship to a needy student.

Civic and community groups also got into the act. The Pasadena Urban Coalition, for example, leased space in the city schools for its tuition-based summer program. For every three paying students, the organization provided two half or full scholarships for needy students. Park and recreation departments also offered "semi-academic" courses—arts and crafts, physical fitness, etc.—on a fee basis.

Implementation of most or all of the ideas discussed thus far could produce major cost savings in public schools. The largest savings, of course, would have to come from reductions in numbers of both teachers and administrators. Yet the reality of the situation is that, between teachers' unions and the tenure system, cuts in personnel are very unlikely to be made. On the contrary, because of the continuing declines in academic achievement, the efforts of both teachers and administrators in the public schools continue to be devoted to obtaining *more personnel and bigger budgets*, in an effort to reverse the declining performance. To find educators willing and able to do more with less, we must look *outside* the public school system.

THE PRIVATE SCHOOL ALTERNATIVE

There *are* schools in America that are still turning out students who can read, write, and compute. And they somehow manage to do so without federal programs, without large administrations, and without a bevy of support personnel. Moreover, they do this for about half the cost of the public schools we've been discussing. The schools in question are America's private schools.

The extent of private education in America is indicated by the figures in Table 6. About 5 million pupils are presently attending private schools, compared with about 42 million in the public schools. The majority of these schools are religiously affiliated, although over half a million of the pupils attend nonsectarian private schools. The vast majority of private schools serve people of lower and middle income while only a small percentage are exclusive day schools and prep schools catering to the wealthy. As can be seen, their cost per pupil is nearly always below $1,000 a year, and sometimes as low as $600. (Note that this is not the *price* charged, which may be zero to members in some church schools; rather, this is the total *cost* of providing the education.) In contrast, the *average* cost of public schooling is $1,740 per pupil, according to the National Center for Educational Statistics.

Although Catholic school enrollments in some parts of the country have been dropping, all other private school groups report vigorous growth. Orthodox Hebrew Day Schools have multiplied from 30 in 1945 to 456 in 1978—a 1,400% increase. The Conservative Jewish Solomon Schechter

Table 6

PRIVATE SCHOOL ENROLLMENT, 1977/78
(Elementary and Secondary)

	NUMBER OF SCHOOLS	NUMBER OF PUPILS	AVERAGE COST PER PUPIL
Catholic	9,822	3,289,000	$ 500 elementary
National Association			1,036 secondary
of Independent			
Schools	760	285,000	2,613
Lutheran	2,200	235,000	600
Episcopal	800	150,000	1,459 (est.)
Baptist	310	87,917	725 elementary
			838 secondary
Orthodox Hebrew	456	83,200	750
Seventh Day			
Adventist	1,095	75,589	N/A
Calvinist	322	62,269	1,100 (est.)
Conservative Jewish	51	10,000	4,125
Miscellaneous	N/A	475,900	N/A

N/A = not available

Day Schools began with one school in 1964 and already have 51. The National Association of Independent Schools (NAIS), whose members include day schools, prep schools, and some independent Quaker and Episcopal schools, reports its membership growing at 5% per year, at a time when public school enrollment is dropping every year. Moreover, 30% of the students attending NAIS boarding schools come from families with incomes of less than $25,000 a year.

Private schools are succeeding where public schools fail for a number of reasons: dedicated teachers, a minimum of frills and administrative overhead, the use of parents and community volunteers, and just plain hard work. And their success is *not* a matter of just avoiding the "hard" cases, especially students who are poor and/or nonwhite. Some of the greatest private school success stories are occurring in just such poor, nonwhite communities.

Take East Palo Alto, California, for instance—a very poor black community of 19,000. Dismayed by the failure of public schools to teach and maintain discipline, Gertrude Wilks founded the Nairobi Day School in 1966. The school's 55 pupils pay only $60 per month tuition—$540 per school year. Students at Nairobi work hard, and nearly all succeed. The school's methods are so successful, in fact, that Wilks offers a money-back guarantee for those who fail to learn to read within a year.

Similarly successful is Marva Collins's Westside Preparatory School in Chicago. Begun in 1975 in a poor, black area, the school teaches minority children, many of whom have been classed as "slow learners." At Westside their achievement levels improve dramatically, thanks to Collins's blend of individual attention, 3-Rs basics, and the classics.

In South Boston, "white flight" from forced-busing programs has led to the creation of a number of private schools, some of which have become full-fledged, permanent educational institutions. One such school is South Boston Heights Academy. Its 410 pupils attend grades 1 through 12, taught by a staff of 17 teachers—about 24 pupils per teacher. But the cost is only $570 per pupil. Teacher salaries start at only $6,500; nevertheless, because of today's surplus of teachers, the school has had no trouble hiring qualified staff. Administration consists solely of a business manager, James McGowan, who reports to a seven-member board of directors.

Although South Boston's private schools are largely white, the private school population in general is not totally white. Some of the best of the newer private schools, such as Nairobi and Westside, operate in mostly black neighborhoods. A great many Catholic schools serve largely minority urban communities; nationwide, 17% of the pupils in Catholic elementary schools are nonwhite, as are 13% in Catholic high schools. In Lutheran schools, the figures are 14% and 20%, respectively.

Among the minority organizations that promote private schools is the Congress of Racial Equality (CORE). In 1977 CORE took over a failing Catholic school in the South Bronx, pledging $50,000 in start-up and initial operating costs. CORE selected the project as a demonstration of its contention that children can be better educated for less money. Tuition at $42 a month ($478 per year) covers 40% of the cost, and CORE picks up the rest. That means that the school's total cost is under $1,000 a year per pupil. According to CORE's educational director, Victor Solomon, the group plans to open a number of similar schools over the next decade.

MAKING CHANGES

In view of the ability of private schools to deliver quality education at low cost, and the strong resistance to cost-cutting on the part of the public schools, many educational reformers—ranging from Senator Alan Cranston to writer John Holt—see a large-scale shift from public to private schooling as the only hope for better and more cost-effective education. But for such a shift to occur, two basic problems must be dealt with.

The first problem is that Americans still believe very strongly in the *idea* of public education—despite the system's runaway costs and its increasingly obvious failure to deliver results. And private schools remain a relatively small fraction of the total number of schools, so it's easy for them to remain relatively invisible. Consequently, most people aren't aware of them as a viable alternative to public schools. Many parents also harbor doubts about whether their children would get "credit" for attending private schools, should they later wish to return to public school or go on to college.

The other problem is economic. For private schools to become a large-scale alternative, the public schools' legislated cost advantage must be removed. Since the public schools are supported by taxes rather than by tuition (user charges), *everybody* has to pay for them—including people who send their children to private schools. Even if private school tuition is a low $600 a year, how many families are going to pay that (for one child) when they are already paying $500 to $1,000 a year in property taxes for schools, plus several hundred dollars more in state taxes?

If the public schools' unfair advantage were removed, public and private schools would, for the first time, be competing on an equal footing for people's educational dollars. Presures for cost effectiveness would be greatly intensified by such a change.

Several methods have been proposed to accomplish this. Professor E. G. West, recognizing the extent to which public schools are entrenched, suggests a gradual method of reducing their cost advantage.[13] His idea is a *marginal user charge*—introducing a small increment of tuition in public schools each year, enough to cover the increase in each year's budget over last year's. Over a period of years, thanks in part to inflation, an increasingly large fraction of the costs of public schooling would be paid directly by the parents whose children were attending public schools, rather than by those patronizing private schools (or no schools).

Another proposal is a *tuition tax credit*. In this plan, those parents choosing to utilize private schools would be able to deduct from their tax bill some fraction of their tuition payment. In its ideal form, the tax credit would cover 100% of tuition payments and would be deducted from those taxes that directly pay for public schools (property taxes, various state taxes, and, to a lesser extent, federal income taxes). In the form in which the plan was debated in the 95th Congress (and nearly passed), the credit applied to only 50% of tuition payments up to a maximum of $500, to be deducted solely from federal income tax payments.

A third approach is *education vouchers*. First proposed by economist Milton Friedman and promoted by sociologist Christopher Jencks, the voucher plan would distribute all school-tax receipts back to parents, in the form of vouchers cashable at *any* school, public or private. Parents would choose *which* school would receive their patronage, and their funds would be spent *only* on that school. After languishing for nearly a decade—during which time public school opposition succeeded in torpedoing every proposal for a full-fledged test of vouchers—the concept has begun to undergo a revival.

In Michigan in November 1978, voters were presented with an initiative measure that would have removed schools from the property tax and set up a statewide voucher system. Although defeated, the measure garnered 30% of the votes, despite relatively little advertising. But the real test of vouchers may occur in California. An initiative petition drive is being organized there, with impressive backing. Its intellectual genesis is the book *Education by Choice* by two liberal law professors.[14] Their case for vouchers includes a new twist: equalizing expenditures among the school districts throughout the state. The authors, John Coons and Stephen Sugarman, were the law professors who provided the arguments supporting a landmark California Supreme Court decision striking down local property-tax funding of public schools because of the large differences in spending among districts. They are now urging liberals to support their voucher plan as the only feasible way to implement the court's decision. Meanwhile, conservative leaders are also backing the measure, as a means of promoting decentralization and individual choice.

It seems likely that vouchers, tax credits, or marginal user charges would lead to a surge of lower-cost schools. Private schools today cannot compete fairly with public schools, despite their nominal cost advantages. But once a competitive market were established, we would likely see an explosive growth of private schooling, as has occurred in the (pre-school) day-care industry. In just ten years day care has burgeoned from a cottage industry to a sophisticated, multimillion-dollar business, with nationwide chains competing for business.

Once the public schools' legislated cost advantage were removed, such a market would develop in schooling as well. The methods developed by innovators such as Gertrude Wilks, Marva Collins, and James McGowan, and modern versions of Lancaster's student tutoring, would be spread across the land by enterprising businesses. Schools of every type, shape, and size would develop, seeking parents' dollars by offering a particular type of educational process, some assurance of results, and reasonable cost. In order to be competitive, public schools would rediscover the need to seek out cost-effective ways of operating.

In education, as in the other public services we've reviewed in this book, privatization and the introduction of competition would lead to both innovative methods and lower costs.

15

Looking Back: How City Hall Withered

This chapter, written from the perspective of the year 2000, shows where the ideas in this book might lead, if applied over a period of years in a typical American city.

Looking back at 1978, who would have believed the revolution that took place in local government! Over a 22-year period, local governments that were overbearing and overburdening became small, compact, and efficient. Services that were previously supplied in one way were provided in multifarious and innovative ways. As local government became smaller, service blossomed. Private firms, volunteer groups, and citizens themselves provided what was needed. Taxes were rescinded right and left (!), and each person had wider choice in deciding what he or she wanted.

Hard as it is to believe, this actually happened in the 22 years since 1978. And it is best illustrated by the events in Cabana Beach, a middle-income city in Southern California.

In the 1970s Cabana Beach had a fairly typical city government for its time. Its 1976/77 budget was $16 million, which supported some 800 full-time employees. The city government was engaged in the usual assortment of service enterprises. It owned and operated an extensive water and sewer system, the city streets, six parking lots and two parking garages, three beaches, 17 parks, a harbor, five fire stations, a police station, a city hall, and a vehicle and equipment yard.

It did not directly provide garbage collection, which was handled by two private companies, each franchised to serve half of the city. And fire protection was provided under contract by the county fire department (using the city-owned fire stations). In addition, welfare and other social services, as well as the court system, are the responsibility of the *county* in California, so the City of Cabana Beach had no direct involvement in these services. Similarly, the school system was operated by a school district, independent of the city government.

Change first came to Cabana Beach in 1978, as an aftermath of labor troubles in the fall of 1977. The county firefighters' union went on strike in October of '77. The strike lasted only five days, with supervisory personnel filling in as best they could, but they were no match for a four-alarm blaze that gutted an old warehouse in downtown Cabana Beach. The death of the night watchman in the blaze was—rightly or not—blamed on the union, in an outcry that went on for 2½ months. That uproar sealed the fate of the city's fire-service contract with the county.

Most of the city council members, reacting to popular sentiment, began to lay plans for a city fire department. But the city manager suggested an alternative: Rather than going to that expense and trouble, why not seek another supplier to replace the county on a contractual basis? By then, nearly everyone in Southern California was aware of Metropolitan Fire Service, Inc., the private firm that served a good portion of Arizona. The company had recently landed its first California contract, in Leisure Lakes, a retirement community in San Diego County. It had submitted a bid 40% lower than that of the county fire department, and so far seemed to be succeeding.

After several months of discussion, studies, and a council junket to Arizona, the city issued a request for proposals for contract fire service. Eager to restore its damaged credibility, the county fire department bid far below cost, but Metropolitan's bid was still 15% less, and the council accepted it. On January 1, 1979, private fire protection came to Cabana Beach.

The service offered by the private company was first rate. Most people didn't notice much change, except that the new trucks were lime-yellow in color, rather than "fire engine red," and sported almost no chrome. More careful observers noted with approval that although just as many firemen turned out at fires, far fewer of them could be seen sitting around the station during the day or playing volleyball out back. A significant fraction held other full-time jobs and constituted a well-trained, paid reserve force. The cost savings, needless to say, were dramatic.

The city had just about gotten used to its yellow fire trucks when crisis once more intervened. In early 1980 the grand jury indicted Cabana Beach's police chief and his top officers in a gambling coverup scandal that rocked the town (and half the surrounding county) to its core. The council met wearily to discuss their options, which boiled down to only two: Replace the entire top echelons of the demoralized department or wipe it out and start from scratch. Since nobody really knew how far down in the ranks the scandal had reached, the first alternative was rejected. But the idea of wiping out the department and starting over raised the politically difficult question, Which of the former officers would be hired back and which ones wouldn't? At long last, the simplest solution was deemed to be, in effect, turning the whole mess over to the county sheriff. The council hurriedly negotiated a contract with the sheriff's department for patrol services, leaving it to the sheriff to decide which former city officers to hire.

Thus, Cabana Beach became California's 59th city to contract with a county sheriff's department for police services. As it turned out, the contract meant cost savings for the city's taxpayers. The sheriff's department, true to its usual practice in contract work, priced its patrol services at the marginal cost of expanding its operations to Cabana Beach. Since the department's existing operations already covered all the shared overhead items (communications, records, jails, etc.), the net cost to Cabana Beach was about 25% less than the cost of its own police force had been. As a result, rather than being a temporary expedient, the contract with the sheriff quickly became accepted as a smart way of doing business.

Despite the *cost* savings produced by the private fire company and the contract policing, no *tax* savings were forthcoming. Indeed, from 1978 to 1982 the city's bureaucracy continued to grow at a rapid pace, leading to much talk of "the betrayal of Proposition 13" and ultimately to the election of a "cut taxes" slate to the city council in the 1982 election. The new council's first priority was a directive to the city department heads to trim the fat from their budgets. But the council didn't stop there. It also hired a consultant to look for ways of saving more in the long run. The consultant took a long, hard look at how the city was managing its various housekeeping functions and proposed turning most of them over to private contractors. This advice went down hard with the city employees, but the daily newspaper backed the idea and the taxpayers kept up their pressure on the council members to make good on their campaign pledges.

As a result, over the next three years, first park maintenance and then street maintenance were let out to bid. The city sold all the vehicles from these two operations and used the money as severance pay for the one-third of the employees who lost their jobs. A further casualty was the city's vehicle-maintenance operation. With the sale of the park and street maintenance vehicles, there was little further need for a vehicle-maintenance division. So the division was abolished and the few remaining city vehicles were maintained on a contract basis by a private garage. Another division eliminated was building inspection. The consultant had pointed out a number of cities where firemen performed this role as an adjunct to their fire-inspection duties. Whereupon the council negotiated an amendment to Metropolitan's fire service contract adding building inspection to the firefighters' duties, and abolished the five-member building-inspection division.

After that, things quieted down for awhile in Cabana Beach. The tax rate dropped three years in a row, much to the amazement of officials in surrounding cities. But in 1987 the city's brand-new multimillion-dollar sewage-treatment plant, five years in construction, was ruled unacceptable by the EPA. The agency demanded return of its grant funds, unless the city could bring the plant's operations within federal specifications within 60 days. The public works department's waste-water division said flatly that the demand was impossible to meet. It was then that the council heard about Eco-Tech, Ltd., a firm that specialized in building and operating advanced-design sewage-treatment facilities. The firm submitted an unsolicited proposal to take over operation of the plant on a five-year contract basis, with payment tied to a guarantee of meeting EPA requirements. The beleaguered council checked the firm's impressive record and accepted the contract. Sewage treatment joined fire protection, park maintenance, street maintenance, vehicle maintenance, and building inspection as provinces of the private sector.

What happened next, in 1988, may at first appear strange, but it is not as paradoxical as it seems. Social scientists are familiar with a phenomenon called "rising expectations." It's what happens when a reform move, instead of satisfying those demanding change, only whets their appetite for more. Something of the sort occurred in Cabana Beach in 1988. Pleased by the efficient service of the private contractors and appreciating the resulting tax cuts (but still beset by ever-rising state and federal taxes), local taxpayer groups demanded more. Despite protests from the previous reform council members, a new group of challengers arose, from the ranks of local professionals—engineers, managers, CPAs—who had gotten involved in the tax-protest movement. Their battle cry was "Get what you pay for and pay for only what you get!" Translated into specifics, they demanded that the remaining city-operated services be put on a self-supporting basis. The message was appealing, and the new reformers obtained a majority on the council.

As a result, more change occurred. The council's first move was to raise the charges for parking, water, sewers, harbor use, and building inspections to cover the fully allocated costs of each operation, reducing the property tax by a corresponding amount. Those who used those services paid the full cost of their use, while those who didn't use a service (like parking) didn't have to pay for it through taxes. Next, the council began examining an expansion of private contracting. Early in 1989 it issued three requests for proposals: one each for operation of the harbor and the water system, and another for police services.

The third one raised quite a few eyebrows. But when the city manager pointed out that some communities in Florida and Arizona had been contracting for police services as early as the mid-1970s, the murmuring subsided. After all, the newspaper editorialized, Cabana Beach had been contracting with the sheriff for nearly a decade; as long as the contending firms could prove they had competent, sworn personnel, and would adhere to the rather stringent provisions of the contract, why shouldn't they be allowed to compete for the city's police business? And so it came about that Wackerton Security Services was hired as the Cabana Beach police department for a three-year term, beginning July 1, 1989, when the sheriff's contract expired. That same day the city's fire department changed hands, as West Coast Fire Protection, Inc., beat out Metropolitan for renewal of the fire-service contract. A provision of the new contract, incidentally, provided for switching to user charges rather than tax support, with the company directly billing the customers on a quarterly basis. Suddenly it was worth it to invest in fire-prevention equipment and an enterprising young entrepreneur opened a store that sold such equipment.

After that things ran pretty smoothly. The International City Management Association (ICMA) sent a study group to Cabana Beach to review the changes the city had made—changes that caused it to show up in ICMA's statistics as having the lowest per-capita cost of government in the nation. The city manager's office began charging a fee for responding to the requests for information that came pouring in, in increasing numbers, from cities across the country.

But in 1994 the combination of a large number of employees' retiring (including many who took early retirement when their city functions were eliminated) and the reduced city tax collections resulted in the city's pension system being seriously underfunded. The city administration was faced with the prospect of sharply *increasing* taxes, just when the citizenry had gotten accustomed to the city's unheard-of low rates. Predictably, the city manager's first trial balloon about a possible major tax increase was greeted with a storm of angry protest. Whereupon the administration went back to the drawing boards and came up with a new approach. Since the money could not be raised out of *income*, it would have to be obtained out of *assets*—hence, they decided to sell off the principal city properties.

It took several years to accomplish, what with appraisals, seeking buyers, writing up contracts of sale with certain restrictive covenants concerning future use, but by 1996 the city had accomplished the following:

- The harbor was sold to General Southwest Corporation, an operator of theme parks and recreational resorts. The company announced it would be investing $3 million in capital improvements and expected the harbor complex to be showing a profit within three years.
- The city's three beaches were sold to three separate bidders, with restrictive covenants guaranteeing continued use as public beaches for 99 years. One parcel was bought by Sun Resorts for use as a commercial nude beach, another by the Disney organization for a family-fun beach park, and the third by the Sierra Club.
- The city parking lots and garages were sold to five different firms.
- The city parks presented a somewhat different problem. Nobody could see the parks as profit-making enterprises, and the land was much more valuable in other uses. But the citizens, for the most part, liked and wanted parks. In the end, it turned out that each park had something of a natural constituency, consisting mostly of people who lived in its neighborhood. The various homeowners associations worked out long-term purchase contracts with the city, to acquire the parks with

payments stretched out over a 30-year period. Local banks provided the financing, so that the city got its money up front and the homeowners got a ruling that the interest expense was tax-deductible, so everyone was happy.

- Last, but not least, since the size of city government had diminished considerably, the city hall was sold for use as an office building, with the city leasing back the space it still needed.

And so it was that when the year 2000 rolled around, the government of Cabana Beach consisted, in toto, of three persons: the city manager, the city attorney, and a secretary. Their main job was administering the contracts under which the various public services were provided. The government still owned the water and sewer lines and the streets (though there were rumblings about turning these, too, over to the private sector).

The revolution in public services that began in Cabana Beach has spread, in varying degrees, across California and on to the rest of the Sunbelt. Some of the ideas are even being adopted by the trustees of bankrupt New York, Cleveland, Boston, Detroit, and Philadelphia. In its own quiet way, creeping capitalism has transformed local government. Public services are now recognized as business activities, like any other business. And increasingly people pay for the services they use, in proportion to their usage, rather than being taxed as much as they can bear. Local government will never be the same.

16

How to Cut
Back City Hall

In the preceding chapters we have seen example after example showing that public services can be provided in less costly and more effective ways. Privatization, user charges, and thinking smarter have been applied to virtually *every* form of local public service, with good results. And we've also seen, in Chapter 15, how combining many individual instances of these changes could lead, over time, to a total restructuring and/or replacement of the municipal monopolies that now dominate local public services.

But it's one thing to show that such measures make sense in theory, or even that many instances were successful. It's something else again to make similar changes in *your* city, when things have *always* been done the way they're done now.

In my years as a consultant and lecturer on public services I've observed that the one characteristic that's most typical of local government is adherence to tradition. The examples of real innovation described in this book are hardly typical—they're very much the exception to the general rule. Department heads, mayors, councils, and city managers are far more likely to tell you why, say, private contracting of fire protection may work in Scottsdale but would *never* work in your town than they are to take a serious look at it as a way of providing more service for less money.

My purpose in this chapter is to offer some suggestions on how to go about making changes (like the ones described in this book) happen in your city—despite the formidable obstacles you're likely to find. Accordingly, the chapter is addressed first of all to the citizen/taxpayer. But it is also addressed to those legislators and administrators who can see an opportunity to cut back on bloated bureaucracy and to respond creatively to people's demands for government to return to being their servant rather than their master.

WHAT LOCAL TAXPAYERS CAN DO

Getting your city to make a commitment to utilize private contracting or to open a specific service to competitive bidding will not be easy. Most likely it will take a combination of generalized tax-cutting pressure and specific, directed action aimed at the specific end goal. While individual action (talking with a council member, writing a letter to the editor) is worthwhile, it will seldom be enough to make anything happen. For that, you have to get organized.

Organized taxpayer activity can take many and varied forms. There can be ad hoc organizations formed to enact one-time tax-cutting measures (Proposition 13), tax-protest groups like the property-tax strikers in Illinois in 1978, ongoing grass-roots organizations watchdogging the spending of local officials, and professional taxpayers' organizations with full-time staff and an ongoing research effort. To enact fundamental tax-saving reforms at the local level, it's useful to have both a grass-roots, activist group *and* a full-time professional organization. Let's discuss each of these briefly.

Grass-Roots Action

The most fundamental component of a local tax-cutting effort is a grass-roots activist taxpayer group. Such a group is, by definition, radical. Its purpose is to *cut taxes and spending*, not to "make government more efficient" or to "keep spending increases within tolerable limits." The grass-roots group must put the pressure on local spenders—and keep it on. When the politicians attempt to buy off one group of voters by cutting a particular tax that hits them hardest—and to "make up the lost revenue" by hiking the taxes of other people—it is the grass-roots group that must blow the whistle. When a permit fee is suddenly increased 400% for no reason other than to obtain more revenue, the grass-roots group must lead the attack and demand its repeal. When the school board promotes a school-construction bond issue as necessary, it is up to the grass-roots group to demand to be told why the existing school buildings couldn't be used year-round so as to provide 25% more capacity at no increase in capital spending.

By making use of the ideas and information in this book, a grass-roots taxpayers' group can arm itself to counteract the arguments for more government spending and higher taxes. It can respond creatively by suggesting ways in which the desired service can be provided, not only without a spending increase but frequently at *less* cost than the present service. By choosing its issues carefully, the group can introduce instances of privatization or user charges as imaginative alternatives to proposals for more taxing and spending.

If there is already such a group in your city, join it and introduce the ideas in this book. But don't be too surprised if you get only a lukewarm reception for the idea of actually *cutting back* on government (as opposed to simply slowing down its rate of growth). Far too many taxpayers' groups are more interested in maintaining an image of respectability than they are in genuinely advancing the interests of taxpayers. If that's the kind of group you find yourself in, you might well consider starting your own—and you may be surprised at how many good people come out of the woodwork once they learn that somebody is really concerned with *cutting* taxes. (That is exactly what made the Proposition 13 movement one of the most successful grass-roots efforts in American history.)

Starting such a group is not as hard as it may seem. Here are some pointers developed by Mark Frazier for a National Taxpayers Union handbook. The organization of a successful grass-roots group does *not* begin with an organizational meeting; on the contrary, it *culminates* in such a meeting. To have a successful opening meeting, there's a host of steps you must take well in advance, to ensure that what develops is what you set out to create. In brief, here's the initial groundwork:

- *Decide on an address.* No organization will be seen as legitimate unless it has at least a post office box address, better yet a street address (which can be your home or office).
- *Obtain reference material*—more copies of this book, materials from the National Taxpayers Union,[1] basic references like the ICMA's *Municipal Yearbook,*[2] copies of your city and/or county government budgets, organization charts, and elective office background data. Subscribe to the Local Government Center's *Fiscal Watchdog*, a monthly newsletter[3] that can be a goldmine of ideas, as can *The Guide to Management Improvement Projects in Local Government.*[4]
- *Order stationery and envelopes* from a local instant printer—or at least a rubber stamp with the organization's name and address for stamping envelopes and stationery.
- *Select interim officers in advance.* There's no need to take up most of the first meeting haggling over officers. Let the people who are doing the organizing hold the initial offices—they've earned it. (You may want to make the chairmanship a largely honorary post if you have a prominent local citizen who'd like to fill it. In that case, the actual chief of operations would be the "executive director" or some such title.)
- *Open a checking account.* Do this right away, with the treasurer and/or executive director as signatory. It's important that contributions be acceptable in the name of the organization right from the start.
- *Try to get a free hall for your meetings.* It shouldn't be too difficult to arrange for a sympathetic local restaurant or savings & loan to give you the use of a room for regular meetings.
- *Publicize the first meeting.* Write a lively, informative press release and send or take it to all the local newspapers, and radio and TV stations. (If nobody in your group has written a press release before, get one or two books on the subject from the library before writing it.) You might also want to take out classified ads about the meeting. And, of course, spread the word personally to everyone you know who might be interested.

With that groundwork laid, you have the basis for a successful kickoff meeting. Your purpose at the meeting will be to obtain agreement on the need for an organization to work aggressively for less government, to lay out some initial plans and priorities, to take stock of your members' interests and capabilities, and to begin work on your group's first projects. If enough willing people show up, you should form committees for such efforts as research, publicity and public relations, and education. If possible, give everyone some sort of responsibility in the division of labor. And by all means end the meeting by agreeing on a specific, realizable goal to be achieved by the next meeting. (It's a good idea to announce the time and place of the next meeting, so that people take more seriously the commitments they have just made to take some immediate action.) Don't forget the coffee and doughnuts after the meeting ends—social ties can be very important in holding the organization together.

After the organizational meeting, subsequent meetings will be largely for reporting progress and attracting new members (via speakers, films, etc.). Most of the real work will be done outside of meetings, by individuals and committees working on assigned tasks.

Professional Tax Cutting

While a hard-core, grass-roots, activist organization is essential to the creation of a climate for cutting back city hall, there are limits to what can be accomplished by an unpaid, volunteer organization. When local officials either purposely attempt to frustrate efforts toward reform or genuinely lack the imagination to know how to respond, it can be invaluable to draw on the services of a full-time, professional taxpayers' organization.

Although supporting such an organization (which requires a minimum of an executive director/researcher and a secretary) may be beyond the means of the taxpayers of a single town or small city, the taxpayers of an entire county may find it an extremely worthwhile investment. Let's take as an example a county of just 100,000 people. Assuming the national average of 2.9 persons per household, that's 34,483 households. If just *one-third* of those households (11,494) contributes $5 a year, that's a $57,471 budget—which can readily support a director ($25,000), secretary ($10,000), rent ($2,400), and leave over $20,000 for literature, public relations efforts, and miscellaneous operating expenses.

There are two principal advantages to a professional taxpayers' group. First, by virtue of having a full-time staff, it can keep on top of what city and county governments in its area are doing. The bureaucrats charged with running the countless local agencies do, after all, work full time, thinking up ways to spend taxpayers' money. When a proposal for cutbacks or other reform measures is made, they typically have access to far more information than do taxpayers about their departments' operation—information with which to construct arguments for the status quo. Fighting this kind of built-in advantage requires comparable information, and getting it requires experience, skill, tenacity, and, above all, time. The best-intentioned volunteer holding down a regular full-time job is simply no match for a seasoned bureaucrat out to defend his or her empire. Even a retired volunteer is very likely to be outclassed—unless perhaps he or she is an ex-bureaucrat, "born again" as a tax cutter. Knowing what questions to ask and having the time to persist until the necessary information is forthcoming *requires* a full-time, skilled researcher.

The second advantage of a professional organization is that it is far more likely to put together imaginative analyses and proposals of its own, than to simply react to the excesses of the local bureaucrats. An organization that simply reacts will earn a reputation for negativism (and it may well be deserved). To accomplish more than cutting out flagrant examples of waste or holding down the rate of government growth, a taxpayers' group must be able to take the initiative. It must be able to show, for example, how and why the county government could abolish its data-processing department and turn the function over to a private contractor. To do this convincingly requires studying the county's existing data-processing operations and their costs, obtaining data from potential contractors, putting together success stories from elsewhere, and projecting the costs and savings that should be possible. Depending on the size of the county and its taxpayers' organization, the result of such a study could be a report of from 20 to 150 pages.

But the job does not end with publication of the report. It must be presented to the county legislative body, the county administrator, the affected department, and, of course, the news media, accompanied by a suitable press release. Follow-up action should be pursued so that the plan cannot simply be reviewed, studied, and forgotten. At this point, the grass-roots groups can get in on the act, lobbying to demand that a proven tax-saving proposal be implemented.

A good example of the kind of professional taxpayers' association we're discussing here—one dedicated to cutting back on government without depriving taxpayers of needed services—is the Contra Costa County Taxpayers Association. In this California county of 600,000 people, it has a staff of two and an annual budget of $90,000. Recently it put together an excellent report on private contracting that explained the advantages of contracting, illustrated its use in four different areas, and recommended specific steps to increase the use of contracting in Contra Costa County.[5]

WHAT ADMINISTRATORS CAN DO

In the previous section we referred rather harshly to "bureaucrats" and "spenders." And unfortunately, the majority of local government department heads and other managers have earned those epithets. Yet that certainly is *not* true of them all. There are conscientious, dedicated *civil servants* in the true sense of the word, who have a sincere concern that taxpayers receive full value for their money. It is to those administrators that this section is addressed.

To begin with, it is important for you to be able to analyze your city's or your department's operations in functional terms, when taxpayers start demanding cutbacks. Do you know how much of the public works budget goes for sweeping streets? How much of the police budget goes for enforcing victimless crime laws? Where particular operations generate revenues, what percentage of their costs are covered by those revenues? And which segments of the community are paying for which services—who is really subsidizing whom? These are the kinds of questions taxpayers are increasingly likely to be asking—and you'd be well advised to develop answers, based on hard data.

The prestige of an administrator has traditionally been measured roughly by the size of the agency—the number of employees and subunits and the size of the budget. The tax revolt has set in motion a fundamental change in the nature of local government—and of its administration. To the extent that taxpayers and their interest in cutting back on government come to dominate the political process (as illustrated in the scenario in Chapter 15), the prestige of an agency head will come to be measured by his or her *ability to do more with less.*

What local government desperately needs is aggressive, innovative managers who can function as facilitators of the shift to smaller government—as *change agents*, to use the sociologists' term. Local governments are appallingly resistant to change. And yet if they fail to respond positively and creatively to the tax revolt, they risk massive alienation of the citizenry, leading to social unrest and possibly chaotic upheavals. By midwifing change to new forms of public-service delivery, of the type described in this book, creative managers can turn a potential crisis into a tremendous opportunity.

We've seen several examples of agencies acting as change agents. Public Service Options was the nonprofit Minneapolis agency that acted as a broker for privatization. It helped local agencies define "packages" of public services suitable for contracting out, convinced prospective suppliers to enter the market, and developed community support for the concept. We also encountered Knoxville's Department of Public Transportation Services, the transit broker that actively involved the private sector in solving the city's transportation problems. These agencies dared to break free from the conventional mold of local government thinking. Each in its own way showed how privatization can provide new solutions—at lower cost—to pressing urban problems. Enlightened administrators can do likewise.

Many of the innovations discussed here—from consolidated police dispatch centers to computerized garbage routes to work-measurement systems—were first introduced to cities by *outside consultants* rather than by city administrators or department heads. Councils or managers interested in making significant cost savings and productivity increases should seriously consider bringing in outside consultants to study their problems and develop solutions.

Instead of hiring expensive consultants, some people suggest just giving the information to department heads and letting them develop solutions. This is less likely to work, for several reasons. First of all, the department head may be one of the reasons why costs are high and productivity is low in the first place. The outside consultant represents a chance to take an objective look at the performance of city departments, one that is not the view of a vested interest.

Second, the consultant's business is *change*, not maintaining the status quo. Experienced consultants invariably have a much broader range of experience in their fields. Chances are they have worked in scores of cities, not in just two or three. They have ready access to the experience of those cities in implementing innovative programs. They can bring to bear all of this experience in dealing full time with the problems to which they are assigned.

Citizens may sometimes ask, If a consultant is so good, why not hire him or her on as a full-time staff member? This question misses an essential point about the use of consultants. Because of greater expertise, the outside consultant commands a higher compensation (per day or per month) than a city staff member of equal years of experience. Hiring the consultant on a *permanent* basis would therefore be costly. Instead, a good consulting contract will ensure the city of a specific, usable result for its money. Thus, when the consultant is finished, the city will be better off, but without the added burden of a new full-time employee position.

Another advantage of using consultants is psychological. Frequently, use of an outside consultant permits a city administration to gain acceptance of innovations more readily than if they had been developed in-house. A reform proposed by a department head may be viewed as part of an internal power struggle between the manager and employees (or as some other kind of political ploy). The same proposal coming from an outside professional may be evaluated much more seriously on its merits. In many cases the department head would rather have sweeping proposals for change originate with outside experts who can shoulder the blame if reaction to the proposals turns out to be negative. In this way, the department head's risk is reduced.

WHAT LEGISLATORS CAN DO

Unfortunately, not all the measures advocated in this book can be accomplished strictly at the city or county level. Some require changes in state laws. The circumstances vary widely from state to state, and it is therefore impossible to give more than very general recommendations here.

The authority of cities, counties, and special districts to contract for service delivery varies considerably, both within states and between states. In one state there may be little or no restriction on contracting for general housekeeping services (park maintenance, building maintenance, garbage collection) but a prohibition on contracting for police or fire protection. In another state cities with home-rule charters may be free to contract but other cities may be prohibited—or vice versa. Local units of government may be forbidden to institute user charges for certain services—or to increase them in order to curtail use or to raise revenue.

Restrictions of these kinds need to be identified in every state and repealed, in order that the shift to new forms of public-service delivery may proceed. This research and lobbying task will probably fall mostly upon taxpayers' organizations. But legislators who wish to cast their lot *with* forces of less government would do well to get their staff people to study the government code for such barriers to change and propose legislation to repeal them.

We have seen how local government can be restructured to cope with the tax revolt. By utilizing the principles discussed in this book—privatization, user charges, and thinking smarter—we can improve the quality and responsiveness of local public services and cut costs substantially.

If you're ready to begin putting these ideas into practice, your first step should be to get more information. The most important books, reports, and articles on which this book is based are listed in Appendix A, keyed to each chapter. That's a good place to start for more details on both the theories and the practical examples. Some of the many firms involved in providing public services are listed in Appendix B. This list is by no means exhaustive. No comprehensive directories of such firms exist, yet. You can probably find quite a few more by checking the telephone book of the nearest metropolitan area. You may want to contact some of the firms listed here for further information. (But remember, these are mostly profit-seeking firms. They don't have the time and money to respond to thousands of curiosity seekers. Unless you're a bona fide potential customer, don't be surprised if you get no reply.) Finally, Appendix C lists a number of research organizations and consultants. Many of these have publication lists dealing with local government studies which they'll be glad to send you. And the consulting firms are available to assist your local government in analyzing problems and devising fresh solutions.

It *is* possible to cut back city hall—and, in the process, to end up with better public services. Doing so will be one of the real challenges of the 1980s.

Appendix A: References

CHAPTER 1: CITIES IN TROUBLE

1. *Public Benefits from Public Choice*, by Robert B. Hawkins, Jr., et al. Sacramento, Calif.: Task Force on Local Government Reform, 1974.

2. *Understanding Urban Government: Metropolitan Reform Reconsidered*, by Robert L. Bish and Vincent Ostrom. Washington, D.C.: American Enterprise Institute, 1973.

3. *Self Government by District: Myth and Reality*, by Robert B. Hawkins, Jr. Stanford, Calif.: Hoover Institution Press, 1976.

CHAPTER 2: KEYS TO CUTTING TAXES

1. *On the Economics of Public Sector Supply*, by Robert Deacon. Santa Barbara, Calif.: University of California, Department of Economics (unpublished working paper), 1977.

2. *Private Provision of Public Services: An Overview*, by Donald Fisk, Herbert Kiesling, and Thomas Muller. Washington, D.C.: The Urban Institute, May 1978.

3. *Public Prices for Public Products*, edited by Selma Mushkin. Washington, D.C.: The Urban Institute, 1972.

4. *Ibid.*, Chapter 13.

CHAPTER 3: POLICE

1. *The Kansas City Preventive Patrol Experiment*, by George L. Kelling et al. Washington, D.C.: Police Foundation, 1976.

2. *Police Response Time: Its Determinants and Effects*, by Tony Pate et al. Washington, D.C.: Police Foundation, 1976.

3. *Criminal Investigation Process. Vol. 1: Summary and Conclusions,* by Peter Greenwood and J. Petersilia. Santa Monica, Calif.: Rand Corporation, 1975. See also: *Criminal Investigation Process—Dialogue on Research Findings,* by Greenwood and Petersilia. Santa Monica, Calif.: Rand Corporation, 1977.

4. *Felony Investigation Decision Model: An Analysis of Investigative Elements of Information.* Palo Alto, Calif.: Stanford Research Institute, 1976.

5. "San Francisco's Hired Guns," by Christine Dorffi. *Reason,* August 1979.

6. *Private Police in the United States: Findings and Recommendations,* by J. S. Kakalik and S. Wildhorn. Santa Monica, Calif.: Rand Corporation, 1971.

7. *Community Organization and the Provision of Police Services,* by Elinor Ostrom et al. Beverly Hills, Calif.: Sage Publications, 1973.

8. *Ibid.*

9. *Ibid.*

10. "On the Fate of Lilliputs in Metropolitan Policing," by Elinor Ostrom and Dennis C. Smith. *Public Administration Review,* Vol. 32, No. 2, Spring 1976.

11. *Patrol Staffing in San Diego: One- or Two-Officer Units,* by John E. Boydstun, Michael E. Sherry, and Nicholas P. Moelter. Washington, D.C.: Police Foundation, 1977.

12. *The Police Patrol Car: Economic Efficiency in Acquisition, Operation, and Disposition,* by Rosalie T. Ruegg. Washington, D.C.: National Bureau of Standards, 1978.

CHAPTER 4: CRIMINAL JUSTICE

1. *What Happens After Arrest?* by Brian Forst, Judith Lucianvic, and Sarah J. Cox. Washington, D.C.: Institute for Law and Social Research, 1977.

2. *Prosecution of Adult Felony Defendants in Los Angeles County,* by Peter Greenwood and Sorrel Wildhorn. Santa Monica, Calif.: Rand Corporation, 1973.

3. "Entrepreneur of Justice," by Robert Poole, Jr. *Reason,* September 1978.

4. *PROMIS/JUSTIS—Prosecutor's Management Information System.* Washington, D.C.: National Institute of Law Enforcement and Criminal Justice, 1977.

CHAPTER 5: FIRE PROTECTION

1. *New Provisions of the ISO Grading Schedule.* Washington, D.C.: Public Technology, Inc., 1974.

2. *The Volunteer Fire Company,* by Ernest Earnest. New York: Stein & Day, 1979.

3. "Volunteer Fire Departments and Community Mobilization," by John Lozier. *Human Organization,* Vol. 35, No. 4, Winter 1976.

4. *Municipal Fire Protection Services: Comparison of Alternative Organizational Forms,* by Roger S. Ahlbrandt, Jr. Beverly Hills, Calif.: Sage Publications, 1973.

5. *Alternatives to Traditional Public Safety Delivery Systems: Civilians in Public Safety Services.* Berkeley, Calif.: Institute for Local Self-Government, 1977.

6. *Municipal Innovations 1: The Mini-Pumper.* Washington, D.C.: International City Management Association, February 1975.

CHAPTER 6: EMERGENCY AMBULANCE SERVICE

1. *Review and Analysis of Santa Barbara Fire Master Plan Recommendations,* by Robert W. Poole, Jr. Santa Barbara, Calif.: Local Government Center, 1979.

CHAPTER 7: GARBAGE AND SOLID WASTE

1. *Evaluating the Organization of Service Delivery: Solid Waste Collection and Disposal,* by E. S. Savas and Barbara J. Stevens. New York: Columbia University Graduate School of Business, 1977. See also *The Organization and Efficiency of Solid Waste Collection,* by E. S. Savas. Lexington, Mass.: Lexington Books, 1977.

2. "Municipal Garbage Collection Survey." *Municipal Yearbook 1975.* Washington, D.C.: International City Management Association, 1975.

3. *Opportunities for Improving Productivity in Solid Waste Collection.* Washington, D.C.: National Commission on Productivity, 1973.

CHAPTER 8: LEISURE AND RECREATIONAL SERVICES

1. *Fees and Charges Handbook: Guidelines for Recreation and Heritage Conservation Agencies.* Washington, D.C.: Heritage Conservation and Recreation Service, 1979.

2. *Contract Services Handbook.* Washington, D.C.: Heritage Conservation and Recreation Service, October 1979.

CHAPTER 9: TRANSIT SYSTEMS

1. "The BART Experience: What Have We Learned?" by Melvin Webber. *The Public Interest*, Fall 1976.

2. "That Old Electric Train's Proving to Be an Unbelievable Luxury." *Washington Star*, March 24, 1976.

3. *Urban Transportation and Energy: The Potential Savings of Different Modes.* Washington, D.C.: Congressional Budget Office, 1977.

4. *Paratransit: Neglected Options for Urban Mobility*, by Ronald F. Kirby et al. Washington, D.C.: The Urban Institute, 1974.

5. "Increasing the Taxi's Role in Urban America," by Martin Wohl, *Technology Review*, July/August 1976.

6. "Taxis and Jitneys: The Case for Deregulation," by Sandi Rosenbloom. *Reason*, February 1972.

7. *An Analysis of Two Privately Owned Shared-Ride Taxi Systems: Executive Summary*, by Kenneth W. Heathington et al. Washington, D.C.: Urban Mass Transportation Administration, 1975.

8. *Guidelines on the Operation of Subscription Bus Service*, by Ronald F. Kirby and Kiran U. Bhatt. Washington, D.C.: The Urban Institute, 1974.

9. "Transit in Smaller Cities: Ride-Sharing Brokerage." *Municipal Innovations 20.* Washington, D.C.: International City Management Association, July 1977.

CHAPTER 10: SOCIAL SERVICES AND HEALTH CARE

1. *Private Provision of Public Services* (see note 2, Chapter 2).

2. *Capitalism and Freedom*, by Milton Friedman. Chicago: University of Chicago Press, 1962.

3. *People Power: An Alternative to 1984*, by Morgan J. Doughton. Bethlehem, Pa.: Media America, Inc., 1976, p. 250.

4. *The Anatomy of AFDC Errors*, by Marc Bendick, Jr., Abe Lavine, and Toby H. Campbell. Washington, D.C.: The Urban Institute, 1977.

CHAPTER 11: PLANNING AND ZONING

1. *The Death and Life of Great American Cities*, by Jane Jacobs. New York: Vintage Books, 1961.

2. *Land Use Without Zoning*, by Bernard H. Siegan. Lexington, Mass.: Lexington Books (D. C. Heath & Co.), 1972.

3. "City Planning in Houston Without Zoning," by Roscoe H. Jones. Houston: City Planning Department, undated.

4. "Houston Defies the Planners and Thrives," by Dick Bjornseth. *Reason*, February 1978.

5. "A Study of Land Use Conflicts in Houston, Texas." Houston: City Planning Department, September 1976.

6. *People Building Neighborhoods: Report of the National Commission on Neighborhoods*. Washington, D.C.: Government Printing Office, March 19, 1979, pp. 204-8.

7. *Alternatives to Traditional Public Safety Delivery Systems: Public Safety Inspection Consolidation*. Berkeley, Calif.: Institute for Local Self-Government, 1977.

CHAPTER 12: PUBLIC WORKS

1. *Municipal Innovations 21: Urban Growth Management*. Washington, D.C.: International City Management Association, September 1977.

2. "Pricing Urban Water," in *Public Prices for Public Products* (see note 3, Chapter 2).

3. *Improving Municipal Productivity: Work Measurement for Better Management*. Washington, D.C.: National Commission on Productivity and Work Quality, November 1975.

CHAPTER 13: CITY MANAGEMENT

1. "Value Determination: The Assessor's Staff vs. the Private Appraisal Firm," by Frederick D. Stocker. *Property Tax Reform: The Role of the Property Tax in the Nation's Revenue System*. Chicago: International Association of Assessing Officers, 1973.

2. *Financial Disclosure Practices of the American Cities*. New York: Coopers & Lybrand, 1976.

3. *Sound Fiscal Management in the Public Sector*. New York: Arthur Andersen & Company, 1976.

4. *Financial Disclosure Practices of the American Cities II: Closing the Communications Gap*. New York: Coopers & Lybrand, 1978.

CHAPTER 14: SCHOOLS

1. *Adult Performance Level Summary Report*, by Norvell Northcutt. Austin, Tex.: University of Texas, Division of Extension, March 1976.

2. "Student Skills Decline Unequalled in History," by Jack McCurdy and Don Speich. *Los Angeles Times*, August 15-16, 1976.

3. *Our Children's Crippled Future: How American Education Has Failed*, by Frank E. Armbruster with Paul Bracken. New York: Quadrangle, 1977.

4. *Violent Schools—Safe Schools*. (HEW: National Institute of Education.) Washington, D.C.: Government Printing Office, January 1978.

5. "Why the Schools Went Public," by Samuel L. Blumenfeld. *Reason*, March 1979.

6. "Effects of High Schools on Their Students," by Christopher S. Jencks and Marsha D. Brown. *Harvard Educational Review*, Vol. 45, No. 3, August 1975.

7. *Peer and Cross-Age Tutoring in the Schools*, by Sophie Bloom. HEW: National Institute of Education. Washington, D.C.: Government Printing Office, December 1976.

8. *Children Teach Children: Learning by Teaching*, by Alan Gartner, Mary Conway Kohler, and Frank Riessman. New York: Harper & Row, 1971.

9. *Federal Programs Supporting Educational Change. Vol. 4: Findings in Review*, by Paul Berman and M. W. McLaughlin. Santa Monica, Calif.: Rand Corporation, April 1975.

10. "Special Education for Poor Has Failed, Studies Indicate," by Grayson Mitchell. *Los Angeles Times*, March 19, 1978.

11. *Ibid.*

12. *Evaluation of the Impact of ESEA Title VII Spanish/English Bilingual Education Program, Overview of Study and Findings*. Palo Alto, Calif.: American Institutes for Research, March 1978.

13. "The Perils of Public Education," by E. G. West. *The Freeman*, November 1977.

14. *Education by Choice: The Case for Family Control*, by John E. Coons and Stephen D. Sugarman. Berkeley, Calif.: University of California Press, 1978.

CHAPTER 16: HOW TO CUT BACK CITY HALL

1. The National Taxpayers Union, 325 Pennsylvania Ave., S.E., Washington, D.C. 20003, publishes a number of handbooks on tax cutting and organizing as well as a monthly newspaper, *Dollars and Sense*.

2. *The Municipal Yearbook* is a hardcover compendium of facts and figures on city government spending, employees, etc., published annually by the International City Management Association, 1140 Connecticut Ave., N.W., Washington, D.C. 20036.

3. *Fiscal Watchdog*, published monthly, is available for $10 a year from the Local Government Center, 221 West Carrillo St., Santa Barbara, CA 93101.

4. *The Guide* is published bimonthly by ICMA (see note 2), for $20 per year.

5. *Private Contracting of Public Services: Opportunities for Contra Costa County*, Martinez, California: Contra Costa County Taxpayers Association, 1979.

Appendix B: Private Service Providers

This appendix lists some of the more important private firms engaged in providing public services, either directly to consumers or on contract to local governments, and it includes all firms mentioned in the chapters in this book.

POLICE AND SECURITY SERVICES

Burns International Security Services, Inc.
320 Old Briarcliff Manor
Briarcliff Manor, NY 10510

California Plant Protection, Inc.
6727 Odessa Avenue
Van Nuys, CA 91406

Guardsmark, Inc.
22 South 2nd Street
Memphis, TN 38103

Pinkerton's, Inc.
100 Church Street
New York, NY 10007

Rural/Metro Fire Department, Inc.
P.O. Drawer F
Scottsdale, AZ 85252

Wackenhut Corporation
1027 Arch Street
Philadelphia, PA 19107

ADJUDICATION

American Arbitration Association
140 West 51st Street
New York, NY 10020

National Private Court
132 Nassau Street
New York, NY 10038

FIRE PROTECTION

American Emergency Services Corporation
825 South Main
Wheaton, IL 60187

East Ridge Fire Department
5341 Ringgold Road
East Ridge, TN 37412

Georgia Rural/Metro Fire
Department
P.O. Box 2743
Gainesville, GA 30501

Grant's Pass Rural Fire Department
and Ambulance Service
4529 Redwood Avenue
Grant's Pass, OR 97526

O'Donnell Fire Service
2401 2nd Avenue North
Billings, MT 59101

Rural/Metro Fire Department, Inc.
P.O. Drawer F
Scottsdale, AZ 85252

Southside Fire Department
P.O. Box 13246
Savannah, GA 31402

West Richmond County Fire
Department
3507 Walton Way Extension
Augusta, GA 30909

EMERGENCY AMBULANCE SERVICE

Acadian Ambulance
Box 52888, OCS
Lafayette, LA 70505
(subscription)

Bethesda-Chevy Chase Rescue Squad
4910 Auburn Avenue
Bethesda, MD 20014
(volunteer)

Central Oklahoma Ambulance Trust
2409 North Broadway
Oklahoma City, OK 73103
(subscription)

Community Ambulance Service
P.O. Box 909
Franklin, PA 16323
(subscription)

Medevac, Inc.
510 North Lake Avenue
Pasadena, CA 91101
(user fee, contract)

Medical Services, Inc.
2100 West 11th Avenue
Eugene, OR 97402
(subscription, user fee)

911 Emergency Services
P.O. Box 3458
Santa Barbara, CA 93105
(user fee)

GARBAGE COLLECTION

Browning-Ferris Industries
Fannin Bank Building
Houston, TX 77025

Golden Gate Disposal Company
900 7th Street
San Francisco, CA 94107

SCA Services, Inc.
99 High Street
Boston, MA 02110

Sunset Scavenger Company
Tunnel Avenue and Beatty Road
Brisbane, CA 94134

Waste Management, Inc.
900 Jorie Boulevard
Oak Brook, IL 60521

SOLID WASTE RECYCLING

Americology Business Unit Company
American Lane
Greenwich, CT 06830

Black Clawson Fibreclaim, Inc.
Parsons & Whittemore
200 Park Avenue
New York, NY 10017

Combustion Equipment Associates
555 Madison Avenue
New York, NY 10022

Energy Systems Division
Wheelabrator-Frye, Inc.
Liberty Lane
Hampton, NH 03842

Garrett Research & Development
  Corporation
Occidental Petroleum
10889 Wilshire Boulevard
Los Angeles, CA 90024

Pyro-Sol, Inc.
775 Harbor Boulevard
Redwood City, CA 94063

Union Carbide Corporation
270 Park Avenue
New York, NY 10017

UOP, Inc.
20 UOP Plaza
Des Plaines, IL 60016

PARK AND RECREATION SERVICES

California Golf
17315 Sunset Boulevard
Pacific Palisades, CA 90272

Environmental Industries, Inc.
21523 Conradia Court
Cupertino, CA 95014

Houston Anti-Litter Team (HALT)
4550 Post Oak Place
Houston, TX 77027

Park Management Systems
151 West Mission Street
San Jose, CA 95110

Resource Ecology Associates
2701 Cottage Way
Sacramento, CA 95825

The William Sherman Company
305 Mission Avenue
San Rafael, CA 94901

TRANSIT SERVICES

American Bus Shelter Company
2900 Pendleton Avenue
Santa Ana, CA 92704

ATE Management and Service
  Company
617 Vine
Cincinnati, OH 45215

Bustop Shelters, Inc.
10 East 53rd Street
New York, NY 10022

Colonial Transit Company
Route 17
Fredericksburg, VA 22401

Com-Bus
16782 Bolero Lane
Huntington Beach, CA 92649

Commuter Bus Lines
6254 Paramount Boulevard
Long Beach, CA 90805

Commuter Computer Van Pool
3440 Wilshire Boulevard, Suite 610
Los Angeles, CA 90010

Convenience and Safety Corporation
919 Third Avenue
New York, NY 10022

New York Bus Line
370 Jay Street
Brooklyn, NY 11201

Reston Commuter Bus Company
11404 Washington Plaza
Reston, VA 22090

Rides for Bay Area Commuters
100 Van Ness Avenue
San Francisco, CA 94102

Specialty Transit Co., Inc.
P.O. Box 253
Wentzville, MO 63385

Transit Shelter of America, Inc.
201 North Wells Street
Chicago, IL 60606

SOCIAL SERVICES

Homemakers International Division
Upjohn Pharmaceuticals
7000 Portage Road
Kalamazoo, MI 49001

Olsten Health Care Services
97-45 Queens Boulevard
Rego Park, NY 11415

Remedy Home & Health Care
Services, Inc.
32122 Camino-Capistrano Boulevard
San Juan Capistrano, CA 92675

Staff Builders Health Care Services
133 East 58th Street
New York, NY 10022

HOSPITALS

American Medical Care International
414 North Camden Drive
Beverly Hills, CA 90210

ARA Services, Inc.
Independence Square West
Philadelphia, PA 19106
(nursing homes)

Hospital Affiliates International, Inc.
4325 Harding Road
Nashville, TN 37205

Hospital Corporation of America
One Oak Plaza
Nashville, TN 37203

Humana, Inc.
1800 First National Tower
Louisville, KY 40201

Intermountain Health Care
36 South State
Salt Lake City, UT 84111

National Medical Enterprises, Inc.
11620 Wilshire Boulevard
Los Angeles, CA 90025

PUBLIC WORKS

Envirotech Systems, Inc.
One Davis Street
Belmont, CA 94002
(waste-water treatment)

ES Environmental Services, Inc.
19101 Villaview Road, Suite 301
Cleveland, OH 44119
(waste-water treatment)

RJA Maintenance Contractors
14291 East 4th Avenue, Suite 270
Aurora, CO 80011
(street maintenance)

SUPPORT SERVICES

ARA Fleet Services
Independence Square West
Philadelphia, PA 19106
(vehicle maintenance)

Bekins Building Maintenance
1335 South Figueroa Street
Los Angeles, CA 90015
(building maintenance)

Boeing Computer Services
7755 East Marginal Way South
Seattle, WA 98108
(data processing)

Computer Sciences Corporation
650 North Sepulveda Boulevard
El Segundo, CA 90245
(data processing)

Electronic Data Systems
7171 Forest Lane
Dallas, TX 75230
(data processing)

Optimum Systems
2801 Northwestern Parkway
Santa Clara, CA 95051
(data processing)

System Development Corporation
2500 Colorado Avenue
Santa Monica, CA 90404
(data processing)

Xerox Computer Services
Stamford, CT 06904
(data processing)

EDUCATION

American Learning Corporation
15562 Graham Street
Huntington Beach, CA 92649
(summer schools)

ARA Services
Independence Square West
Philadelphia, PA 19106
(school busing)

Behavioral Research Laboratories
3280 Alpine Road
Menlo Park, CA 94025
(programmed learning)

Dorsett Educational Systems
P.O. Box 1226
Norman, OK 73070
(programmed learning)

South Boston Heights Academy
486 East Third Street
South Boston, MA 02127
(franchised schools)

Appendix C: Consulting and Research Organizations

MANAGEMENT AND FINANCIAL CONSULTING

Booz, Allen, Hamilton, Inc.
135 South LaSalle Street
Chicago, IL 60603

Haskins & Sells
1114 Avenue of the Americas
New York, NY 10036

Arthur D. Little, Inc.
25 Acorn Park
Cambridge, MA 02140

Peat, Marwick & Mitchell
345 Park Avenue
New York, NY 10017

SRI International
333 Ravenswood Avenue
Menlo Park, CA 94025

Arthur Young & Company
277 Park Avenue
New York, NY 10017

WORK-MEASUREMENT STUDIES

Case & Company, Inc.
30 Rockefeller Plaza
New York, NY 10020

Kapner, Dull & Wolfberg, Inc.
13455 Ventura Boulevard
Sherman Oaks, CA 91423

LABOR RELATIONS ASSISTANCE

Labor-Management Relations
  Service
1620 Eye Street, NW
Washington, DC 20006

PRODUCTIVITY IMPROVEMENT RESEARCH

Council for International Urban
  Liaison
818 18th Street, NW, Room 820
Washington, DC 20006

Diebold Institute for Public Policy
  Studies, Inc.
430 Park Avenue
New York, NY 10022

Institute for Law and Social Research
1125 15th Street, NW, Suite 600
Washington, DC 20006

Institute for Local Self-Government
Claremont Hotel Building
Berkeley, CA 94705

Institute for Sub/Urban Governance
Pace University
Bedford Road
Pleasantville, NY 10570

International City Management
  Association
1140 Connecticut Avenue, NW
Washington, DC 20036

Local Government Center
221 West Carrillo Street
Santa Barbara, CA 93101

Public Technology, Inc.
1140 Connecticut Avenue, NW
Washington, DC 20036

Rand Corporation
1700 Main Street
Santa Monica, CA 90406

PRIVATE CONTRACTING RESEARCH

California Contract Cities
  Association
2468 Huntington Drive
San Marino, CA 91108

Center for Government Studies
Uris Hall
Columbia University
New York, N.Y. 10027

Local Government Center
221 West Carrillo Street
Santa Barbara, CA 93101

Public Service Options
c/o Minneapolis Citizens League
84 South 6th Street
Minneapolis, MN 55402

The Urban Institute
2100 M Street, NW
Washington, DC 20037

Index